How to
Make It Big
as a
Consultant

Third Edition

COHEN'S MAXIMS

compensation Compensation, whether in the form of profit, salary, or job satisfaction, is the by-product of your contribution to society and is in direct proportion to this contribution. It is an error to make compensation the focus of your life's work. You will not reach your full potential, and you will have cheated society of the full benefits of your talent and ability.

duty Whatever your occupation, you have a duty to the society of which you are a member. If you are a soldier, your duty is to protect that society. If you are in business or industry, your duty is to create and manage the jobs, wealth, and products of that society. Therefore, failure will be harmful not only to you but to society, just as success will be beneficial not only to you but also to society.

individual ability Every individual has the potential to do great things. To reach this potential, you must discover your special abilities and qualifications. This means that you should always attempt new tasks and accept responsibility for untried assignments whenever they are offered.

leadership A leader accepts responsibility. This means that the welfare of those you lead must always come before your own well-being. Therefore, while your primary duty is the accomplishment of your organization's mission, the welfare of your subordinates comes second, and your own welfare last.

planning Successful actions are results not of accidents or luck but rather of an analysis of the situation and the preparation and proper execution of plans. Because of a changing environment and other variables, plans will not always succeed as originally conceived. But planning will maximize your successes and minimize your failures.

responsibility If you are assigned a task, you are responsible for its successful completion. There are no acceptable excuses for failing to fulfill this responsibility, and this responsibility cannot be shifted to others.

risk Never be afraid to take risks. If you work for someone, risks are part of what you are getting paid for. If you work for yourself, taking risks is the only way you can become successful.

self-confidence Self-confidence comes from successfully completing increasingly difficult tasks and assignments. Give your maximum to every project, no matter how insignificant or formidable.

success Success does not come from working hard. Success comes from playing hard. Therefore, if you want success, you must position yourself so that the duties you perform, no matter how difficult or challenging, are considered play by you and not work. If you do this, not only will you gain success, you will have fun doing it.

How to
Make It Big
as a
Consultant

Third Edition

William A. Cohen, Ph.D.

AMACOM
American Management Association
New York • Atlanta • Boston • Chicago • Kansas City • San Francisco • Washington, D.C.
Brussels • Mexico City • Tokyo • Toronto

This publication is designed to provide accurate and authoritative
information in regard to the subject matter covered. It is sold with the
understanding that the publisher is not engaged in redering legal,
accounting, or other professional service. If legal advice or other expert
assistance is required, the services of a competent professional person
should be sought.

Library of Congress Cataloging-in-Publication Data

Cohen, William A., 1937–
    How to make it big as a consultant / William A. Cohen—3rd ed.
        p.   cm.
    Includes bibliographical references and index.
    ISBN 0-8144-7073-4
    1. Business consultants.   I. Title.

HD69.C6 C57 2001
001'.023'73—dc21   2001022196

Printing number

10   9   8   7   6   5   4   3   2   1

This book is dedicated to
my mother, who taught me that I could do anything I wanted
to do if I worked hard enough

and

my father, who taught me that the purpose of all work is to
contribute to a better society

CONTENTS

*Practice—How the Computer Can Double or Triple
Your Productivity—Proposals and Desktop
Publishing—Need Overhead Transparencies? No
Problem!—Managing Your Practice—Direct
Marketing—Correcting Your Writing—Naming
Products and Services—Making Forecasts and
Plans—Evaluating Potential Employees—Simplifying
Marketing Research—Voice-Activated Word
Processing—Gaining Access to Information the
World Over from Your Office—What You Need to
Know about Computers—What Kind of Computer
Should You Buy?—Desktop, Laptop, or Palmtop?—
What Kind of Printer Should You Buy?*

*What Is the Internet?—What Do You Need to Get
Online?—Researching on the Internet—The Search
Engines—How to Use the Search Engines—
Evaluating and Using Your Results—Some Books on
Researching on the Internet—Marketing on the
Internet—Internet "Freeways" for Marketing—The
World Wide Web—Usenet Marketing—E-Mail
Marketing—Books on Internet Marketing*

*Selecting the Legal Structure for Your Consulting
Firm—The Sole Proprietorship—The Partnership—
The Corporation—The S Corporation—Other Legal
Necessities—Obtaining a Business License—The
Resale Permit—Fictitious Name Registration—
Clients' Use of Credit Cards—Stationery and
Business Cards—Insurance and Personal Liability—
Keeping Overhead Low—The Telephone—Fax
Machines—Anticipating Expenses—Necessary
Records and Their Maintenance—Tax Obligations—
Income Taxes—Withholding Income Taxes—
Withholding Social Security Taxes—Remitting
Federal Taxes—Excise Taxes—Unemployment*

*Taxes—Obtaining an Employer Identification
Number—State and Local Taxes—Minimizing Tax
Paperwork—Sources of Additional Information*

ACKNOWLEDGMENTS

I want to acknowledge and thank the hundreds of consultants who have worked with me in helping clients and the dozens of other consultants who have contributed their knowledge toward helping my students over the years in learning what it means to consult.

PREFACE

Several months ago, a friend and experienced consultant, attended a seminar on consulting. The seminar leader divided the attendees into four groups. Each group was asked to agree on the top three actions that a consultant should take to become successful. My friend was very excited about the results and that's why he called me. Although the book you now have in your hands was never mentioned during the seminar, three out of the four groups independently decided that getting a copy of *How to Make It Big as a Consultant* was one of the three things every consultant should do to reach success! That's quite a testimonial. Knowing that the book was having such an impact helped convince me that updating it was akin to a public service, and I accepted the task from my publisher with a great deal of enthusiasm.

Before we get into the nitty-gritty of consulting, there is one thing you need to understand. Like most others, I didn't start out in life with a burning desire to become a consultant. I know that I am not alone in this, because I have spoken to hundreds of other full- and part-time consultants and very few started out with that intention. Most of them may have had an early experience like mine. My entrance into the consulting field was unplanned, and the first time I performed consulting services I had no one to ask for advice.

This is true for perhaps the world's foremost independent consultant, Peter F. Drucker. He didn't plan on becoming a consultant. I know this because Peter, still my friend, was my professor when I studied for my Ph.D. at Claremont Graduate University. Peter told me that his first experience in consulting was shortly after arriving in this country. Previously, he had been a newspaper correspondent. However, having a doctorate, Peter's services were mobilized for World War II and he was placed under the command of an army colonel. "You're going to be a management consultant," stated the colonel. "What's a management consultant?" asked Peter Drucker. "Don't be impertinent, young man," answered the colonel. "By which," Drucker told me, "I knew the colonel didn't know what a management consultant was either."

Experience in other fields had taught me that whenever I lacked knowledge about something, my first step should be to find a book on the subject. So I did just that. I visited several bookstores; I checked with the libraries. But I found no books with the information I needed. The few books on consulting were all about consulting by the large consulting firms. They contained none of the specifics I needed.

How much should I charge? Was a contract absolutely necessary? Did I need a business license or some other kind of license? What could I do as a part-time consultant without running into a conflict of interest with my full-time employer? How much could I make if I decided to work full-time at consulting? Also, if I consulted full-time, how much time would I need to spend marketing my services versus actually consulting, and how should I go about marketing my services, anyway? These and numerous other questions plagued me, but I had nowhere to turn for answers.

Eventually I learned, but mainly it was the hard way: through experience. I made numerous mistakes, which in some cases cost me money and in all cases wasted time and brought frustration. However, I did finally learn what to do and how to do it, and I began to make money. I consulted for Fortune 500 companies, for small businesses, for start-up companies, and for the government, and this endeavor continues to this day.

Then some years ago, within a few months of each other, I received my Ph.D. and became a full-time university professor. (I might interject here that becoming a successful business consultant in many specialties does not require a Ph.D., an MBA, or in fact, any business degree at all. But more about that later.) In any case, becoming a business professor did not curtail my consulting activities. If anything, it intensified them.

At my university, I noticed that many students had a tremendous interest in business consulting—and not just business students. I was persuaded to develop an interdisciplinary course at California State University at Los Angeles on the subject of consulting for business. As this course developed, we did not stop at theory; every quarter I invited practicing consultants from many fields to share their experiences. The speakers ranged from those in small one-person operations to staff consultants employed by multimillion-dollar corporations. My speakers included full- and part-time consultants, both men and women.

This course became so popular that it attracted not only business students from all disciplines but also psychologists, chemists, anthropologists, attorneys, and English majors. Many of those who took the course were older students from outside the university, including engineers, pilots, and many company executives and professionals who wanted to leave their corporate jobs or to consult part-time. We even attracted a number of professors who sat in on these lectures at various times to pick up what they could.

Partially due to the success of the business consulting course, another program for which I had responsibility also prospered. This was the Small Business Institute at the university, of which I was the director. The Small Business Institute program, conducted at universities around the country under the sponsorship of the U.S. Small Business Administration, furnishes consulting services to small businesses. Business students, supervised by professors, did the consulting. Over a period of years, we developed one of the largest Small Business Institutes in the country and several times won district, regional, and national awards for the top performance among participating universities. The Small Business Institute program allowed students in the consulting course to do hands-on projects as a part of their education. Unfortunately, this fine program fell victim to budget cuts by the federal government in 1994. However, many universities continued it, asking small business clients to pay for the consulting work accomplished, which I have to say, is still a bargain for the small businesses that choose to participate in the program.

Meanwhile, the success of our program led to many requests for help from outside the university. In order to make this program mobile, we developed a consulting seminar that I gave several times a year. These seminars were attended not only by neophyte and would-be consultants but also by many consultants with considerable experience in their various professions. They generously shared their experiences and knowledge with other seminar students, and with me.

As a result, this book is based not only on my own experience but also on that of many others—including numerous guest lecturers, professors, and students who have accomplished more than five hundred different consulting engagements for as many different small businesses. It is also based on the face-to-face interchange of ideas from consultants in many different fields and geographic locations.

Had I had this book in my hands when I first started out, I would have saved myself thousands of wasted hours and much frustration. I would have avoided countless blunders, including journeys down blind alleys, while I struggled to learn how to promote my practice, develop long-term client relationships, and, in one case, get paid for services performed.

This book contains the collective experiences of hundreds who have endeavored to earn or supplement their livelihood through the practice, either full- or part-time, of business consulting. Its aim is to help you to build a successful, rewarding business consultancy.

This edition not only updates every chapter but also contains extensively modified appendices and several new chapters, two from expanding the former single chapter on marketing your practice and a brand-new chapter on how to use the Internet in all phases of your practice.

I truly believe that this book can have a major impact on your ability to succeed as a consultant. But in the final analysis, how you apply this information is up to you, so your success will be your victory. Good luck!

William A. Cohen
Pasadena, California

How to
Make It Big
as a
Consultant

Third Edition

1

THE BUSINESS OF CONSULTING

Independent consulting has to be one of the most incredible businesses around, with advantages found in no other way of making a living. Consider working hours. You probably have some time of the day when you work best. Most people do. Some people work better early in the morning, others late in the evening, and a very few people work equally well all day, at any time. But in independent consulting, it doesn't make any difference, because you can pick your own hours. You can decide when you work and when you do not. You can always work at your best time.

Are you in a job where you don't like your boss? Must you work with people whom you just do not care to be around? Well, in independent consulting you decide whom you wish to work for and whom you do not wish to work for, as well as whom you do and do not work with. Whether you do or do not work for a particular client or others who may help you with a project is entirely up to you.

Are you dissatisfied with your current income? Do you feel you are underpaid? In consulting you set your own fees; you decide how much you're worth and how much you want to make. If you are worth more right now, today, you can immediately give yourself a raise.

Do you prefer to work at home? In consulting you can make $100,000 or more working out of your own home without worrying about parking, driving, or the expense of an outside office. In fact, the office in your own home will probably be tax-deductible.

Finally, are you concerned about taking the big plunge of

going into your own full-time consulting practice? No need to risk
your time, career, or a large monetary investment. You can start
consulting part-time and ease your way in. Many successful consultants have started with part-time work after their full-time jobs,
at nights and on weekends. And if you follow the instructions in
this book, you will soon be able to build a successful consulting
practice; you will not have to quit your full-time job until you are
fully ready and certain that you will be successful.

What Is Consulting?

Consultants operate in many, many different fields. Import-export,
management, human resources, engineering, and marketing are
some of the more common ones. There are consultants in archeol-
ogy and consultants in clothes selection. There are even consultants
to help authors overcome writer's block. In my classes and in seminars around the country, I have met experts from all those fields
and more. All had become or had the potential for becoming successful consultants. They had widely varying backgrounds and
consulted in many different business areas. As I was writing the
first edition of this book, my wife called my attention to an article
in the *Los Angeles Times* that told the story of an enormously successful consulting business run by a young mother. She worked
about six days every month, advising businesses on which records
to keep and which to throw away.

A consultant is simply anyone who gives advice or performs
other services of a professional or semiprofessional nature in return for compensation. This means that regardless of your area of
interest or expertise, you can become a consultant. Everyone has a
unique background, with special experiences and interests that are
duplicated by few others and that are in demand by certain individuals or companies at certain times.

Many of my students have asked whether it is necessary to
have an advanced degree in order to be a consultant. The answer
is definitely no. Although the orientation of a consultant is clearly
professional, I have known many successful consultants with limited formal academic training. The important thing is that you have
the necessary experience, qualifications, and skills to help with a

task that an individual or company wants performed. Where you obtained these skills is of far less importance. I must add, however, that if it is your intent to work as a management consultant for a major consulting firm and not on your own, a masters of business administration (MBA) will probably be required.

Sometimes those employed in the large corporate firms may even be a little miffed about being compared with independent consultants. When I wrote the first edition of *How to Make It Big as a Consultant*, I received a call from a consultant at one of the prestigious consulting companies who had read my book. "I consider consulting a profession, not an entrepreneurial opportunity," he said. I reminded him that his own multibillion-dollar firm was started by a single entrepreneurial consultant.

If you are on your own, whether or not you obtained your expertise from a university is not crucial. I know of a successful import-export consultant with no degree and an expensive consultant to top management of major corporations who has only an undergraduate degree in sociology.

How Big Is the Consulting Industry?

Because consulting encompasses so many different aspects of work life, it is very difficult to measure precisely the total dollar volume for consulting services currently performed in the United States. Most people are able only to estimate the value of consulting services being performed for business. Ten years ago various sources estimated that the size of the consulting industry had reached $10 to $15 billion annually.[1, 2] Today it is likely that worldwide consulting revenues have reach $100 billion annually. This explosion has been fueled by technological advances such as the Internet, which not only facilitates the consulting process but creates the demand for an entirely new class of consultants.

Consulting for Business

Even business consulting encompasses a very wide area of activities. Jerome H. Fuchs, author of *Making the Most of Management*

Consulting Services, categorizes consulting activities into eleven different areas.

1. General management, encompassing organizational planning, strategy, and other general management tasks
2. Manufacturing, including production control and facilities management
3. Personnel, having to do with development and training, recruitment, selection, management of employee benefits programs, and similar activities
4. Marketing, covering such topics as new product introduction, pricing, promotion, and development of distribution channels
5. Finance and accounting, including cost accounting, valuation, tax advice, and investment programs
6. Procurement and purchasing
7. Research and development and potential product selection and screening
8. Packaging, including aspects such as packaging machinery, design, and testing
9. Administration, including office management and administrative procedures
10. International operations, which has to do with import, export, licensing, tariffs, and joint ventures
11. Specialized services, which catches all the many other areas, such as executive recruiting or telecommunications

Some years ago, *Consultants News,* a newsletter for the consulting industry, surveyed 583 companies to find out what types of consulting expertise they offered. (Appendix A contains the address for *Consultants News* as well as a list of other references helpful to consultants.) Here are the results:

Consulting Expertise Offered	*Number of Firms Offering*
General management	219
Personnel	143
Marketing	126

Organizational planning	113
Manufacturing	112
Management development	100
Strategic business planning	97
Administration	96
Finance and accounting	89
Marketing strategy and organization	82

Types of Consulting Firms

Other aspects of their business may also define consulting firms, including size, location, and the types of clients they serve. These include:

1. *National general management firms.* These are large firms such as McKinsey and Company, Booz-Allen & Hamilton, or Arthur D. Little, which do millions and millions of dollars in consulting business every single year. How much is millions and millions? It is estimated that in one year, these firms can produce a billion dollars or more in annual revenue.

2. *Major accounting firms with consulting divisions.* Most national CPA firms today, including all of the Big Five, perform management consulting in addition to their regular accounting activities. Last year, Arthur Andersen did more than $8 billion annually in business revenue, much of it from consulting, and primarily as a result of its information systems work.[3]

3. *Functionally specialized firms.* These organizations specialize in certain particular areas of business. Such a firm might deal only in market research or in strategic planning.

4. *Industry-specific firms.* These are large national or international firms dealing only with certain industries or certain types of operations. An example would be Theodore Barry & Associates, known primarily for its work as consultants in the utility industry.

5. *Public sector firms.* These firms specialize in consulting primarily with the government—national, state, and local—or nonprofit organizations such as universities or hospitals.

6. *The so-called think tanks.* These very large firms, such as Rand and SRI International, may have many or very few customers.

The Aerospace Corporation, located in Los Angeles, consults mainly for the U.S. Air Force.

7. *Regional and local firms.* There are numerous consulting firms that operate in a single and limited geographic area, even though their annual sales may be quite large.

8. *Sole practitioners.* This is an area many new consultants seek, and for good reason: There are more than fifty thousand such consulting businesses in the United States; more than half of these are one-person operations, and another 20 to 25 percent have between two and ten employees.

9. *Specialty firms outside of business.* This may actually be one of the largest areas of consulting, although it is rarely counted because the focus is outside the area of business. Such firms may consult on health, etiquette, dress, or even personal behavioral management.

This wide variety indicates that the opportunities in the consulting business are tremendous. Many of the local or regional firms, and even the larger firms, started with a sole practitioner and grew to be multimillion-dollar giants.

Why Does Anyone Need a Consultant Anyway?

You may ask yourself why it is that a large company hires a consultant, at sometimes very high compensation, when it already has staffs of experts who, one would think, should be even more qualified than the consultant. In a television broadcast several years ago, *60 Minutes* asked this very question about consultants to the government. After all, if the government employees themselves are qualified, why the need to hire consultants? And why pay them more than the employees themselves are being paid?

Actually there are very good reasons why both the government and business organizations use consultants. In fact, not only are they hired but they are hired again and again and held in considerable esteem. Because it is good business to find a need and then fill it, it is very important for you to understand exactly what these reasons are. Let's look at each of them in turn.

1. *The need for personnel.* Sometimes even the largest companies lack personnel at specific periods of time or for specific tasks. They may need assistance during a temporary work overload, or they may require unique expertise that is not needed on an ongoing basis every day of the year. Temporary assistance might be needed, for example, when a company bids for a government contract. During this period, it is required to put out a great amount of work over a short period of time. The staff personnel may not be available to do this without stopping other important projects, so consultants are hired, or a company may need unique expertise on a short-term or project basis. Take direct marketing, an area I frequently consult in. Even today with the amazing growth in direct marketing and database management, many businesses use direct marketing only occasionally. So it does not make sense to hire a full-time expert whose salary could easily exceed $75,000 per year. Therefore, a company is perfectly happy to hire a consultant at fees of from $50 to $300 an hour (or more) to accomplish a specific task.

The large revenues in executive search consulting, another unique area of consulting, also demonstrate the need for personnel and their importance to a firm. According to *Executive Search Review*, the large search firms had the following revenues (in millions of dollars):

Korn/Ferry International	$301.1
Heidrick & Struggles	$258.1
Spencer Stuart	$223.3
Russell Reynolds Associates	$184.3
LAI Amrop International	$182.2
Egon Zehnder International	$181.9[4]

2. *The need for fresh ideas.* Not infrequently, a company has a problem, and management feels the employees are too close to it to understand all the ramifications. It makes sense to bring in someone from outside, someone with competent problem-solving skills but not necessarily knowledge of the business. In fact, sometimes the individual's very ignorance (assuming, of course, a talent for problem solving) helps to provide the answer. Peter F. Drucker, one of the most famous independent management consultants,

says that he brings to the problem not so much his knowledge about a certain problem but his ignorance. Drucker has a tremendous ability to penetrate through a confusion of factors and recognize the main issue, and thus he is able to recommend ways to solve the problem. I believe his services are well worth the fees he charges.

3. *Company politics.* At times the solution to a problem may actually be known. However, for various political reasons those who understand the problem are not allowed present it. For example, a division of a major company once proposed that the company enter a new market with one of its products, which would have required an investment of millions of dollars. The potential in this new market was highly controversial within this company. Because the new product would come from the division that suggested it, the division's recommendations would be considered prejudiced. However, by hiring an outside consultant to study the same issues, the division succeeded in accomplishing the same thing. The consultant was assumed to be more impartial and less likely to be influenced by company politics.

4. *The need for improved sales.* No business can exist without sales. This is true no matter how knowledgeable its president or senior staff, how skilled its financial people and accountants, or how innovative its engineers in developing or manufacturing new products. A company that needs to increase sales in a short time frame will sometimes look outside its own marketing or sales staff for help.

5. *The need for capital.* Every company needs money. The need for capital is extremely common in start-ups. But it is also very common in successful companies. In fact, the more successful a company, the more capital it needs. The need for capital is a continuing problem with many companies. An individual who has expertise in finding sources of capital will be in continual demand.

6. *Government regulations.* Government regulations, if not obeyed, can result in fines, imprisonment, or even the closing of the business. No company is immune to government regulations, and all companies need to ensure that they fulfill these regulations in the most efficient and effective manner. At the same time, they wish to minimize any negative impact on their business and, if

possible, use the regulations to help the operation of their business. These regulation concerns may involve a variety of areas: equal employment opportunity, age discrimination, consumer credit protection, safety standards, veterans' rights, and numerous others. If you have knowledge in any of these regulatory areas or can become an expert in them, there is a real market for your consulting services.

7. *The need for maximum efficiency.* All organizations need to operate in as efficient a manner as possible. An organization that operates at lower efficiency than it is capable of will eventually have problems. More efficient competitors will take away its market and drive it out of business. Inefficiency leads to high costs, making prices noncompetitive. Slippages, delays, and low productivity all result from inefficiency. If you know how to increase the efficiency of an organization, you have something important to sell as a consultant.

8. *The need to diagnose problems and find solutions.* One reason that the consultant with an MBA degree is so sought after by many businesses is these graduates are supposed to be very adept at diagnosing problems faced by business and developing solutions for them. Anyone who can do this is in demand. The more general problem solving you do and the better you become at it, the more your name will get around. Large consulting firms have capitalized on the need of businesses to have their problems diagnosed and recommendations for solutions made. For this reason, these firms have sought to hire MBAs from the top schools at extremely high starting salaries in order to build and maintain a reputation for problem solving. Even some individual practitioners such as Peter F. Drucker are nationally and sometimes internationally known for their problem-solving talents, which means that they are in great demand.

9. *The need to train employees.* The operation of any business is becoming more and more complex, and today many employees are continually trained throughout their careers. Managers need different types of training for leadership, organizational, and planning skills; computer operators need additional training with the latest equipment, techniques, software, and programming. In fact, developments are occurring so rapidly that virtually every single

functional area of business needs continual training. If you are an expert and can teach skills in any area that is in demand, you have a niche in a type of consulting that commands large fees from industry.

10. *The need for a complete turnaround.* A friend of mine, who made a worldwide consulting reputation as a "workout specialist," was often called in by a bank or a group of investors to take over a company in danger of bankruptcy. He would come in as president and do whatever was necessary to turn the company around. Sometimes he was president of several companies simultaneously, when he'd spend a good deal of time in flight, continually going from one distressed company to another. Once the company was in shape, off he would go to the next project. Because many companies find themselves in extreme conditions, when the investors are willing to put up a fight, there is a need for a troubleshooting consultant who can pull off a complete turnaround. Turnaround specialists command heavy-duty fees, as much as $2,000 per day or more.[5] William Brandt became a turnaround consultant while working on a doctorate in sociology. A friend asked him to help a failing coal mine. Once involved as a consultant, he never stopped. Brandt, then only thirty-nine years old, built his Development Specialists, Inc., into a $4 million practice.[6]

11. *Computers and data processing.* Data processing specialists have been with us for a long time. But the technological advancement in computers has opened up opportunities at many levels for those who know their stuff. These consultants are earning big fees, too. For example, when my computer had some problems, a business friend recommended a computer consultant. She turned out to be a young lady in her early twenties who had never entered college. She billed at $100 an hour and was worth every penny because every hour without my computer was costing me money.

Actually, the types of consulting are probably unlimited. Flying across country recently, I picked up a copy of *American Way*. One article asked: "Are you losing ground at work? A personal coach can help you devise a game plan to regain your competitive edge." The article went on to describe personal coaching, an unusual type of one-on-one business consulting that is generally done

over the phone. The article stated that more than ten thousand coaches now offer their services this way.[7]

Signals Indicating the Need for a Consultant

According to James E. Svatko, the senior editor of *Small Business Reports,* the following situations signal the need for outside expertise from a consultant:

- Lack of a written business plan
- Unexplained low morale
- Steady, constant increases in costs
- Regular cash shortages
- Chronic delays or late deliveries of products
- Loss of market position
- Overworked staff
- Excessive rework without achieving objectives
- Continual supply deficiencies
- Lack of information about the competition or market[8]

Remember, these are the reasons that businesses normally need consultants. There are also thousands of other areas in which both businesspeople and nonbusinesspeople may need assistance. For example, consultants are making millions of dollars today by teaching people how to manage their time, control stress, lose weight, and keep fit. If you have specific knowledge in almost any area—from handicrafts to hypnotism, mathematics to merchandising—you may have skills that are in demand by some segment of the population. In fact, *Fortune Magazine* wrote an exposé called "In Search of Suckers" in which well-known author and consultant Tom Peters was quoted as saying, "We're the only society that believes it can keep getting better and better. So we keep on getting suckered in by people like Emerson . . . and me."[9] I believe Peters was speaking somewhat tongue-in-cheek. After all, he includes the world-famous nineteenth-century philosopher Ralph Waldo Emerson in the same category as a huckster. Also, given the worldwide demand for consulting in all of these fields, I doubt that we Americans are the only ones seeking improvement.

How Potential Clients Analyze Consultants for Hire

James Svatko's analysis of the consultant-client relationship led him to recommend that companies answer the following questions before deciding whether to hire a consultant. As a consultant, you should answer these five questions yourself before submitting your formal proposal to a client:

1. Can you add something worthwhile to the company's total output?
2. Will your expertise bring the company any closer to its goals?
3. Can you make the company work more effectively?
4. Will you save the company time?
5. With the budget available, can you do a comprehensive and effective job?[10]

If your proposal doesn't prove that you can do these things for your client, either rework your proposal or don't submit one.

What Makes an Outstanding Consultant?

Being a consultant and being an outstanding consultant are two different things. After talking with many top-flight consultants around the country, I have identified seven areas that make the difference.

1. *Bedside manner.* This refers to your ability to get along with your client. Here it's not so much what you say but how you say it. Doctors with much knowledge but poor bedside manners often find that their patients prefer to go to doctors with much less experience or ability. Developing a pleasant bedside manner so that your clients have confidence in what you *say* can be as important as your technical knowledge.

2. *The ability to diagnose problems.* To stay with the doctor analogy, we know that the doctor has access to all sorts of medicines to help cure a patient. But if he or she makes an incorrect diagnosis,

the medicine may hurt more than it helps. Similarly your ability to diagnose the problem correctly is extremely important. It is one of the most significant criteria of an outstanding consultant.

3. *The ability to find solutions.* Of course, having diagnosed a problem, you are expected to recommend the proper actions to correct the situation. Chapter 11 is devoted entirely to problem solving. With practice you will be able to solve complex problems consistently by suggesting the right course of action for your client to take.

4. *Technical expertise and knowledge.* Perhaps you expected this would be the most important skill for a good consultant, and it is true that technical expertise in a field is important. Expertise comes from your education, your experience, and the personal skills you have developed. But it may be in any one of a variety of areas, and it may develop in a variety of ways. G. Gordon Liddy, known primarily for his association with the Watergate break-in, today commands a six-figure income as a security consultant. Note that even a background that includes incarceration in a penitentiary does not affect your ability to be a good consultant and to make a major contribution to the benefit of your client.

5. *Communication skills.* Charles Garvin, from the well-known Boston Consulting Group, has done extensive consulting in the area of business strategy since the early 1960s. From more than forty years' experience, Garvin has identified three major attributes that every good consultant needs. He believes the number one attribute is superior communication abilities. (Analytical skill is second, and the ability to work under pressure is third.)

Some years ago, a study of how companies viewed recent business school graduates was conducted by Dr. Allen Blitstein. Dr. Blitstein wanted to know two things: the most important factors in why new graduates were hired, and the major factors that indicated success on the job after hiring. You may have thought that such factors as grade point average or perhaps the school attended would be of primary importance. But not so. According to the employers who did the hiring, the ability to communicate was far more important. And that was true both for getting hired and for success on the job. You should study Chapter 14, on presentations, with particular interest.

6. *Marketing and selling abilities.* Regardless of the technical area you are interested in, whether it is a functional area in business or something entirely different, you must learn to be a good marketer and a good salesperson. Not only do consultants sell an intangible product, they also must sell themselves. Chapters 2, 3, and 4 discuss how to market your consulting practice; every secret I have learned from my own experiences or from other consultants I reveal to you in these chapters.

7. *Management skills.* Last, but not the least in importance, is the ability to manage a business or a practice and to run projects. In my mind, an outstanding consultant must also be a good manager. As with other skills, the ability to manage can be learned. To assist you in this process, Chapter 7 shows you how to manage your business efficiently. In addition, throughout the book I give step-by-step instructions for many processes that will help you perform as a skilled manager.

Dick Brodkorb is the former chairman and chief executive officer of a consulting company in Costa Mesa, California, called Decision Planning Corporation. Dick frequently spoke to my classes on consulting. He identified two groups of skills that he feels are most important in making a good consultant. He calls them The Big Three and The Big Four. The Big Three are (1) communication skills, both written and oral, (2) technical command of a subject, and (3) the ability to get along with others.

He suggests that neophyte consultants first master The Big Three and then move on to The Big Four. The first of The Big Four is analytical skills (not necessarily quantitative). The second, sensitivity to others, is extremely important. The third is that you should have a tolerance for the consulting life-style, which may require intensive hours of work on some projects; and fourth, you need to have a strong personal drive to be successful.

In summary, there are certain things you must know in order to be a consultant. These are:

○ How to use your expertise to be a consultant
○ How to get clients

  ○ How to diagnose and solve problems
  ○ How to run your practice

All these topics, and a lot more, are covered in this book.

It's important to recognize that you may not need actual hands-on experience in your technical area of interest at first. One of my MBA students went to work for one of the largest consulting firms in the country with no hands-on experience at all, using solely what he had learned as a student. Peter F. Drucker once said that although he consults internationally for major corporations, he has never been a practicing manager, with the single exception of serving as dean at Bennington School for approximately two years in the 1940s.

How Much Money Can You Make as a Consultant?

No one should embark on a career as a consultant primarily to make money. Still, money is needed to live, and it can provide the freedom to choose what one wishes to do in life and for whom, so this is a valid question.

Albert Vicere and Robert Fulmer, two management professors at Pennsylvania State University, estimated that consultants are commanding daily fees that range as high as $10,000—and even higher.[11] Of course, the larger fees tend to be charged by the larger well-known consulting firms, which are themselves consulting to larger well-known organizations. In fact, a very large consulting firm doing a major project may charge millions of dollars or more for their work.[12] Another important variable is the field in which you are consulting and for whom you are consulting. If you are consulting for an individual in a field where your client isn't making much money, you can't charge very much either. But no matter what your fees are, you can make much more than you could doing the same work for someone else as an employee.

Remember that computer consultant with a high school education I mentioned earlier? Well, because she's billing at $100 an hour, at eight hours per day, that's $4,000 per workweek, or well over $200,000 per year!

But wait. Though it is true that at $100 an hour, you can sure make a lot of money over the course of a year, it is important to realize that you will not be able to bill for every minute of every day. Some time must be spent in marketing your services. Therefore, it's important to consider the ratio of billable time to time spent marketing, which is not billable.

Howard L. Shenson, who gave seminars around the country on consulting, estimated that new consultants should plan to spend at least one-third of their time the first year marketing their services, and only two-thirds in actual billable time. After the first year, marketing time can be reduced to 15 or 20 percent. Other estimates for marketing time have ranged as high as 40 to 50 percent. Many independent consultants note that, once established, they spend almost no time marketing, because they either receive additional clients through referrals or spend all their available time on established clients.

When you are estimating how much you can actually make as a consultant, it is better to start with the assumption that in the first year you will spend about half of your time marketing your services. You may not actually need that much, but it's safer than expecting to spend most of your time on work billed to your clients and then finding that you have grossly overestimated your first year's sales.

How Do People Become Consultants?

Individuals get into consulting in many strange ways, and no two stories are exactly alike. You may be interested in hearing how some consultants got their start.

Howard L. Shenson was a Ph.D. student at the same time he was teaching and serving as department head at California State University at Northridge. He received numerous requests from companies in the local area, and he soon was engaged in a variety of consulting activities in addition to his teaching and research. As the months went by, he realized he was spending more and more time consulting, and he was finding it more fascinating than his academic work. Finally he decided to devote himself entirely to full-time consulting, and he found not only better job satisfaction but far greater compensation than he could ever earn as a professor.

Hurbert Bermont, author of the self-published *How to Become a Successful Consultant in Your Own Field* and a successful consultant in the publishing industry as well as a consultant's consultant today, got his start when his boss called him in one day and fired him. Bermont said he went through total shock at the time, but he later realized it was a favor in disguise. In desperation Bermont called around and found a friend who agreed to let him use his office, secretary, and telephone for a nominal sum in exchange for training his friend's new secretary. He was able to attain as a client the most prestigious and successful name in his business by working for the company at the right price: nothing. This door opener eventually led to a paying contract with the company and, more important, gave him a major client with which to impress other prospective clients. At the end of six months, he was earning almost as much as it had taken him twenty years to reach in his previous career.

Phil Ross started out as an actor who worked as a salesperson with a manufacturing company between jobs. Because of his unique abilities not only to sell but also to educate and motivate, he soon became national sales director. When he became dissatisfied with company policies, he began looking for another job, using a national executive search firm. In the process, he was recruited by that same search firm to become an executive recruiter, or "head-hunter." Search consulting probably calls for more sales skills than any other type of consulting. This is because the consultant must be able to convince a company to become a client *and* persuade a fully satisfied employee to consider leaving his or her current organization and become a candidate for a job with a different company. Phil mastered these skills and excelled as a search consultant, and soon he was appointed national training director. After several years, Phil left to start his own executive search firm and eventually founded The Pros, a consulting firm that assists corporations worldwide with their personnel and recruitment problems.

Luis Espinosa was born in Mexico and was my student at California State University at Los Angeles. He wanted to become a consultant for a major consulting firm. Using special job-finding techniques that got him face-to-face interviews with principals of top consulting firms, he was soon hired by Theodore Barry, International. After only two years, he was recruited as a top-level strategic planner for a bank in Mexico City with $20 billion in assets. He then went on to a similar high position as an internal strategic planning consultant with an American bank.

This points out yet another advantage of consulting. Not infrequently, consultants who are highly visible to top management so impress their clients with their performance that they are catapulted immediately into senior executive ranks at extremely high salaries. Several years ago, *Business Week* carried the story of Ilene Gordon Bluestein, who became director of corporate planning at the Signode Corporation in Glenview, Illinois, at age twenty-eight, only four years after leaving school. The point here is that those four years were spent in consulting. Bluestein wasn't the only success mentioned. This article told of others who used consulting as a springboard to corporate success. All were young, held senior positions, and made large salaries. And every single one had been a consultant.

John Diebold opened a consulting operation in his parent's house in Weehawken, New Jersey. Had he prepared a résumé, the most recent item would have been the fact that he had been fired from another consulting group. The reason? He had tried too hard to convince a company to buy a computer. That was in 1954. Three years later, he bought the company that had fired him. Eventually, his firm, The Diebold Group, had branches around the world, and he was called "The Prince of Gurus."[13]

I've given you so many stories about how others became consultants, that I might as well give you mine. I was in the U.S. Air Force where my primary duties were flying. However, after a tour of duty in Vietnam, I was put in charge of the development of personal body armor systems for aircrew in the air force. After leaving the air force, I wrote an article about personal body armor for a magazine called *Ordnance*. Meanwhile, a company that made pilots' helmets and oxygen masks hired me to direct their company's research and development activities. After reading my article, the vice-president of a major aerospace company in California that had developed a lightweight infantry helmet wanted me to help market it. He asked me to lunch and offered me a job on the spot. I explained that I was happy in my current job. He then asked if I would do the work as a consultant, because it did not conflict with the product line of the company I was working for. I got permission from my regular boss, and thus a new consultant was born. I didn't know anything about consulting then. I learned the hard way. I certainly wish *How to Make It Big as a Consultant* was available then!

In this chapter, I've supplied an overview of the entire consulting business. I hope I've opened your eyes to some of the potential—both in the lifestyle of a consultant and in the compensation you might receive—as well as to different consulting areas that you might enjoy. Finally, although I've mentioned stories of several individuals who have become consultants, it's important for you to realize that it is not so important *how* you become a consultant as that you actually *become* one. There are many routes to becoming a consultant, but the bottom line is that becoming a successful consultant is what counts. The process of making it big as a consultant starts in Chapter 2 with your learning how to get clients using direct marketing methods, because they don't always fall into your lap unintentionally as my first client did.

Notes

1. Anne B. Fisher, "The Ever-Bigger Boom in Consulting," *Fortune* (April 24, 1989), p. 113.

2. Gregory J. Miliman, "Taking the Con Out of Consultants," *Business Month* (February 1990), p. 44.

3. Taken from the Arthur Anderson Web site: www.arthuranderson.com, December 9, 2000.

4. *Executive Search Review* (March 1998), www.kornferry.com/leading/html, May 14, 1999.

5. Susan Carey, "Turnaround Consultants Make a Living Fighting Fires," *Wall Street Journal* Interactive Edition, www.collegejournal.com, December 9, 2000.

6. Lois Therrien, "William Brandt: Putting Small Businesses Back in the Black," *Business Week* (August 21, 1989), p. 99.

7. Janet G. Sullivan, "Kick The 'Buts,'" *American Way* (May 1999), p. 58.

8. James E. Svatko, "Working with Consultants," *Small Business Reports* (February 1989), p. 61.

9. Tom Peters quoted in Alan Farnham and Amy Kover, "In Search of Suckers," *Fortune* (October 14, 1996), www.pathfinder.com.

10. Svatho, p. 59.

11. Farnham and Kover; E. Svatho.

12. Howard P. Allen, "Are Management Consultants Worth Their Hire?" *Business Forum* (Fall 1988/Winter 1989), p. 31.

13. Frank Rose, "The Prince of Gurus," *Business Month* (April 1989), p. 67.

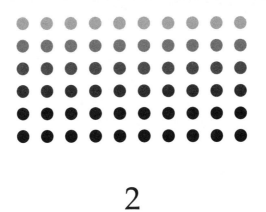

2

HOW TO GET CLIENTS: DIRECT MARKETING METHODS

Marketing is one of the most important areas in consulting, because without marketing you will have no clients and, therefore, no sales. Without sales there can be no consulting practice. No matter how expert you are or how much demand there is for your field of expertise, without clients, the business and the practice cannot exist. In this chapter and the next, you will find both direct and indirect methods of marketing your practice and obtaining clients. Both are important. The indirect method takes longer, but it can greatly expand your practice. To build a dynamic practice, you should integrate both direct and indirect methods into your marketing program. In this chapter, we'll cover the direct methods, and we'll cover the indirect methods in the next chapter. Finally, in Chapter 4, we'll cover a special case: marketing your services to government agencies.

Direct Methods of Marketing

With the following seven direct methods of marketing, you approach potential clients directly and let them know that you are available:

1. Direct mail
2. Cold calls

3. Direct response advertising
4. Directory listings
5. Yellow Pages listings
6. Former employers
7. The Internet

I'll cover the first six methods in this chapter. The Internet is useful to a consultant in so many ways that I'm going to cover this relatively new technology in a separate chapter (Chapter 16). I will also cover brochures in this chapter. Brochures are an important tool in marketing that may be used with any of the above methods.

Direct Mail

With direct mail, you send potential clients a letter or a brochure, or both, advertising your services. An example of a direct mail piece is shown in Figure 2-1. Note that this letter talks directly to the client's needs and tries to avoid sounding pompous or distant. The key is to establish personal communication with the potential client. By suggesting the firm's past accomplishments, the writer implies the kinds of things that can be done for this potential new client in the future. Finally, the piece doesn't leave things hanging; at the very end, the prospective client is asked to call at once for additional information or to set up a consulting appointment.

Direct Mail Letters

Writing direct mail letters for any purpose is an art. Not everyone can write compelling copy for direct mail letters. However, it is not necessary that you be able to do so. There are plenty of good copywriters around who make this their business, and plenty of very successful consultants have their advertising copy written by someone else. The cost may be several hundred to several thousand dollars, but for a good direct mail letter, it is an investment well made.

To find a good copywriter, look for one who already has a track record in direct response work. He or she knows how to write copy for direct results, and that's what you're looking for.

Where can you find someone like this? Try the English or ad-

Figure 2-1. Example of an effective direct mail letter.

William A. Cohen, PhD, Major General, USAFR, Ret.
1556 NORTH SIERRA MADRE VILLA ~ PASADENA, CALIFORNIA 91107
Tel. (323) 343-2972/Fax (626) 794-5998
Email: wcohen@calstatela.edu
Website: www.stuffofheroes.com

January 10, 2002

Mr. James W. West, President
Consolidated International, Inc.
3456 Avenue of the Americas
New York, New York 10158

Dear Mr. West:

"Our productivity increased 35% in less than three months after your one-day 'Stuff of Heroes' workshop for our general managers. This is the most significant increase I've witnessed since I became president." That's what the CEO of the Albright Corporation wrote me after a one-day leadership seminar we gave last month.

I'm writing to you because you may be looking for a way to dramatically increase your company's productivity, or customer service, or sales. I have had the privilege of helping some of the finest organizations in America, such as the Cheesecake Factory Restaurants, Hobart Corporation, FBI, U.S. Marine Corps, National Management Association, Hughes Aircraft Company, the National Association of Accountants, American Business Women's Association, Boeing Aircraft Company, Contel Corporation and many more.

Why do such prestigious organizations engage us? Because, quite frankly, we produce for them. These speeches, seminars, and workshops are not ordinary:

(continues)

Figure 2-1. *(continued)*

• Every presentation is individually tailored especially for the organization and it's individual needs.

• As a university professor of both leadership and marketing, I combine research from both of these disciplines and present it in a dramatic way for maximum impact.

• Backed by hard research, our concepts have been endorsed by world famous individuals like Senator Barry Goldwater; General H. Norman Schwarzkopf; astronaut Frank Borman; Secretary of State Alexander Haig, Jr.; Barry Gordon, the longest serving president of the Screen Actors Guild; management thinker Peter F. Drucker; and CEOs from around the country.

For complete information, call me at my personal number (323) 343-2972.

Sincerely,

William C. Cohen, Ph.D.
Consultant

P.S. I am the only consultant I know of who offers a money back guarantee if you are not satisfied, no questions asked. Call me right away, the number of dates available is limited. You have nothing to lose and everything to gain.

WAC

vertising department of your local college or university. Sometimes you'll find outstanding freelancers masquerading as professors or graduate students. Direct marketing clubs or associations of copywriters can sometimes recommend candidates for you to check out; check for the associations in your telephone book. You can also consult the Yellow Pages; look under "Copywriters." Other good sources are the direct marketing professional magazines: *Direct Marketing, DM News, Target Marketing,* and *Direct.* Their classified and space advertisements contain listings of many freelance copywriters. Your local library either has or can get these publications for you. In all cases, ask for a sample of the copywriter's work before you contract with him or her.

If you don't mind dealing with someone who may not be local, let me recommend Dr. Luther Brock, "The Letter Doctor." Dr. Brock has been in the business of writing direct response copy for years, and his expertise has brought him deserved renown. He can be reached at 2911 Nottingham, Denton, Texas 76201. His telephone number is 940-387-8058.

Writing Your Own Direct Mail Copy

You can write your own direct mail copy, but you must be a competent writer and be willing to work at doing this special type of selling in print.

There are numerous formulas around to help you write direct mail copy. My own formula consists of five steps:

1. Get attention.
2. Develop interest.
3. Demonstrate benefits.
4. Show credibility.
5. Deliver a call to action.

Write in the first person. Write simply, with your potential client in mind. And keep it personal. Define your target audience exactly. Focus on that individual reader as you write your copy.

Let's say you are consultant John Smith. We'll create a direct mail piece, going through it step-by-step.

Getting attention. First, you want to get attention. You do this with a headline. However, usually it isn't written as a headline. Instead make it the first paragraph in your letter. It is an extremely important paragraph because it must "hook" your prospective client instantly. If it fails to do this, your letter goes right into the trash can unread.

To construct this paragraph, try to think of the most important thing you've done that would be important to your target audience. Let's say you're a marketing consultant specializing in increasing sales for small- to medium-size companies. Think through the assignments you've had and what happened as a result of your work. Look for five to ten great accomplishments and then pick the most important. If you are a new consultant, you might consider what you did while working for someone else. It really doesn't matter whether these accomplishments were achieved for a client or a boss or even while working for no pay in a volunteer organization. What is critical is that good results came about due to your work.

Finally, craft your attention getter. Keep reworking the paragraph to minimize the number and complexity of words and maximize the dramatic effect.

Let's say you finally come up with the following:

A few weeks ago, a client called to thank me. He's the president of a $5 million export company. The sales plan I put into effect for him caused his sales to increase by 541 percent in two months. And he told me that this increase in sales came with no increase in costs. No wonder he was so excited!

Can you imagine the president of a small company throwing that letter away without reading further? I can't. Not if it's written on high-quality bond paper with an impressive letterhead, and the letter is addressed to him or her by name. Every company of that size wants to increase sales. If you've increased a similar company's sales by 541 percent at no cost increase in such a short time, maybe you can do the same for the prospect's company. He or she would have to be a fool not to at least read further.

Now that you have your prospective client's attention, develop his or her interest.

Developing interest and demonstrating benefits. You can develop interest and demonstrate benefits at the same time. All you need to do is state the reason for your letter and list some more of your accomplishments from the five to ten that you selected earlier.

I am writing to you because I am a marketing consultant specializing in increasing sales for companies like yours. If you are interested in increasing your company's sales dramatically at low cost, you may be interested in some other things I have done:

- Trained 7 salespeople of a $20 million clothing manufacturing company. Their sales increased by an average of 46.3 percent after 6 months.
- Conducted a marketing audit for a $2 million company making small industrial parts. This company increased its sales by $441,000 the first year and cut selling costs by 4 percent at the same time.
- Developed and helped implement a marketing plan for a new product for a $75 million pharmaceutical company. First-year sales were $11 million—twice that of new products introduced in the past.
- Created a sales and promotional plan for a start-up newsletter for a small publishing company. The newsletter was profitable after only 8 months. Second-year profit objectives set prior to my plan were exceeded by 111 percent.

Note that there are few adjectives but a great many numbers. Numbers add credibility as you develop interest and show your prospective client some of the benefits he or she could receive. Also note that you use Arabic numerals, not words. You're not looking for an *A* in English. You want an *A* in response so you can turn prospects into clients. Arabic numbers let your figures really stand out. These accomplishments are like your attention-getting paragraph. Your prospective client knows that if you can do these kinds of things for other organizations, you can probably do similar things for his or hers.

Showing credibility. Up to now, everything you've stated consists only of *your* words. It's important to have a third party confirm your abilities. The best way I've found is to quote from letters from clients and former clients or from former bosses if you are a new consultant. After you have been a consultant for a while, you're going to get letters of thanks. Then all you need to do is ask if you can quote the writer in your sales literature. But how do you get endorsements when you are just starting out? The best way is simply to ask for them.

If you've done a good job for someone, telephone and ask him what he thought about your work. Was he happy with the results? Did anything good happen? If your client was pleased, ask if he'd be willing to write a letter from which you can quote. You might even offer to supply ideas and figures that would help him write it. Once you collect four or five good quotes, you are ready to confirm your credibility in your sales letter.

Here is what some of my clients have said about my work:

John Smith is the World's Best Consultant for small- and medium-size companies.—*George Able,* president, ABC Service Company.

You tripled my sales in three months and saved my company.—*Hugo Mondesto,* president, Q. T. Limousine Service.

Your sales training really did wonders. Now all of my salespeople are superstars.—*Joe Fine,* The Cutting Edge, Inc.

In some cases, you may not be able to get permission to extract from a letter for your direct mail. In that case, use initials only and disguise the company name like this:

The ROI for your services was 500 percent plus. Thanks. —*A. A.* president, a medium-size travel agency.

Another way of showing credibility is with a brief statement of your educational and technical or consultant experiences:

I have a B.S. in engineering from California State University at Los Angeles and an MBA from the University of Michigan. I

have managed marketing activities and consulted in marketing for twelve years.

Delivering a call to action. **Research has demonstrated conclu-**
sively that if your prospective client doesn't act immediately, he or
she will probably never act. So the final part of your direct mail
letter should be a call for immediate action. To do this, be very clear
and explicit about what you want your prospective client to do.
Usually you'd like him or her to call or write you to set up a face-to-
face interview. You can call your prospective client to action like this:

> Please call or write me at no cost or obligation for a face-to-
> face interview so you can judge for yourself whether I can help
> you. One cautionary note: Please call or write immediately.
> The majority of the work I do is done by me personally; I be-
> lieve that's one of the secrets of my success. But I get booked
> early. Even if your ideas are not firmed up yet, I recommend
> calling or writing now. That way it is more likely that I will
> have the time available to help you.

I recommend using a P.S. as well. The reason is that a P.S. is
almost always read. Some people read the P.S. even before they
read the rest of the letter. Use the P.S. to stimulate the action you
want. If you can, it helps to offer something free in return for action:

> P.S. I have prepared a special booklet, *How to Get the Most Out*
> *of Marketing Consultants*, for my clients. If you call or write, I
> will send you a copy with my compliments, while they last.

The free offer and the "while they last" provide additional
incentives for your prospective client to respond right away.

Of course there are many ways of writing a direct mail letter
to get clients. To help you, I recommend the following books:

- *The Copywriter's Handbook: A Step-by-Step Guide to Writing*
  Copy That Sells by Robert W. Bly (Henry Holt)
- *Persuading on Paper: The Complete Guide to Writing Copy That*
  Pulls in Business by Marcia Yudkin (Plume)

Locating the Right Mailing List

Producing your letter, your brochure, and their first-class envelope is not inexpensive. You can expect to spend as much as fifty cents or more including postage to get each direct mail package to a potential client. Therefore, you do not want to waste your mailing on individuals who have only a slight chance of being interested in your services. You want to reach those who are real potential customers, who have the authority to hire you and would probably be interested in what you have to offer.

Some sources of help are those professionals who handle mailing lists: list brokers, managers, or compilers. These experts can be found in most Yellow Pages under the heading "Mailing Lists." They will discuss your needs with you and help you rent lists of potential clients interested in the particular services you offer. Usually you pay nothing for this advice on lists. The list broker gets paid a commission from the list owner when you rent the lists.

If you are located in a small-size town, the potential size of your market, depending on your specialty, may be so small that a direct mail campaign is not advisable. On the other hand, you could do a direct mail campaign with the idea of promoting a national or international business. This, of course, may require travel on your part, unless you consult through the mail or by telephone, both of which are possible.

Large firms spend a lot of money on this effort, as much as $100,000 a year on their direct mail campaigns. These companies, with client lists numbering in the thousands, stay in touch by mailing out multiple first-class packages (each containing a letter, a card, and a small brochure) in the span of a single year. But even a response rate of 1 to 2 percent can result in millions of sales.

If you would like to receive additional information or catalogs of lists, here are some representative companies to contact:

America List Counsel, 88 Orchard Road, CN-5219, Princeton, N.J. 08543 (toll-free: 1-800-ALC-LIST)
America on the Move, 1889 Palmer Avenue, Suite 3, Larchmont, N.Y. 10538 (toll-free: 1-800-752-5083)
American Business Information, 5711 South 86th Circle, P.O.

Box 27347, Omaha, Nebr. 68127-0347 (toll-free: 1-800-249-6902)

Best Mailing Lists, Inc., 7505 East Tanque Verde Road, Tucson, Ariz. 85715 (toll-free: 1-800-692-2378)

The Dartnell Corporation, 4660 North Ravenwood Avenue, Chicago, Ill. 60640 (toll-free: 1-800-621-5463)

Dependable Lists, Inc., 1450 East American Lane, Suite 1545, Schaumburg, Ill. 60173 (toll free: 1-800-532-3638)

The Destination Group, Inc., 2137 Espey Court, Suites 1 & 2, Crofton, Md. 21114-2487 (toll free: 1-888-405-5225)

Dun and Bradstreet, One Diamond Hill Road, Murray Hill, N.J. 07974 (toll-free: 1-800-234-3867)

Dunhill International List, Inc., 1951 19th Street, NW, Boca Raton, Fla. 33064 (toll-free: 1-800-386-4455)

WorldData, 3000 North Military Trail, Boca Raton, Fla. 33431-6375 (toll-free: 1-800-331-8102)

Cold Calls

Cold calls are those made to prospects with whom you have had no prior contact. This method can be extremely effective in obtaining clients. However, it is time-consuming, and it involves significant rejection, which you must learn to cope with if you are to use this method.

Let's say you've decided to devote a single day to obtaining clients through cold calls. That means you should make from twenty-five to thirty actual contacts with individuals who have the authority to hire you. If even half this number retained your services, you would soon be extremely wealthy from consulting. As a matter of fact, you would have more consulting work than you could possibly handle. But the reality is that if one of these calls leads to a one-time engagement worth $3,000 to $5,000, the day has been well worth your time. If you consider that this is a satisfied client who will hire you again and again, this single success out of many calls was really worthwhile. However, twenty-five to thirty calls with one success usually means twenty-four to twenty-nine rejections, some of which will be rude and abrupt. Therefore, if you wish to use cold calling, you must train yourself to be prepared for the rejection that accompanies its use.

You can maximize your success in using the cold-call method by doing the following:

1. *Write out exactly what you want to say ahead of time.* Usually you should follow the outline of a good direct mail letter. That is, you should speak about benefits to your potential client and sell yourself by describing past accomplishments. (These could be things you did while employed full-time for someone else. The important thing is that you were the one responsible and actually did whatever it is you claim.) While planning what you are going to say, never forget that the object is not to make a sale over the phone, which is almost impossible to accomplish, but to get a face-to-face interview in which you can close the sale. (I show you how to do that in Chapter 5.) So now you know how to tell when you've had a successful cold call: It always ends with an appointment for a face-to-face interview.

2. *Use creative ways to get around the secretary.* One of the most bothersome aspects about the cold-call method is that frequently executives who may wish to hire you have secretaries in place between you and them. Part of a secretary's job is to screen out job seekers and those wanting to sell something to the boss. Therefore, it is essential that you get through the secretary. One method is simply to avoid the secretary altogether. Call before 8:00 A.M. or after 5:00 P.M., and chances are the manager will answer the call directly. Another technique is to identify yourself by name and ask for the individual you wish to speak with, using his or her full name. If you do not have this name, call the company and ask the receptionist for the individual's full name, not just Mr. Smith but Don Smith. When the receptionist connects you with his secretary, say firmly, "This is Jane Black for Don Smith. Would you connect me please?" Or you can say, "This is Jane Black, president of the XYZ Consulting Group, for Don Smith. Would you connect me please?" If the secretary asks the nature of your call, say that it is a private business matter. If he or she refuses to connect you without having this information, ask the secretary to forward the information to the boss and leave your number for him to call you back. The chances of getting through are better this way than if you say that you are calling to see if Mr. Smith is interested in hiring you as a consultant.

3. *Combine your calls with a direct mail campaign.* This one-two combination punch can work very well. Do the direct mail campaign first, and then wait several weeks. This gives the executive time to call you directly if he or she wishes, and you will have a greater chance of setting up an interview. After several weeks have gone by, you cold-call those who have not responded to your mailing. Now if the secretary asks the reason for the call, you can say that it has to do with a letter you wrote previously to Don Smith. If you're wondering whether to include in the letter a statement that you will call, my recommendation is not to do so. For one thing, if you indicate that you will call, the executive who may otherwise have called may not. It's always much better if he or she calls you rather than the other way around. Second, consulting is a little unstable. You can have little to do for a period and then get extremely busy with contracted work. If this happens, you may delay calling when it is expected and you could lose the sale. The direct mail campaign, combined with a cold-call follow-up, works well because some executives who desperately need your services may not realize it from your letter. In a personal conversation, they may recognize that you can fulfill their need and will make an appointment for an interview.

Direct Response Space Advertising

Until fairly recently, the advertising of consulting services was not particularly common. Today, a number of different types of consultants are using it successfully. Executive search consultants, for instance, advertise in magazines or trade journals in their areas of specialty. Because potential clients in certain industries prefer to deal with specialists, these ads are often successful. However, advertisements for other consulting services are less successful; some are even prohibited by professional consulting associations. Consultants tend to be equated with attorneys and doctors in terms of confidentiality and standards of professionalism. Because the ethics codes of these two professions have only recently permitted advertising, it is no wonder that the same has been generally true for consulting.

However, depending on the type of services you offer, advertising may be effective and acceptable. If you decide to advertise, it is important that the ad be well written, which means written with your potential clients in mind. Also, be certain to place your ad in a medium likely to be read by your target audience. Don't be fooled by the total number of people reached by your ad. It is only likely clients who count. For this reason, don't advertise in your local newspaper unless everyone in the general population is a potential client for the services you offer.

Advertising is expensive. Further, learning how to write the copy that makes such advertising work is not easy. The type of advertising that you are interested in is *direct response space advertising*. Like a direct mail letter or cold calling by telephone, this type of advertising is intended to bring a direct response. At the very least, such an ad should result in inquiries that will lead to consulting engagements.

Even some professional writers cannot write this kind of copy. The copy must be so compelling that prospective clients needing your services would be foolish not to contact you. Most such advertisements use the AIDA formula—attention, interest, desire, and action. A dramatic headline is used to attract people's attention. Their interest is immediately aroused in the lead-in paragraphs through the statement of specific benefit. Additional benefits are stated and talked about until their desire to respond to the ad is at a peak. At this point, the ad calls on them to respond at once by taking specific action. Figure 2-2 shows an example of an effective direct response ad.

Here are three books that may help:

- *Building* a *Mail Order Business: A Complete Manual for Success*, 4th ed., by William A. Cohen (John Wiley & Sons)
- *How to Write a Good Advertisement* by Victor O. Schwab (Wilshire Book Co.).
- *Tested Advertising Methods*, 4th ed., by John Caples (Prentice Hall)

Directory Listings

There are many directories that list consultants and the particular services they provide. Some are free; some charge for listings. Usually this method of advertising is not very effective for a simple rea-

Figure 2-2. Example of an effective direct response ad.

AN OVERVIEW OF
SALES AND MARKETING CONSULTING
WITH STEVEN WEST AND HIS GROUP

There are many occasions in which the complexity or importance of a problem or a situation mandates the use of an outside consultant.

Outside consultants maintain a detached objectivity. They don't get emotionally involved in the internal politics or fixed way of thinking of the past. Consultants bring with them fresh ideas. They are emissaries of new information. Often, they will cross-pollinate ideas between clients and act as a conduit for new technology. Consultants bring with them specialized talent. This highly specialized talent can be hired to solve a particular problem, define a particular opportunity and then that assignment can be completed. Consultants become part-time, pro tempore members of your staff. They give you depth and allow you to maintain a lean and mean payroll. And consultants will often work on a fixed fee basis, so that you know exactly what your costs will be. There are no guesses and no equivocation.

Steven West and the New York Marketing Group are considered to be the world's leading sales and marketing consultants. Their 7 operating divisions can bring sharpness of focus and expertise to bear upon unique and complex problems at your company. They combine a no-nonsense, real-life experience with the most sophisticated cutting-edge technology. Their unique blending of a pragmatic, straight-line thinking, coupled with advanced strategies and tactics in sales and marketing, are fitted to your company's needs to find solutions to problems. But their solutions are focused on reality—not in graphs-charts-philosophies-models.

New York Marketing Group and its affiliates are the largest private sales and marketing consulting company in the world. More than 50 specialists each focus in on specific areas of sales and marketing consultation. Under the direction and leadership of Steven West, this group can marshal its resources to assist you in solving your unique corporate problems.

More than 1/8 of the Fortune 500 companies and half of America's largest banks utilize Steven West and his associates to help solve their unique consulting problems. Companies such as Revlon, Sears, Wang, Citicorp, Manufacturers Hanover, Data General, GTE, Nynex Telephone Company, and Bell South are just a few of the clients who utilize Steven West's services.

Many smaller companies whose names, no doubt, would mean nothing to you, are active users of Steven West and his company's services. You need not be a multi-billion dollar, multi-national company to take advantage of the expertise of this group.

Fees, seniority, and experience level can be adjusted to suit your respective budgets. This group can readily undertake projects in the millions of dollars. Conversely, projects of a few thousand dollars are welcome with the same level of enthusiasm.

Whether your requirements are for a few days of consultation, or an in-depth, on-going relationship, Steven West and his associates will be happy to explore working with your company.

A Word of Caution—The New York Marketing Group and Steven West will not accept any assignments that they feel would not be fruitful for their clients. If what you have in mind is not going to work, or if there is a probability that it is unlikely to work, your project will not be accepted.

Recently, a top executive at Baush & Lomb said, "In talking to my friends in the business community, what sets aside Steven West and his group from all other sales and marketing consultants, is their batting average. 96% of the time they will find the solution that you are looking for. If they don't think that you are barking up the right tree, they'll politely reject the assignment." This is professionalism in its ultimate development. For information call:

(718) 479-3700

There are 7 specialized areas of consultation in which you can utilize Steven West and his group.
THE NEW YORK MARKETING GROUP
61-47 188th Street
Fresh Meadows, NY 11365

Courtesy of The New York Marketing Group.

son: Few potential clients use directories when seeking consultants. As a test, I once paid $300 to be listed in one of these directories. Over the period of a year, I received numerous letters about my listing, but every single one was from someone seeking to sell *me* something! Directory listings are not recommended unless the listing is free. Here's one on the Internet that's free. Let me know whether it works for you: http://www.expert-market.com/index.html.

Yellow Pages Listings

Listings in the Yellow Pages of your telephone book may be effective for certain types of consulting practices. Clients who have never used a consultant before may turn to the Yellow Pages in search of services. If you decide to advertise this way, it is important that you buy a large ad. The psychology of this is simple: A larger ad will attract readership over a competitor's smaller ad. Second, many people assume that a large ad is placed by a large company and a small ad by a small company. A large advertisement for a small business may actually outpull a small ad placed by a multibillion-dollar organization. Try such an ad for one year. If it brings in clients, continue to use it. If not, simply maintain a listing in the Yellow Pages, without an ad.

Former Employers

Many consultants get their initial cash flow going by selling their services to former employers. They are able to do this because no matter what the circumstances of your departure (unless you were fired for incompetence) you have something to offer that company in expertise and experience. Retaining you as a consultant allows your former employer to use that expertise without the large overhead of an annual salary and benefits, even though as a consultant, you may get a much higher hourly rate than when you were an employee. A former employer may also wish to hire you simply to ensure that you will not go to work for a competitor, either as a consultant or as a full-time employee. In any case, it is certainly worth exploring. Approach your former employer, explain that you are now going into full-time consulting and that you would be happy to do for the company what you did in the past, as well as other related work.

Brochures

The basic purpose of any brochure is, first, to advertise your type of work and, second, to convince the reader that you are the most capable individual available to do this work. Therefore, if you are going to develop your own brochure, write it to answer two questions: "What is it that I do?" and "Why am I the best?" Answering these questions may require that your brochure have different sections. Sections might include:

o Descriptions of the kind of work you do.
o Specific examples of problems you have solved for clients in the past, along with benefits they have accrued from using your services.
o Reasons why your services are better than those offered by competitors.
o Your experience, background, and special qualifications that make you unique.
o A list of previous clients (if available).
o Testimonials from previous clients. As mentioned earlier, if you haven't done any consulting previously, you can write down accomplishments that you attained when you were an employee working for someone else. As long as these accomplishments were in your area of consulting expertise and benefited whomever you were working for at the time, it is unimportant whether the beneficiary was an employer or a client.

There are a number of good books available to help you in preparing your own brochure. Here are a few:

o *Better Brochures, Catalogs, and Mailing Pieces* by Jane Maas (St. Martin's Press)
o *Brochures That Work* by David E. Carter (Hearst Books International)

○ *Creating Brochures & Booklets (Graphic Design Basics)* by Val Adkins (Northlight Books)

Designing Your Brochure

Before you even begin to design your brochure, decide what it is supposed to do and who your target market is. Consultant brochures can have very different objectives. One consultant whose area was strategic planning wanted her brochure to continually remind her clients and prospective clients of her expertise. Her brochure was a twenty-page manual on strategic planning printed on glossy paper. It cost a fortune, but she maintained that it was well worth the investment.

Another consultant I knew produced a multicolor glossy brochure with numerous photos. It cost him $20,000 for 1,000 copies. He told me that most of his prospective clients barely looked at his brochure and few read any of it. Yet he was entirely satisfied. His consulting practice was in a highly technical area of composites and composite structures. The brochure demonstrated conclusively that he was a force in the industry, and he said that the brochure enabled him to capture significant business that he previously could not obtain.

However, most of us want something simple that we can use with our direct mail letter or get to prospective clients in other ways. We would like a brochure that will help us get in the door for a face-to-face interview or reinforce our capability and help close the sale of the engagement during or after the interview.

The target market is also important. An expensive brochure says that you are high priced. That's fine if your market has the money. That's why the big consulting houses have fancy, expensive brochures. But if your clients are small businesses and your pricing is anything but high, you may scare off prospective clients.

Deciding on the objective for your brochure as well as your target market will help you to decide on type of printing, paper, size, and other factors. It will also help you to decide what should go in your brochure.

The basic contents of a brochure include who you are, what you do, how you work, what you've done, and how to contact you. Who you are can be handled by your qualifications and a photo. I like to include a photo because it lets people know there is a real person behind the name. A list of the kinds of things you do gives your prospective clients some idea of how they can profit from using you. How you work can be in the form of a case history of an assignment or just a description of your method of operation from initial meeting to assignment completion. In the section on what you've done, you can list your accomplishments as described for your direct mail letter. Just remember to use few adjectives but lots of numbers, dollar figures, and percentages. You can also include a client list and a page with quotes regarding your performance, as in your direct mail letter. Finally, make certain you include your address and phone number.

Once you know what your brochure is going to contain and its approximate size, you can begin to work out a rough layout. It is important to do this before you begin to write copy. If you have only the equivalent of two sides of an $8^1/2$- by 11-inch sheet of paper, there may not be sufficient space for everything you want to include. Do a rough layout and you'll know.

Only after the layout is done should you begin to write copy. As with direct mail, you can get a professional designer and copywriter to do all of this for you—or you can do it on your own. In the old days, I did everything myself except the final typesetting. But nowadays, with the numerous computer software programs available, you can probably do everything yourself and produce a very professional brochure.

Your direct mail letter should accompany your brochure. The format of your brochure could be anything from a simple one-page flier to a slick, many-page booklet. Small consulting operations often get good results with a modest brochure, perhaps an $8^1/2$- by 11-inch sheet folded twice, that describes the background of the company, the type of work it does, and the qualifications of the principal or principals. Many of the very large firms produce quite elaborate brochures covering all aspects of their practices, which are designed to impress clients with the stature, size, and accomplishments of the firms simply by the brochures themselves.

I have also included an example of one of my own current brochures in Appendix B. In recent years, the emphasis of my work has been on my speeches, seminars, and workshops. So this brochure is really a media kit. It emphasizes my background for leader development. It is a folder, the front and inside pockets of which you can see in Appendix B. The front describes what I offer. Inside, on both sides of the folder, are pockets for inserting additional material. In the left folder pocket, I put articles about me, or that I have written, which have appeared in newspapers or magazines. In the right pocket, I put a description of my background, the various services I offer, letters I have received from satisfied clients, a list of my clients, and a black-and-white photograph.

What I particularly like about this brochure is that I did everything on my computer using desktop publishing. So my brochure is never outdated, nor do I waste money in printing up copies that are never used.

It's important to remember that clients will not automatically come to you. You must market your consulting service. But if you do this well, in accordance with the guidelines in this and the next two chapters, you will soon build a successful consulting practice. In Chapter 3, we'll look at indirect methods of marketing your consulting practice.

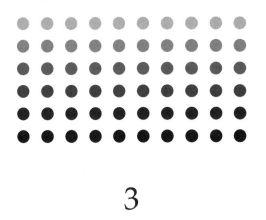

3

HOW TO GET CLIENTS: INDIRECT MARKETING METHODS

Indirect selling methods must be a significant part of your overall marketing program. They will usually not bring in instant clients as can direct marketing methods. However, over the long term, the benefits of indirect methods are considerable. Many times you are so busy consulting that you may forget about your marketing. That's when the benefits of indirect methods are really clear, because they go on working even when you may have let the marketing part of your business slip. So make no mistake about it, indirect methods may not work instantaneously, but they are necessary for any consulting practice.

The Basic Indirect Methods of Marketing

Indirect methods of getting clients include:

1. Speaking before groups
2. Sending out newsletters
3. Joining and being active in professional associations
4. Joining and being active in social organizations
5. Writing articles
6. Writing a book
7. Writing letters to the editor
8. Teaching a course

    9. Giving seminars
   10. Distributing publicity releases
   11. Exchanging information, leads, and referrals with non-competing consultants

Let's look at each of these in more detail.

Speaking before Groups

Speaking in public is an excellent way of building your consulting practice. In your community, there are probably numerous groups that use guest speakers, sometimes on a monthly or even a weekly basis. If the type of consulting you do is something associated with their needs and is of interest to members of these groups, you can benefit from speaking to them.

Dr. Pedro Chan, an immigrant from Macao, China, used this method to build his acupuncture consultancy for physicians. You can do the same thing. Simply pick a topic having to do with the services you offer, whether it's tax consulting, starting a new business, direct response marketing, or some other subject of potential interest. Then prepare a forty-five-minute talk that would be of interest and value to your audience. If you consult in direct marketing, you could speak on the topic, "Five Ways to Increase Direct Mail Response." If you consult in personnel matters, you might choose "How to Decrease Personnel Turnover" as your topic.

Now go to your telephone book, and look for local organizations that appear to have meetings and therefore may use guest speakers. Call and ask to speak to the program chair. Explain what you have to offer and how the membership can benefit from your presentation.

After your speech, let your listeners know how to contact you for additional information. A business card is good, but a prepared handout, with useful information pertaining to your presentation together with your telephone number and address, is even better. In the bio that you supply to the organization (which will be used to promote your appearance and to introduce you when you speak), make certain to include the fact that you are a consultant. In some cases, you will actually get paid for your presentation, but this is only a bonus. Your major objective is to gain exposure and eventually get additional clients.

Three books that will help you are:

- *101 Secrets of Highly Effective Speakers: Controlling Fear, Commanding Attention* by Caryl Rae Krannich (Impact Publishing)
- *Inspire Any Audience* by Tony Jeary (Trophy Publishing)
- *Speak and Grow Rich* by Dottie Walters and Lilly Walters (Prentice Hall)

You may also want to join the National Speakers Association and participate in their many programs for helping speakers. The association even has a professional emphasis group for consultants. For membership information, contact the National Speakers Association, 1500 South Priest Drive, Tempe, Arizona 85281 (tel.: 602-968-2552).

In the front of this book, you will see "Cohen's Maxims." This is one of many handouts that I give my attendees at many of my courses and seminars.

Sending Out Newsletters

The way to use a newsletter to get clients is not simply to dispense news but to dispense news of interest and value to potential clients and to remind those that have already been your clients that you are still around. Every time a client or potential client receives one of these newsletters with your name on it, he or she thinks of you. One method is to use newsletters written by someone else. These newsletters may be either printer or online. They may be prepared especially for you or syndicated newsletters that can be mailed out with your firm's name imprinted on each copy. Here are a couple organizations that can provide this service:

- Company Newsletters, 18593 Jasper Way, Lakeville, Minn. 55044-9681 (tel.: 612-892-6943; Web site: www.company newsletters.com)
- Newsletter Only Co., 4418 Meridian Avenue, N, Suite C, Se-

attle, Wash. 98103 (tel.: 206-634-3031; e-mail: Newsonly@
MSN.com)
○ NF Communications, Inc., 1700 North Broadway, Suite 405,
Walnut Creek, CA 94596 (tel.: (800) 980-0192; Web site: www.
ntcom.com)

A sample of a generic or private label newsletter from NF
Communications, Inc. is shown in Figure 3-1. Of course, you can
write your own newsletter with specialized information pertaining
directly to services you offer. It doesn't have to be elaborate; you
can type a master directly onto your business letterhead and have
it reproduced by a quick printing service. If the material is of value
to your readers, you can be sure it will increase your credibility
and help to build your practice.

A sample of one of my own newsletters is shown in Figure
3-2. Note how useful information and promotional materials are
combined.

Figure 3-3 is a newsletter published by consultant Dr. Robert
Swette. His excellent newsletter has helped build his popular consulting practice, and I don't mind a bit that he reviews one of my
books in this issue.

If you'd like to attend a seminar on the editing, design, and
production of newsletters, or want consulting help with your newsletter, contact Put It In Writing, 1517 Buckeye Court, Pinole, California 94564, tel.: 510-724-9507, e-mail: jeff@put-it-in-writing.
com.

See also:

○ *Home-Based Newsletter Publishing: A Success Guide for Entre-*
  preneurs by William J. Bond (McGraw-Hill)
○ *Marketing with Newsletters: How to Boost Sales, Add Members &*
  Raise Funds with a Printed, Faxed, or Web-Site Newsletter by
  Elaine Floyd (EF Communications)
○ *Producing a First-Class Newsletter: A Guide to Planning, Writ-*
  ing, Editing, Designing, Photography, Production, and Printing
  by Barbara A. Fanson (Self-Counsel Press)

Let me tell you a story about effective use of a newsletter. I
was the head of a rapidly growing organization and had been hiring

Figure 3-1. Example of a generic newsletter.

Your Picture Here!

Your Name Here.

Larry Klein,
Publisher

SeniorFinances

SPECIALIZING IN INVESTMENT MANAGEMENT AND ASSET PROTECTION
For Those Age 55 and Better
August 1999

It Used to Be Bonds For Income But Take a Look at This Idea

Historically, if you desired income, you purchased income investments such as bonds or preferred shares. However, the data suggests that stocks may be a better source of income. Although most stocks do not have very significant dividends (the average dividend on the S&P 500 stands at 1.28%), their appreciation over time can be used as a substantial source of income.

A study published in the AAII Journal (February 1998) indicated that a portfolio heavier in stocks provided a better chance of a retiree meeting their income needs than a portfolio of bonds.

For the period analyzed of 1926 to 1995, the data showed that if an investor wanted to draw 7% annually on their portfolio for 20 years after retiring, a 100% bond portfolio would have been successful in delivering the necessary income only 47% of the time. On the other hand, a portfolio of stocks would have been successful at delivering the required income 92% of the time.

If we look at the same data but only for the period since World War II, stocks show up even better than bonds as a retirement income source. Stocks would have been successful 100% of the time in producing a 7% annual income while bonds would have been successful only 42% of time.

The best part about this study is that it takes into account that stocks can be more volatile than bonds. The study accounted for the fact that a retiree would need to take their 7% income even in years when their portfolio was declining in value and thus tests these hypothetical portfolios under a real life scenario.

If you've been staying away from the stock market, worrying that it's "too high" and relying on income investments to supply your retirement income, this article suggests that you are taking the more financially risky path. I know that stocks seem more risky because many investors focus on the *short term.* But when you look at the *long term*

as this article does, you can more clearly see that bonds have been the more risky income alternatives as they *have failed to deliver a 7% income more than half of the time.*

If you'd like details on how to design a stock portfolio that has provided an investor's income needs comfortably at 8% annually for the past 25 years, please check off the attached coupon.

Health-adjusted SPIAs—Poor Health Can Be a Factor in Producing More Income

There's a type of annuity that pays you more if your health profile is not good. This may sound strange, but here's how it works:

SPIA, which stands for Single Premium Immediate Annuity, has long been a popular investment for obtaining a fixed income which cannot be outlived. With the life option, a SPIA pays you a fixed monthly income for life. Insurance companies calculate the size of your monthly payment based on standard life expectancy tables. Once calculated at the beginning, you continue to receive the same monthly amount, regardless of how long you live. It's almost like getting a second social security check.

Some companies take into account your individual health condition and use that information to calculate your life expectancy. If your health records indicate conditions that could lower your life expectancy, this is factored into the monthly payment you receive and increases the monthly payment. You then receive this fixed monthly amount no matter how long you live.

Take this hypothetical example. A man age 70 decides to obtain a SPIA. He deposits a $100,000 premium and based on his standard life expectancy of 16 years, his monthly payment is $871.05 (a 10.4% annual payout rate). He will receive this fixed monthly amount regardless of how long he lives.

Your Office Address and Phone Number Here

(continues)

Figure 3-1. *(continued)*

However, if he has a negative health profile and the insurance companies calculate his life expectancy at only 10 years, his monthly payment will jump to $1393.68. Because of the negative health history, this annuitant receives more income.

SPIAs have been most popular with single individuals who are not concerned with leaving an inheritance. That's because, once the initial premium is paid, the SPIA cannot be surrendered for value. Rather, you receive a fixed monthly income for life. For those people who like the idea of increasing their monthly income and do want to leave funds to heirs, remember that you would use only a part of your assets for a SPIA and other assets can be designated for heirs.

If you would like a quote on how much monthly income you could get from a SPIA, complete the attached coupon. If you have poor health history, please call to make an appointment, as we will need your written permission to release this information to insurance companies in order to obtain quotations.

Additionally, if you've been relying on municipal bonds for tax sheltered income, please call for an appointment and we'll show you how some previous mini-bond investors use SPIAs to increase their monthly tax sheltered income.

What About Asia (and Other Investor Mistakes)?

In the October 1998 issue of this newsletter I wrote an article explaining the difference between the rich and the not-as-rich. The not-so-rich people tend to focus on the next few days or weeks, while wealthier people tend to have much longer time horizons. They invest in real estate and stocks and wait until they rise.

Similarly, it's my observation that investors with short time horizons do not do as well. They tend to buy items when popular (like Internet stocks) and sell items that are unpopular. I suggest rather that buying low and selling high is a much better method of making money. In this light, I wrote in October of 1998,

"If you were to adopt such a strategy with some of your funds, where would you put money to work now? Into Asia, into gold, into beat-up technology stocks and into Eastern Europe."

In fact, for the first part of 1999, the best performing mutual funds according to CDA/Weisenberger

were emerging growth funds, reflecting rapid increases of stock prices in Asia and Eastern Europe (Emerging Market Equity 33.23). The second best sector was technology/communications (up 30.7%). Please note that the price of gold is still very weak and this "buy low sell high strategy" is not for someone with a short time horizon and is not guaranteed to produce profits.

But these results do indicate as they have many times in the past, that if you listen to the current news of the day, you're likely to make poor investment decisions. In fact, a recent example would be the rising of interest rates. Many investors believe or have been taught that when interest rates rise, stocks go down. In fact, the Dow Jones average hit a new high after the recent increase in interest rates by the Federal Reserve. This provides yet another lesson not to invest based on today's news.

If you like the idea of a buy low/sell high system, on which we base our client's portfolios, we're happy to show you how to use a system to do that. Not only have we found it more lucrative, but it frees up the time you otherwise waste listening to the latest forecast on CNBC, CNN or your other favorite financial show.

Check off the coupon for details.

Space for your individual announcement or paste in another article from our web-based article database accessible by newsletter subscribers

Your Office Address and Phone Number Here

Figure 3-2. Example of a newsletter promoting consulting seminars.

The Stuff of Heroes Newsletter

Publisher, William A. Cohen, PhD

Editor-In-Chief, Lan Banh

Volume 1   Special Issue 3   *December 1998*

"Stuff of Heroes" Biggest Business Book Signing Ever, Says Oldest California Bookstore

Vromans Bookstore in Pasadena is the oldest bookstore in Southern California. On Saturday, October 10th, Dr. Cohen set a new record when he autographed his new book, *The Stuff of Heroes: The Eight Universal Laws of Leadership* (Longstreet Press). Roughly 150 Vromans' customers crowded the store to participate in an autograph signing session unlike any other. Linda Urban, Special Events Manager, said, "This is the largest business book signing we have ever had at Vromans. For a business book, we feel lucky to get twenty people to come in."

A three-time Emmy award nominee by the name of Michael Teilman conducted the ceremonies like a Hollywood production. Teilman, who is currently the Director of the Hollywood Museum, is also a full colonel in the Army Reserve. As you will see, this fact was significant. Cohen received acknowledgments, congratulations, and awards from Governor of California Pete Wilson, Mayor of Los Angeles Richard Riordan, and other well-known politicians. We should also note that there was a singer and guitarist, and about 15 former Russian officers, complete with accents and medals. It was unclear whether more than one or two spoke English, but they all seemed quite enthusiastic and were eager to have their pictures taken with the author. It turns out all were members of an organization called Russian War Veterans of World War II in Los Angeles, for which Cohen had once been a guest speaker with the help of a translator.

Cohen's book is supposed to be about business leadership, but he claims there is much more to it because of the message. He got his data by researching what he says is the most challenging of leadership environments . . . in which both followers and leaders would rather be somewhere else: battle. Seemingly to prove that he knew what he was talking about, Cohen led his own effort to promote the signing. Even Linda Urban of Vromans Bookstore said, "For a business book, we usually get so few customers that we really don't even like to have them anymore."

What is this message which seems to attract so much support for Cohen's book? I asked his campaign manager, Misty Iwasu. "Dr. Cohen has touched a nerve with *The Stuff of Heroes*," she said. "He's got us looking at leadership in a different way, not for the benefit of the leader, but for the benefit of the followers and the organization." According to Dr. Cohen, most of us are in leadership roles whether we like it or not. This includes a parent, salesperson, coach, or teacher. The eight universal laws enable us to succeed in these roles. Who can argue with the campaign manager or the author of the book that drew the biggest audience in history at the oldest bookstore in California?

THE STUFF OF HEROES NEWSLETTER CONTENTS . . .

(continues)

Figure 3-2. *(continued)*

From the Editor . . .
How a Chef Taught Me a Little Chinese and a Lot of Leadership

When we left Vietnam for the U.S., we came with almost nothing. So, during my high school days I had to find a job to help support my family. Back then, I lived in Utah so there wasn't a great selection of jobs available to teenagers. I had my share of babysitting, mowing lawns, and washing cars. But now that I was grown-up, I needed a "real" job that paid more money. Most of my friends were in the fast food business and they had convinced me to look for something in the restaurant business. I had several interviews and landed a job working as a hostess for a Chinese restaurant. There was just one problem. I was Chinese from Vietnam. But, I didn't speak Chinese.

On my first day of work, Jonathan, the manager, explained to me the proper ways to greet customers, techniques to use in describing lunch and dinner specials, and how to properly handle the cash register. But, because of my inability to read or write Chinese, my duties were limited to bookkeeping. During the first few weeks, I felt that my job was important because I was responsible for tabulating the restaurant's daily income/loss. At the end of each day, I knew exactly how much sales the restaurant had made. But after a few months, the restaurant started to get busy and I found myself wanting to assist the waiters and the waitresses. Their jobs seemed more exciting and demanding than mine. It seemed like a challenge to me. All I could do during those busy hours was to stand behind the cash register and smile. But since I was a shy person, I didn't tell anyone. Weeks went by and I found myself disliking my work more and more. I felt like an outsider.

To my good fortune, one of the chefs asked me if I would be interested in being a waitress. Thomas had some say in the matter, because he was part-owner of the restaurant. I was speechless since I knew that I had to learn Chinese. It was my chance to make things happen but I was hesitant since I didn't know whether I could master Chinese or not. Thomas said that if I was interested, he would teach me how to read and write enough Chinese to get by. That was a commitment, he promised. I thought it over and finally agreed. His training was not easy. I don't think Thomas learned how to teach Chinese at a Berlitz School. Moreover, the other workers at the restaurant made fun of everything. They laughed at my punctuation, and writing. I felt helpless and stupid. Here I was, a Chinese girl in a new country who could not even read or write in a language that everyone thought I knew. But every day, Thomas would reassure me that I was going to succeed. By constant practice, repetition, and hard work on both our parts, I slowly progressed. Exactly two months later, Thomas said it was time. I began my career as a waitress. Some people might smile and not think that becoming a waitress was any big thing. They may think that anyone can do waitress work. Maybe, but try it in a foreign language with customers who are most unforgiving about complicated orders wrong. I've seen senior corporate executives that would have never been able to pull it off. I was as proud as I could be. Not only did I enjoy my new job, but also I was able to earned extra money in tips. My parents and friends even came by the restaurant to see me in action.

To this day, I am very thankful to Thomas for believing in me and most important, for teaching me the tools to succeed in life. In my view, Thomas possessed the qualities inherent in "The Stuff of Heroes." Here's what he did: **1) Maintain Absolute Integrity.** Thomas kept his word. He knew that my lack of language skills was going to make things happen. When he hired me, he said he would work with me until I was successful. He did. **2) Know his Stuff.** Thomas was an expert at operating restaurants and he was also a great chef. In addition, he knew what it takes to be a good waiter and from him, I learned what I needed to succeed. **3) Declare his Expectations.** Thomas told me that in order to do well as a waitress, I had to be on my toes and be ready to assist customers. Thomas' expectations that I would succeed help motivate me to success. **4) Show Uncommon Commitment.** Thomas' vision for me to become a waitress seemed impossible when we started. But because he stayed committed until we succeeded, so did I. **5) Expect Results.** Thomas visualized the result he wanted to achieve and he maintained enthusiasm. Whenever I felt tired, Thomas would remind me that if I wanted something, I must never quit. He used to say, "nothing in life comes easy and if it did, you probably wouldn't want it." **6) Take care of your People.** Thomas told the other owners that if I did not succeed, he would no longer be a part of the hiring process. To me, this meant that he really cared about me and he would assume responsibility if things went wrong. **7) Put Duty Before Self.** Not only did Thomas practice this law, but he lived by it. After a busy, tiring and hot day behind the kitchen, he spent two to three hours tutoring me. **8) Get out in Front.** Thomas wanted to see me succeed not just by talking or dreaming about it, instead he spent countless hours coaching me. He demonstrated high moral courage and had never put himself first and that to me is what makes a great hero! So, thank you Thomas. Whatever I achieve I owe much to you.

New *"Stuff of the Heroes"* Web Site

If you are looking for a new and informative place to surf, you should visit us at our new web site—www.stuffofheroes.com. The web site covers Dr. Cohen's eight universal laws of leadership and it also includes the latest news on the book. There is also a page comprised of quotes and thoughts from several experts regarding "The Stuff of Heroes."

We are still in the process of building it, and haven't begun to promote it yet. But you can tell your customers about it and invite them to check it out. Right now, it contains a link to amazon.com. However, we will be happy to list booksellers that carry "The Stuff of Heroes and request it. Feel free to check out our web site and enjoy surfing! If you have any comments or suggestions, please contact me at Ibanh@18.aol or Dr. Cohen at wcohen@calstatela.edu.

Feel free to check out our web site and enjoy surfing! If you have any comments or suggestions, please contact me at Ibanh@18.aol or Dr. Cohen at wcohen@calstatela.edu.

Cohen Spreads "The Word"

Did you know that Dr. Cohen speaks nationally and has spoken to groups of up to 15,000 people? For example, over the last few months, he has spoken on *"The Stuff of Heroes"* to groups of up to 1,000 salespeople and sales managers around the country plus 700 Air Force officers at Squadron Officers School in Alabama and many other groups of executives, managers, and entrepreneurs. Next month he is a guest speaker at the FBI Academy in Quantico, Virginia and will conduct a workshop on *"The Stuff of Heroes"* for 40 chiefs of police from major cities around the country.

Dr. Cohen's latest seminar is based on the principles he discusses in *"The Stuff of Heroes."* Through his seminars, Dr. Cohen will show how the 8 universal laws can be applied not only in business and sales, but by teachers, coaches, parents and anyone who wants to put *The Stuff of Heroes* to work in their lives. These seminars last from three to six hours and provide principles to last a lifetime.

Whatever the size of your group, whether they're trainees, CEOs or people wanting to be better parents, they can get *The Stuff of Heroes!* For additional information on reserving Dr. Cohen for a special training session, please e-mail him at wcohen@calstatela.edu.

A 70-Year-Old Leader Takes Care of His People When Times are Tough

You either take care of your people, no matter how bad the situation, or you do not. Age or civilian clothes have little to do with this concept of taking care of people. A man from Lawrence, Massachusetts, named Aaron Feuerstein did the former. On the night of December 11, 1995, while Feuerstein was celebrating his 70th birthday, his factory, Malden Mills, burned down.

Malden Mills was a complex of nine buildings, and it employed 2,400 semi-skilled workers. Most of them were immigrants. The manufacturer of upholstery and synthetic winter wear fabrics was a $400 million company and one of the largest employers in the region.

Feuerstein pledge to continue paychecks and health benefits for as long as it took to rebuild. It cost him $1.5 million a week just to meet his payroll. He even paid the previously announced holiday bonus of $275 to each employee. Rather than take the insurance money and run, he vowed to rebuild on the same spot.

Eventually, it cost Feuerstein $15 million to rebuild. But he opened a $100 million factory on the site of the destruction. At the factory opening, U.S. Representative Martin Meehan commented, "Feuerstein showed the difference when you have somebody who is passionately committed to his workers. It would have been easier for him to retire."

Again, bean-counting managers at large companies said he should have pocketed the insurance company, and if not, then rebuild further south where labor costs were lower. That would be a good business decision, they said. Feuerstein instead replied. "Why would I go south to cut costs when the advantage that I have is quality? And that comes from focusing on people, not cutting costs."
And how are Feuerstein's people performing today? As an example, Feuerstein says, "The fourth plant, which prior to the fire had never produced more than 130,000 yards a week, is producing more than 200,000 yards."

Dr. Cohen on TV and Radio Around the Country

Since the publishing of his new book, *"The Stuff of Heroes,"* Dr. Cohen has been the highlight of many TV and radio shows all around the country. Dr. Cohen has mentioned that during his visits, he has enjoyed meeting new people. The following is a list of shows that Dr. Cohen has been a guest star on:

Sept. 27	KSCI TV - Phil Blazer Show	Los Angeles, CA
Oct. 1	KACD Radio - John Darrell Show	Santa Monica, CA
Oct. 5	KALI Radio - Gary Mercer Show	Pasadena, CA
Oct. 6	WPBR Radio - Dan Gregory Politics	Palm Beach, FL
Oct. 9	KDKA Radio - Mary After Midnight	Pittsburgh, PA
Oct. 9	WOLB Radio - Jay Cottrell	Baltimore, MD
Oct. 13	KURV Radio - Darin Rankin Show	Brownsville, TX
Oct. 14	KIEV Radio - Larry Merino Show	Glendale, CA
Oct. 21	KDOC TV - Michelle Merker Show	Irvine, CA
Oct. 27	KINA Radio - Rick Mack Show	Salinas, KA
Oct. 28	KOST Radio - Tobi Knight Show	Los Angeles, CA
Oct. 30	KWHY TV - Richard Saxton	Los Angeles, CA
Nov. 1	KPCC - Gerta Govine	Pasadena, CA
Nov. 4	KLON - Nick Roman	Long Beach, CA
Nov. 5	KCBS TV - Bob Navarro's Journal	Los Angeles, CA
Nov. 11	WFTD Radio - Gary Harris Show	Toledo, OH
Dec. 8	KCEP Radio - Enterprising People	Las Vegas, NV

Retired Hero from *"The Stuff of Heroes"* Does Book Signing in Pennsylvania

Brig. General George K. Patterson, USAF Ret., who is prominently featured in the book, *The Stuff of Heroes: The Eight Universal Laws of Leadership* by fellow general officer, William A. Cohen, has obtained special permission from the author, his publisher, and Barnes and Noble Bookstores to do a special autograph book signing. The signing was held at Barnes and Noble Bookstore in Town Square Mall on Veterans' Day, Wednesday, November 11, 1998, at 7:00 p.m. (1900 hours).

General Patterson is a former General Manager at Singer Link and a member of the Southern Tier Chapter of the Retired Officers Association (TROC). Major General Cohen, the author, was a student of General Patterson at West Point in the late 1950s and is now a Professor at California State University in Los Angeles.

During General Patterson's thirty-year Air Force career, he flew 100 combat missions in the Korean War, taught jet fighter combat tactics, instructed in weapon systems engineering at West Point, modernized the Flight Test Center's research simulators and flight test range at Edwards AFB, led the construction and operation of five range tracking ships for the Apollo program, commanded the AF Human Resources Lab, was program manager for the SRAM nuclear missile and many other weapon programs and was Commander of the Defense Electronics Supply Center. He was awarded 17 medals, including the Distinguished Service Medal, Legion of Merit, Distinguished Flying Cross and Air Medals.

(continues)

Figure 3-2. *(continued)*

GREAT LEADERS ARE MADE, NOT BORN

There are many well-educated and motivated people who lack the knowledge of how to lead others. So they don't assume leadership positions, or if they do, they don't do very well in them. They and others too, assume that these individuals just weren't born to be leaders. And since salespeople are leaders, there are a large number of salespeople in this category that could be doing a much better job in leading.

That's really a tragedy, because every country in the world needs good leaders. Corporations, associations, and athletic teams all need good leaders. Even parents must be good leaders or their families can become dysfunctional. Success in any endeavor is dependent on good leadership. But my research shows conclusively that effectiveness as a leader depends not on some innate trait you are born with, and much more on the universal laws of leadership that anyone can follow.

One of the greatest American military leaders was General Hoyt S. Vandenberg. He eventually became the U.S. Air Force's second Chief of Staff. General Robert Danforth who was Commander of Cadets at West Point when General Vandenberg was a cadet told me an amazing story. General Vandenberg was not a natural leader. In fact, we almost dismissed him from the Academy for lack of leadership ability at the end of his first year. Instead, we counseled him. He took note and applied himself. He was a very competent leader by the time he graduated. Clearly he continued to develop himself afterwards.

The last few months, a number of sales organizations have asked me to speak on leadership. They recognize that salespeople are leaders, too. Good salespeople influence others to purchase products and services, some of which can change the world. As book salespeople, you are in that category. So if you want to sell like a hero, I sure wouldn't worry about whether you are a "born salesman" or not. As General Sherman of Civil War fame once said, "I have heard that they are individuals peculiarly qualified by birth to be a general, but I have never encountered one." If you want to increase your productivity, I recommend you to take a few minutes to read over the eight universal laws of leadership: Maintain absolute integrity. Know your stuff. Declare your expectations. Show uncommon commitment. Expect positive results. Take care of your customers. Put duty (your customers and your mission) before yourself. Finally, get out in front. That is, take the responsibility and show the initiative in helping your customers. Follow these eight laws and I personally guarantee your increased success, and you can tell me about it in Los Angeles at the BEA next year.

WITHOUT ACTION THE UNIVERSAL LAWS ARE WORTHLESS

From the past to as far as we can see into the future, the universal laws of leadership are immutable. Over the millennia, they have not changed. They are as true today as they were in the times of the ancients, and they will be as true thousands of years from now for those who come after us. But unless leaders take action on their knowledge, the laws are without value.

The mere knowledge of the eight universal laws alone is not power. But the laws of leadership do constitute potential or stored power. If knowledge of the universal laws is acted upon, the resulting plowshares are exceedingly powerful. If not, they are worthless. Leaders who apply the eight universal laws to their actions will lead more effectively. The organizations they lead will be more productive. There will be fewer failures and more and greater success. Those who lead and those who follow will be happier, wealthier, and more content in the work they produce and in the tasks in which they are engaged. My research of combat leaders now serving as leaders in all types of organizations proves this. Seven thousand years of recorded history confirm it. There is no possibility of error. But to repeat, to reap the power in the universal laws, they must be acted upon.

Figure 3-3. A newsletter published by consultant Dr. Robert Swette.

CONTRIBUTIONS
"to give in common with others"

Robert F. Swette Associates
partners in business growth   **Winter 1999**

GETTING SPIRIT INTO YOUR COMPANY
Managing Employees like Volunteers
by Robert F. Swette

When I reflect upon my time spent as a businessman on the one hand and a non-profit volunteer on the other, I am often struck by the vast differences between the two. Most of my volunteer time is enjoyable, rewarding and worthwhile, while much of my business career feels tense, competitive, political, and at times trivial. In retrospect, I also feel some of my most rewarding work came as a volunteer, and more significantly, that I have usually felt that I wanted to be there, as opposed to feeling that I had to be there, which is often the case in business. In sharing my thoughts, I hope to prompt reflection on way to make our work environment a better place.

THE ROLE OF MISSION

To begin with, most non-profits have a mission that really means something. The non-profit mission is typically clearly unique and in fact qualifies as a mission, like providing food, shelter or education for the poor; providing reconstructive surgery for children who are born with birth defects; or caring for the sick or elderly, and so on. From my professional work and observations, many executives claim their real mission is "making a profit and providing above average returns to stockholders" - the basis for executive compensation. These mission statements are supplemented with slogans like, "customer service is number one, we are the leader, our employees are our greatest asset, etc." These phrases are vague to the point of being meaningless. While the importance of profitability is self evident, I quite frankly do not find these goals motivating or having any inherent importance or compelling uniqueness. Personally, it is hard to get motivated about making someone else more money and trying to find meaning in it through empty slogans.

Furthermore, the true spirit of a mission statement is only felt through the daily interactions between the members of the organization and those they serve. In contrast to what happens in most companies, in non-profits you somehow feel "connected" to the mission and "catch its spirit." Whether it is

Continued on page 2

LETTER FROM THE PUBLISHER

Although I feel that the term leadership is grossly over used, to me it fits the theme of this newsletter. To me, it is interesting that leadership is noticed more often when it is absent and it is difficult to describe what it means to have it. We confuse leadership with charisma, heroics, tough mindedness, eloquent speeches, skillful debate, etc. What I have found to be more day to day leadership is helping people care about themselves, their work, and their treatment of others. Leadership motivates people to discover themselves and their talents, to do their best, and to take responsibility and share recognition for achievement and failure. This has become evident to me in the volunteer work that I have participated in over the years.

In my opinion, Dave Lehman and Bill Cohen, two friends of mine, illustrate exemplary leadership. Dave is Vice President and General Manager of Manufacturing for Solar Turbines and was instrumental in the company receiving the Malcolm Baldridge Quality Award in 1998. To hear him tell the story is incredibly interesting. Dave articulates a framework for how the team should approach a problem and then everyone else develops their own means to accomplish that end. He goes to great lengths to make sure all employees have the

Continued on page 4

Inside This Issue

1 Getting Spirit into Your Company - *Managing Employees like Volunteers*

2 Book Review - The Stuff of Heroes, by William A. Cohen, Ph.D.

3 Observations

(continues)

Figure 3-3. *(continued)*

Continued from page 1

GETTING SPIRIT INTO YOUR COMPANY
Managing Employees like Volunteers

through front-line involvement, working behind the scenes and hearing the stories and meeting those you serve, or organizing people and experiencing accomplishment through their work, you live the mission and see it manifested through the work. Within business, connecting employees with customers is less common for various reasons. Sometimes the benefits of these efforts can not be justified quantifiably, so why do it? Sometimes companies claim they can not afford the employee downtime, or are possibly afraid of risks of direct dialogue between employees and customers - who knows what someone will say? Periodically, programs focusing on customer interaction are created to motivate employees, but such programs do not alter the company's "way of life." The mission must become alive in the culture of the organization, and that happens best when you are "connected" to the mission - and non-profits do that because it is part of what keeps people coming back - the glory and importance of the work.

Developing a simple, clear mission and making it "real and compelling" is not an easy chore. It takes an incredible amount of work to clarify something into simple terms, that is not simpleminded. The process of creating a true mission can be a powerful factor in motivating, involving and empowering people.

LEARNING AND PROFESSIONAL DEVELOPMENT

A second aspect of volunteering is learning while you participate. A recent Gallup study revealed that one of the major reasons people volunteer is to learn. When volunteering you not only learn more about the community you serve, but also how to apply your skills in ways that you may not have imagined. For example, volunteer organizations may let you stretch by taking on an assignment that you might think goes beyond your capabilities, and they are there to support you because they want you to succeed. There is a support net. In business, people are typically hired for what they know and left to prove themselves. Very few corporations see these same reason for what they can be by helping them discover their skills and interests. Non-profit volunteer management not only looks at the person for what they can offer, but also tries to develop projects and activities that allow individuals to use their skills to contribute, learn, grow and discover.

When I was first introduced to my work as a volunteer in Tijuana, Mexico many of the other volunteers encouraged me to try different things to "find my place." I must say, I have learned about caring for orphaned, abandoned or troubled young girls, the poor and poverty, about a

different country, about construction, about healthcare, among many other things that subtly crept into my awareness. The same is true with Fresh Start Surgical Gifts, in the treatment and care of children with birth defects, burns, abuse, etc. This organization opened a whole new world for me. As president of the Drucker Management Center Alumni Association I learned about higher education and its marketing. In each of these situations, I have been able to not only contribute management and marketing expertise, but to learn an incredible amount in the process, helping me grow as a person.

AS A SOCIAL COMMUNITY

From my experience, the way people interact in business environments and non-profits is extremely different. Quite commonly in business there is a sense of tension. Many times the tension is intentional to "get the most out of people." I believe this environment is the result of incredible over emphasis on short-term results. The consequences of this pressure are manifested by employees constantly positioning themselves for leverage, continually passing judgment on others, and seeing "the game" as a competition among themselves, rather than creating and keeping customers. In general, I believe competition is beneficial, but the trend in "over-competition" is destructive. If not mitigated, competition can destroy the creative, risk taking, and collaborative spirit that corporate executives claim is what makes a company great.

Contrast this with most volunteer work where there is camaraderie in the accomplishment of a task, and co-workers become friends, not the competition. I have developed deep and lasting friendships from my volunteer work; where peers genuinely are pulling for you and want the best for you as you do for them. Your co-workers do not stand in judgment of your skills or lack of them, but try to teach, help and support patiently, knowing we all have unique strengths and weaknesses. In the end your success is theirs and interaction is pleasant, sincere, and helpful. Like business, results are expected, but they are also appreciated because non-profits can not exist without volunteers. Receiving recognition is great for our self esteem, but is often elusive in fast-paced business situations. In the non-profit community, I find a willingness for people to stand up and take on an extra task, share leadership and grunt work, and take joy in accomplishing a task. Businesses often complain that employees need to take ownership and responsibility - which for many employees is a euphemism for placing blame. Responsibility in any organization is fundamental, its a matter of how it is

Continued on page 3

CONTRIBUTIONS   3

Continued from page 2

GETTING SPIRIT INTO YOUR COMPANY
Managing Employees like Volunteers

delegated and managed.

CONCLUDING THOUGHTS

Like so many things, these generalities are susceptible to contrary experiences. These thoughts are not meant to be criticisms or prescriptions, but ideas that businessman can use to instill a volunteering spirit in their organizations. We all want a work environment where employees are excited, enthused and convinced of the importance and value of their work; where collaboration is as important as competition and the balance is evident in practice; and where employees learn and grow through contributions and management creates an environment where this happens. As professionals continue to be more mobile and have more choices about who, how, and where they work, they will act more like volunteers.

Changing company cultures is not simple or easy. It is complex and difficult. It requires compassionate thought, consistency and action. In my opinion, it will be well worth starting a discussion with the goal of making it unnecessary to state that "our employees are our greatest asset" - it will be evident in the intangible spirit of the organization.

The Stuff of Heroes, by William A. Cohen, Ph.D.

Reviewed by Robert F. Swette

The Stuff of Heroes, is one of the best leadership books I have read. It demonstrates that leadership is not something we are born with but something that can be learned, and it illustrates how. It does this because it is written from a unique perspective that is a well-balanced combination of theory, contemporary anecdotes, and history. Cohen researches over 200 military leaders who have transitioned to industry careers and identifies leadership characteristics that transcend the two. His conclusions are supported through analysis of dozens of corporate situations and in-depth study of military history. From this vast research emerges eight universal and timeless laws of leadership that Cohen clearly and persuasively describes. The Stuff of Heroes is thought provoking, inspiring and useful in developing leadership skills in practical ways. „

These eight universal laws are systematically defined and characterized, then supported and illustrated through numerous examples. The first law is *"Maintain Absolute Integrity."* Cohen describes integrity; "In simple terms, integrity means adherence to a set of values that distinguish honesty and freedom from deception. But it is more than honesty. Integrity means doing the right thing regardless of the circumstances or benefits to the leader or the organization." Cohen goes on to describe four ways to develop integrity; *Keep your word, Chose the harder right than the easier wrong, Guard your principles, and Do the right thing.* Each of these ways is further developed through individual stories illustrating straying from and keeping to integrity, ranging from seemingly "small things" to crucial and complex decisions.

When reading The Stuff of Heroes, I found my feelings ranged from questioning how I might have handled situations differently to being inspired to achieve more. For example, the second law is *"Know Your Stuff"* and Earl Nightingale, the famous motivational speaker who spent his life researching success, says that one can become an expert at something within five years or less regardless of your field - if you make the effort. Becoming an expert requires doing a little each day - reading, writing, taking classes or talking with peers. It is a matter of getting involved. For me, this and other stories in the chapter reinforced the need for persistence and continuous learning.

I highly recommend this book for anyone who is interested in leadership. Despite the seriousness of the topic, The Stuff of Heroes is an easy and enjoyable read. It is one that I am recommending to our book club because it is thoughtful, stimulating and of practical value when we take on leadership roles at work and within our community.

(continues)

Figure 3-3. *(continued)*

4   **CONTRIBUTIONS**

Continued from page 1

LETTER FROM THE PUBLISHER

opportunity to understand the business and their roles in it, on the one hand, while providing them with the tools for doing an outstanding job on the other. In other words, he helps people excel. He is totally and genuinely unselfish and humble about his contribution, and prefers to recognize others. The other friend, Bill Cohen's recently published book is reviewed in this newsletter. I am not exactly sure, but I believe his books number about 30. He is totally committed to whatever he does, always encourages you to just try and is there to provide genuine support. As you will read in the book review, he has explored the concept of leadership and his work provides thought provoking insight and practical advice.

By the way, both Dave and Bill received their Ph.D.'s from the Drucker Management Center, Claremont Graduate University, and like myself were heavily influenced by the practical leadership displayed by Peter Drucker. I have also had the pleasure of getting to know Doris Drucker who is a wonderful person and a true leader in her own right.

I hope your new year is off to a tremendous start and I wish you the best. Please let us know if we can be of service to you.

Rob

OBSERVATIONS

• Thank you, thank you, thank you to all of those who supported me on the 100 hole golf marathon for Big Brothers of Los Angeles. I completed all 100 holes and wasn't sore, but very tired the next day. In all the golfers raised $60,000. *Rob Swette*

• A response to a previous article on the role of business development, "As far as resolving the conflicting roles of business development, sales and marketing, I believe it takes a very structured approach. Most companies do not manage their idea generation process (especially given they only formally plan once a year) well enough to manage the conflict. Business Development roles are more likely checking out everyone else's good ideas versus a structured approach." *Walt Matwejic, Director of Planning, Rogers Group*

<u>Robert F. Swette Associates</u>   (760)930-9257
partners in business growth   E-Mail Robswette@aol.com

CONSULTATION TO MANAGEMENT
Specializing in Marketing ♦ Business Development ♦ Strategic Management
6810 Vianda Court ♦ LaCosta, CA 92009

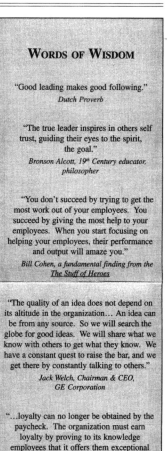

WORDS OF WISDOM

"Good leading makes good following."
Dutch Proverb

"The true leader inspires in others self trust, guiding their eyes to the spirit, the goal."
Bronson Alcott, 19th Century educator, philosopher

"You don't succeed by trying to get the most work out of your employees. You succeed by giving the most help to your employees. When you start focusing on helping your employees, their performance and output will amaze you."
Bill Cohen, a fundamental finding from the The Stuff of Heroes

"The quality of an idea does not depend on its altitude in the organization... An idea can be from any source. So we will search the globe for good ideas. We will share what we know with others to get what they know. We have a constant quest to raise the bar, and we get there by constantly talking to others."
Jack Welch, Chairman & CEO, GE Corporation

"...loyalty can no longer be obtained by the paycheck. The organization must earn loyalty by proving to its knowledge employees that it offers them exceptional opportunities for putting their knowledge to work."
Peter F. Drucker, The Information Based Organization

new people every few months, mostly through advertisements in *The Wall Street Journal*. Every time one of my ads appeared, headhunters would call offering to find the needed candidate for me; because I had never dealt with headhunters and knew that they were expensive (fees up to 30 percent of an executive's annual salary), I turned them all down. However, one day I received a friendly letter from a recruiter, along with a free subscription to his newsletter. Over the next two to three months, I continued to receive this newsletter, which I found useful. When I next needed to recruit, I hired this headhunter to help me. That newsletter helped earn the headhunter a $7,500 fee on that one placement, not to mention the potential for future business.

Joining and Being Active in Professional Associations

Membership in professional associations can be an excellent way to obtain clients over the long term for two reasons: First, your participation lends you the credibility of the association even if you yourself are unknown; second, professional associations are excellent for making contacts, especially if you take an active role. Plan to participate actively in programs, for example, hold an office. Over the years, many clients have come to me because of my active role in associations.

Joining and Being Active in Social Organizations

Social organizations are more for contacts than credibility. They include alumni associations, tennis or bowling clubs, or health studios. I have even obtained clients from fellow members of a martial arts club. When a social relationship is established, a client relationship often follows. Individuals see you, get to know you, and begin to trust you. If they happen to have a need in an area you are consulting in, they may think of you. With very little direct effort, you may acquire a contact.

Organizations, both social and professional, are a basis on which you can build long-term relationships. It's no wonder that "relationship marketing" is now considered an important idea for all businesses.

Writing Articles

Naturally, if you are going to write an article, it must pertain to the type of consulting you do, and it must be interesting and valuable to the reader. Perhaps most important of all, the biographical information that you include with the article should note that you are a consultant.

Management consultant trainer Howard L. Shenson used to tell the story of a consultant who wrote a single article and syndicated it to ninety different in-house publications. It resulted in so many requests for his services that he had to go into business as a consultant broker, brokering the offers that came his way, because he simply could not handle so much business on his own.

I've used this marketing method to promote not only my consulting services but other activities as well. One example concerns a book that I wrote, *Building a Mail Order Business,* published in its first edition by John Wiley & Sons in 1982. To assist the promotion of this book, I wrote an article entitled "Can Anyone Make a Million Dollars in Mail Order?" and self-syndicated it around the country to magazines and newspapers, offering each an exclusive in its geographic area or industry. (As long as the publications know what kind of rights you are offering, this is entirely legal and ethical.) In this manner, I multiplied my readership for this one article many times over. You can see a sample of my cover letter as well as a sample article printed under the title, "Imagination is the key to making a million," in Figures 3-4 and 3-5. That book is currently in its fourth edition and has sold almost 100,000 copies!

One day my publisher called and asked if I would be willing to go on radio station KLBJ in Austin, Texas, the station started by President Lyndon B. Johnson. Naturally I agreed. This radio appearance, which was actually done from my office in California through a telephone hookup, led to additional radio and television appearances around the country and in Canada. But the interesting thing is that this first appearance resulted from the article I had written. Someone in Austin had read the article, requested a copy of the book, and felt that it might be an interesting subject for a half-hour talk show.

Another technique you can use is to rewrite articles on the

Figure 3-4. Cover letter sent to an editor promoting article about mail order books.

Dear _____:

Recent research that I completed has uncovered a business that can be run out of the home on a part-time basis, yet which can and has produced a number of millionaires. In fact, its current sales volume exceeds $100 billion every year, and it is so lucrative that more than half of the "Fortune 500" companies are engaged in it.

The business that I am referring to is the mail order business . . . and readership demand for information about the subject is so great that many major book publishers, including McGraw-Hill, Prentice-Hall, and Harper & Row, have published books on the subject. Interestingly, almost every one of these books stays in print over the years and continues to sell. For example, one of Prentice-Hall's books on mail order is in its twenty-fourth printing. John Wiley has just published my book entitled BUILDING A MAIL ORDER BUSINESS: A COMPLETE MANUAL FOR SUCCESS.

The reason that I am writing to you is that I have just completed a short article that explores the question, "Can Anyone Make a Million Dollars in the Mail Order Business?" I know that the answer, which is based on the research that I did for my book, will surprise you. It certainly surprised me . . . and I know that it will surprise and interest your readers as well.

I am enclosing this article for your review. I can offer it to you on an exclusive basis to your newspaper in your city. However, like many hot items that may be due in part to present economic conditions, the demand for this information is time-sensitive. Therefore, I can only reserve my offer to you for 30 days. Please let me hear from you as soon as possible.

Sincerely,

William A. Cohen, Ph.D.
Professor of Marketing
California State University,
    Los Angeles

Figure 3-5. Article about mail order books in *Salem Evening News*.

living   THE SALEM, MASS., EVENING NEWS—FRIDAY, JUNE 25, 1982   **19**

Imagination is the key to making a million

By DR. WILLIAM A. COHEN

More than eighty years ago, Richard Sears and Julius Rosenwald got together to build Sears, Roebuck & Co. into what would eventually become a $10 billion corporation. In the process, these two entrepreneurs built themselves into the world's first mail order millionaires.

Since the time of Sears' beginning, countless part-time and full-time entrepreneurs have been attracted by the apparent ease with which inexperienced business people could enter this profession of selling products through the mail and emerge with a fortune. What is surprising is not that many have failed. Many have. But the unexpected fact is that in both good times and bad, many have succeeded.

Just before the depression of 1929, a young man by the name of Robert Collier wrote a book in less than two months called, "The Secret of the Ages." In the first six months after writing the book, Collier made more than a million dollars selling the book solely through the mail. He went right on selling the book through the 1929 depression. In fact, although the book has never appeared on any best seller list, it wouldn't surprise me if "The Secret of the Ages" was one of the biggest sellars of all time since it has never been withdrawn and is still being sold through the mail today.

Now it could be that Collier's achievement was a fluke . . . if so many others hadn't done the same thing with similar products.

Brainerd Mellinger, famous for his self-published course on import-export, built a huge multi-million dollar business around his product. Joe Karbo wrote his book, "The Lazy Man's Way to Riches," in 1973. Before he died in 1980, he sold more than a million copies at ten dollars each. His family continues to sell the book today.

Melvin Powers, a famous mail order publisher in North Hollywood, started with a single small book on hypnotism. Today he has more than 400 books in print and has sold millions of books in the interim.

Of course, there are a great many products besides books which are sold through the mail. In a recent year, more than $2.7 billion in general merchandise including home furnishings, housewares and gifts were sold as well as another billion dollars each in ready to wear clothing and collectibles. This is the stamping ground of mail order wizards like Joe Sugarman in Chicago who built a $50 million a year business selling electronic products in only seven years right out of his garage.

Sixty-nine-year-old A. J. Masuen of LeMars, Iowa, went from door-to-door salesman to more than $1 million a year selling first aid kits and supplies through a mail order catalog. Two high school boys, Len and Rick Hornick, started their multi-million dollar mail order business selling hand-carved, wooden ducks to hunters and collectors. Today they employ more than 100 expert craftsmen to make their ducks, and they mail out a 32-page catalog to almost a million customers four times a year.

What qualities does the would-be mail order entrepreneur need? Three qualities are absolutely essential: imagination, persistence, and a high degree of honesty. Imagination is needed in order to be able to visualize the special appeal which will compel a potential customer to buy your product. If you have imagination, you can sell almost anything by mail.

Mail order pro Ed McLean proved this by selling thousands of an unpopular model of a Mercedes-Benz automobile which conventional automobile dealers hadn't been able to sell. Mail order experts Hank Burnett, Christopher Stagg, and Dick Benson proved it by selling sixty airplane tickets at $10,000 each for an around-the-world flight. But perhaps the king is Joe Cossman. With no more business experience than being an ex-serviceman, Cossman sold 2,118,000 ant farms, 1,583,000 potato spud guns, 1,600,000 imitation shrunken heads, and 1,508,000 home garden sprinklers and many other products . . . all by mail.

Persistence is required because success is rarely instantaneous and there are always obstacles and set-backs. Cossman spent over a year working on his kitchen table encountering false leads, problems, and failures at the same time holding down a full-time job during normal working hours before he finally hit his first success. And even that first successful project required hard work and numerous obstacles that had to be overcome. Less persistent entrepreneurs would have quit long before.

Absolute honesty is required because a successful mail order business is built on trust, repeat sales, and satisfied customers. After all, you are asking your customers to send money, sometimes a great deal of money, to someone he does not know and cannot see. Cheat your customer even a little, and you've lost that customer forever. Without repeat customers, you might just as well invest your time and energy in a dried up oil well. The potential for a successful enterprise might have existed once, but now its gone for good.

The basic principles which you must understand to be successful in mail order have to do with product selection, structuring your offer, testing, where and when to advertise, and what to put into your advertisements. It takes a book to do justice to all of these subjects in detail, so we'll look only at the rudiments.

While it is true that a mail order expert can sell just about anything through the mail, some products just naturally make better mail order products than others. To increase your chances of picking a winner, look for a product that is light weight, nearly unbreakable, has a broad appeal to a large segment of the population, and has a large margin for profit. This last requirement means you have to be able to buy low, and sell high. Believe me, you are going to need this high profit margin in order to pay for your advertising costs, and at first to pay for your mistakes during the learning process.

You should try to get a product which allows you to sell it at three or four times the cost of the product to you. Now clearly you can't do this with a high priced product. But for most products under $25 this should be your goal.

This brings us to the important subject of testing. Successful mail order dealers test almost everything. They test which offer is best. They test different types of appeals. They test different prices. And they test different media in which to advertise. Testing is mail order's secret weapon. It is also the secret which allows a mail order operator to fail with four products out of five and still walk away with a million dollars or more.

How is it done? You spend a little money for a test. A complete failure tells you to drop the whole project. A marginal failure or a marginal success says to experiment and rework some aspect of the project. A major success gives you the green light for a larger investment. In this way you can afford to lose a little money on several dismal failures. But when your testing indicates a clear success, you can move immediately to capitalize on what you know to be a winner. The idea is not to risk a lot of money until you are certain of success.

While there are no guarantees, the potential does exist for just about anyone to make a million dollars or more in this business if they have imagination, persistence, and honesty and if they follow the basic principles that have proven to be successful.

(Dr. Cohen is a professor of marketing at California State University, Los Angeles. He has just published a book entitled, "Building a Mail Order Business: A Complete Manual for Success," which is in its second printing.)

same subject matter. I learned this from a very famous individual in his field: Captain P. V. H. Weems. Now retired from the U.S. Navy, Weems is considered the father of aerial navigation. When I was a young Air Force officer in 1961, I had the good fortune to catch the attention of Captain Weems, who invited me to his home in Annapolis, Maryland, to visit during a leave of absence from navigating B-52E aircraft in Oklahoma. During this visit, Captain Weems taught me to rewrite a single article many times to gain increased publicity for my ideas. "If you just write about your topic once, you will miss a good deal of your potential reader-ship," he told me. I have used this technique many times since. A recent example is Figure 3-6 (see page 61), which was published in eight different magazines and journals in various forms to promote my books on leadership, *The Stuff of Heroes* (Longstreet Press, 1998) and *The New Art of the Leader* (Prentice Hall Press, 2000).

Three books that may be helpful in the area of marketing and publishing articles are:

- *How to Write Articles for Newspapers and Magazines* by Dawn B. Sova (Arco Publishing)
- *Sell and Resell Your Magazine Articles* by Gordon Burgett (Writers Digest Books)

Writing a Book

Writing a book is much like writing an article except, obviously, there is more to it. Having your book published demonstrates ex-pertise in a certain area because the reader knows that your writing has passed a rigorous screening by the publisher. Publication gives you a credibility edge over your competitors who do not write. I continue to receive a considerable number of requests for consult-ing that result from my books. Recently I had a most unusual re-quest. The president of a small company read both *The Executive's Guide to Finding a Superior Job* (published by AMACOM in 1978 and released in its second edition in 1983 but now out of print) and the mail order book mentioned previously. He asked if I would locate a senior director of marketing for his company. Although I indi-cated that I hadn't done headhunting in some years, this potential client said that he had read both my books and felt that the combi-

Figure 3-6. Example of article promoting book on leadership.

WILLIAM A. COHEN

Laws of Leadership

If you don't maintain your integrity, you will never be fully trusted by those you lead.

I HAVE TRIED TO IDENTIFY principles of leadership that are universal in all situations. The basis of my research was a survey sent to more than 200 former combat leaders and conversations with hundreds more. I sought those who had become successful in other organizations after leaving the armed forces. I asked them to list what they considered to be the three most important principles.

Their responses confirm there are universal principles that successful leaders follow to boost productivity and achieve extraordinary success.

The strength of the results of my investigation motivated me to name these principles the *eight universal laws of leadership*.

1. Maintain absolute integrity. Without basic trust between leader and followers, the leader is forever suspect. Integrity means doing the right thing. Lack of integrity can have terrible consequences. Even if a leader loses a fight, by maintaining absolute integrity, he or she retains his or her mandate to lead. Others will still follow, while leaders who violate this law are never fully trusted, no matter their abilities or accomplishments.

2. Know your stuff. Those who follow you want to know whether you know your stuff. Followers want you to be good at what it takes to get the job done.

3. Declare your expectations. This law includes planning, goal setting, and communicating. You can't get "there" until you know where "there" is, and let your followers know.

4. Show uncommon commitment. To show uncommon commitment, you've got to take risks. "No guts, no glory." Ask yourself, what is the worst that can

happen? Accept that, and press on. If you aren't committed, no one else will be.

5. Expect positive results. The higher your goals, the higher goals you will achieve. There is a direct relationship between the goals you expect and what you get. Successful leaders expect positive results and maintain a positive attitude regardless of external realities. If you expect to succeed or expect to fail, you're right. So, although it makes sense to be ready for the worst, expect the best.

6. Take care of your people. If you take care of your people, they will take care of you. Loyalty is a two-way street. You cannot expect others to support your interests if you ignore theirs. J.W. Marriott once said: "We take care of our people, and they take care of our guests."

7. Put duty before self. If you are a leader, your duty encompasses accomplishing your mission and taking care of your people. Usually, the mission must come first. Sometimes, you must take care of your people first, or you may never accomplish your mission. All leaders must put the interests of the mission and their followers before their own. If your mission and your people don't come before you, you are not the leader.

8. Get out in front. The only way to lead is to get in front. You lead by pulling, not pushing. Get out where you can see and be seen. That way, not only will you know what's going on, but those who follow will know you are committed.

Review these eight laws of leadership every morning and look for opportunities to implement them. At the end of the day, review your actions. Note where you succeeded and where you did not. When you fall short, replay the events in your mind. See the new outcome as a result of applying these concepts. The success you will achieve will be dramatic. **EE**

William A. Cohen is professor of marketing at Cal State University, Los Angeles, and author of The Art of the Leader. 323-343-2972.

Excellence in Action: Start thinking today about ways in which you can apply these eight concepts.

> *Get out in front where you can see and be seen.*

nation of a former headhunter and an expert in direct response marketing was just what he needed. The result was my first search assignment in years.

For more information on writing books, see:

- o *2001 Writer's Market: 8,000 Editors Who Buy What You Write* edited by Kirsten C. Holm (Writers Digest Books)
- o *The Art of Creative Nonfiction: Writing and Selling the Literature of Reality* by Lee Gutkind (Wiley)
- o *How to Write Books That Sell* by L. Perry Wilbur (Allworth Press)

Writing Letters to the Editor

Letters to the editor can have the same result as other types of writing: building credibility. These are frequently called "op-ed" pieces because they appear opposite editorials in the newspaper in which they appear. To be effective as a marketing tool, the letters and magazines should contain comments resulting from your expertise in a certain field, and you should identify yourself as a consultant in the area on which you are commenting. However, you should understand beforehand that the editor makes the decision on whether to publish your letter. Far more letters are received than could ever be published. To maximize your chances, make sure your letter is timely and well written. But when this technique works, it really works. A colleague of mine recently said that he received 110 letters of inquiry after his recent op-ed piece in the *Wall Street Journal*.

Teaching a Course

Teaching a course at a community college or a university can also lead to consulting assignments. Naturally, the course must be in your area of expertise. Also make sure you teach this course at night because this is when business executives are more likely to be continuing their education. My own teaching has led to major consulting assignments with large companies, locally as well as internationally. My only cautionary note here is that you must not consult with individuals while they are your students. This would be a conflict of interest. When I am asked about consulting while I am also serving as an instructor, I indicate that I would be happy to talk about the student's becoming a client after the course is over.

Giving Seminars

Giving seminars is much the same as teaching a course. Attendees at seminars tend to be responsible individuals interested in the topic. If your seminar has to do with the area of your consulting services, this can easily lead to additional assignments. I know of several consultants who depend solely on this method to promote their practice; the fees they receive for giving the seminar are only a secondary consideration. You don't even need to do the administrative work of setting up your own seminars. Contact any local community college or university. Many offer seminars and are on the lookout for new talent. They will require an outline of the seminar that you wish to give, its target market, the hours of attendance, the price, and a strong description of your background and expertise.

Here are some books that can help you:

- *How to Develop and Promote Successful Seminars and Workshops* by Howard L. Shenson (Wiley)
- *How to Run Seminars and Workshops: Presentation Skills for Consultants, Trainers, and Teachers* by Robert L. Jolles (Wiley)
- *Marketing with Speeches and Seminars: Your Key to More Clients and Referrals* by Miriam Otte (Zest)

Distributing Publicity Releases

Every newspaper, trade journal, magazine, or other publication depends on a constant flow of news. They are interested in what you have to say, as long as what you have to say is of potential interest to their readership. Anytime something of importance happens in your field, there is probably a story in it for some publication. Many times you will be surprised that what you consider common knowledge is new and quite interesting to many people, including potential clients. It is easy to write a publicity release. Just tell your story in a terse, straightforward style like that used in a newspaper article. A potential mailing list for your publicity release should include newspapers and other media such as trade journals whose target readership contains potential candidates for your services. Directories that list such media are available in your local library. The librarian will be happy to help you find what you need.

Here are some additional sources of information that will help you:

- *Bulletproof News Releases: Help at Last for the Publicity Deficient* by Kay Borden (Franklin Sarrett)
- *The Consultants Guide to Publicity: How to Make a Name for Yourself by Promoting Your Expertise* by Reece Franklin (Wiley)
- *The Publicity Handbook: How to Maximize Publicity for Products, Services, and Organizations* by David R. Yale (NTC Business Books)

Exchanging Information, Leads, and Referrals with Noncompeting Consultants

Once you have established your area of expertise in consulting, you will find that there is a noncompeting consultant network made up of other consultants who provide different services, much like doctors who deal in only one specialty and refer their patients to other specialists when required. Let's say that you specialize in organizational development, and a client is seeking marketing consulting. You can recommend another consultant who will be able to help your client. In turn, this marketing consultant can recommend your organizational development services to his or her clients when needed. To participate in this kind of network, use the cold-call or direct mail techniques described earlier in this chapter, only this time target noncompeting consultants. Offer these other consultants an exchange in which you will recommend their services to your clients or potential clients if they will do the same for you. Make certain that they have a good supply of your business cards and brochures, and ask for the same from them.

Of course, before you make such an arrangement, you must

be sure that this consultant will do a good job in the area in which you refer clients to him or her. You won't build much of a practice by referring people to consultants who fail to do a good job.

It is always important when clients contact you to find out how they happened to get your name. In many cases, this will be a referral, and once referrals begin coming in, it is a sure sign that you are well on your way to a successful practice. But in order to know which of the direct methods or indirect methods to continue and which to eliminate, you should always ask the question, "Can you tell me how you got my name?"

You may be tempted to ignore the indirect methods of marketing your consulting practice, especially when your direct methods start to pay off and you feel you have more than enough work to last for the foreseeable future. Be forewarned. The work situation can change in consulting very rapidly. A client's sales may suddenly fall off, forcing him to delay work you had anticipated. Other prospective work—thought to be a sure thing—can suddenly disappear. All of a sudden, you are finished with your current work and no other engagements are scheduled. It is then, while you are just beginning to reinstitute your direct campaigns, that you'll be glad you implemented and continued these indirect methods.

In the next chapter we're going to look at a somewhat different market for consulting: the public sector. There are tremendous opportunities for such consulting with local, state, and national governments, and you'll see exactly how to approach this market and take advantage of the opportunities it offers.

4

Marketing Consultant Services to the Public Sector

There is a tremendous opportunity for consultant services in the public sector. For the same reasons that large businesses use consultants, federal, state, and local governments have a real need for external consulting services and will probably continue to spend millions or even billions of dollars to obtain them. In my career, I have consulted for the Federal Bureau of Investigation; the U.S. Postal Service; the United States Air Force, Navy, and Marine Corps; a number of state universities; various police departments; and other governmental organizations. No consultant should dismiss the public sector market because the potential for work is big.

Different Types of Government Consulting Services

Some of the many consulting services used by the government are listed below:

- Advice on, or evaluation of, agency administration and management in such areas as organizational structures and reorganization plans
- Management methods
- Zero-base budgeting procedures

- Mail-handling procedures
- Record and file organization
- Personnel procedures
- Discriminatory labor practices
- Agency publications
- Internal policies, directives, orders, manuals, and procedures
- Management information systems
- Program management, such as program plans
- Acquisition strategies
- Regulation development
- Assistance with procurement of solicited or unsolicited technical and cost proposals
- Legal questions
- Economic impact
- Program impact
- Mission and program analysis

There are also various research and development and technology assessments done by external consultants even though the government officially does not classify these areas as consulting services.

Consulting for the Government

Bernard Ungar, deputy director of the General Accounting Office, the congressional "watchdog" of the U.S. Government, wrote that consulting services were being accomplished in eleven categories of federal product/service codes. While these may vary from year to year, this list gives some idea of the wide range of consulting services desired. These were:

1. Management and professional services
2. Special studies and analyses
3. Technical assistance
4. Management reviews of program-funded organizations
5. Management and support services for research and development

6. Technical representatives
7. Quality controls
8. Special medical services
9. Public relations
10. Training
11. Engineering development and operation systems development stages of research and development[1]

Checking with *A Citizen's Guide to the Federal Budget: Budget of the United States Government Fiscal Year 2001* confirms that these opportunities for consultant work have not disappeared.[2]

How to Get on the Government Bandwagon

The basic method of locating opportunities to sell to the government is to use the *Commerce Business Daily* (*CBD*), a newspaper published by the U.S. Government five days a week. It's expensive; a yearly subscription by mail will cost you several hundred dollars—so I don't recommend that you order a subscription until your business in the government sector is high enough to warrant it. Fortunately, the *CBD* is also available in many public libraries online. There is a guest account that's free, so you can try it out. Its Web site address is: www.cbdweb.com.

Many states also publish business opportunities periodically (for example, California provides the *California State Contracts Register*). Contact the contracting office of the state you would like to do business with to see if such a publication is available.

With regard to using the *CBD* or state publications, I recommend that you not bid directly on consulting opportunities unless you have had prior contact with the government agency. Simply responding to an advertisement in the *CBD* or a similar publication usually produces nothing but the wasted time and money in putting the proposal together. You need face-to-face contact with your prospective customers to convince them that you are better than the competition, and rarely can you do this with a proposal alone. The way to use these publications effectively is to consider the advertisements as a source of future clients and to make appointments for face-to-face meetings so that a later Request for Proposal (see below) will find you well-prepared.

Another method of locating opportunities in the government is to contact the Small Business Administration (SBA) in your area. Almost every government agency needs some type of consulting service. Whether it needs *your* services is another story. That you must investigate. Your local SBA office can help. Let them know that you are a business consultant and explain your area of expertise. Frequently, someone can refer you to somebody within the agency who can help you find government contracts. The SBA also hires small-business consultants to help counsel its own small-business clients.

The Buying Process

The government buying process usually begins with an Invitation for Bid (IFB) or Request for Proposal (RFP). With an IFB, usually you just state a price for whatever is wanted; with an RFP, in addition to a price, you must submit a technical proposal documenting your method for accomplishing whatever services are requested. It is important to recognize that submitting an IFB or an RFP does not guarantee you a contract. Usually other firms are competing for the same work. Low price is always of importance; in fact, with the IFB, low price determines who wins the contract, assuming that the firm is otherwise qualified. With the RFP, however, other factors may be of equal or even more importance. This is the reason that preproposal marketing is so important.

The Importance of Preproposal Marketing

Some years ago, I completed several research projects seeking the primary factors that influence the winning of small ($2 million or less) government research and development contracts. Two popular theories seemed to indicate that marketing was more important than technical approach or even the price attached to a particular proposal. One of these was consumer acceptance theory.

According to consumer acceptance theory, the consumer may achieve three levels of intensity in his or her relationship with any product or service: acceptance, preference, and insistence. Consumer acceptance, the lowest level of intensity, means that the customer may have had some contact with the product or with some promotional effort. This contact leads to a decision on acceptability. Customer preference suggests a more satisfactory experience over a competing product and implies that the product will be favored over the competition's. Insistence, the highest level of intensity, is the stage in which the customer will take the product almost regardless of price or hardship and will brook no substitution. This stage, according to the theory, can be reached by a full knowledge of the product based on considerable experience.

The other idea that was important to this application of marketing was the merchandising theory. Merchandising here means fitting the product to the potential customer's wants and needs. According to the main aspect of this theory, merchandising must be the central part of any marketing program. The market must be segmented in order to zero in on a specific customer, and the approach must accommodate the fact that this customer has a number of sometimes conflicting wants and needs that must be satisfied. These wants and needs are influenced by the customer's physical or mental state, his or her background or conditioning, the immediate situation that confronts him or her, and, most importantly, what he or she knows about the product either directly through its use or vicariously through communication with others. These wants and needs are of different relative values and may change. The desire for a particular product is influenced by its accessibility, including such factors as price, the customer funds available, and the effort required to get it. Suppliers are likely to see a product from an entirely different perspective than the customer's. Yet the potential exists for presenting the product in such a fashion that it does satisfy the most important of the customer's wants, needs, and desires, or for altering the product within certain limits in order to accomplish the same purpose. To do this requires presentation to the customer; feedback from the customer; analysis of the customer's wants, needs, and desires; and calculation of the best way to satisfy them.

Thus, both theories, based on practice in the industrial consumer world, argued for heavy investment in preproposal marketing for small government research contracts. And in fact, actual research with several different companies indicated the tremendous importance of the marketing done before the proposal was ever submitted. During this preproposal marketing, not only would the product or service be sold but also critical information would be learned and ideas shared between the company and its potential government customer. This included how much the customer had to spend, the scope of the activities, and the kind of product or service the customer expected he or she would receive. In some cases, win ratios increased from 0 to 100 percent by the simple influence of preproposal marketing. Preproposal marketing activities are absolutely critical for selling consulting services to any organization. Unfortunately, many consultants forget this when attempting to deal with the government.

The Marketing Sequence for Government Consulting

The sequence of marketing to the government involves six steps. All of these are built around the notion of preproposal marketing.

1. Locate potential clients.
2. Screen.
3. Visit and make the initial presentation.
4. Maintain contact and gather intelligence.
5. Prepare the proposal.
6. Negotiate the contract.

Locating Potential Clients

Potential clients can be located through the *CBD*, the state register of opportunities, the SBA, or other government directories, and through government sources on the Internet. You should use all of these sources to develop a list that includes every potential client in the government.

Screening

The initial screening should be accomplished by telephone. Go right down your list and call each potential client one after the other. Indicate what types of consulting services you provide and try to pinpoint the interests of the potential client. If there is no interest, it is better to establish this now, when the only cost is a telephone call. Finally, try to establish an appointment for a face-to-face presentation. If this must be done at some other location, such as out of state, these visits should be coordinated so that you can make several on one trip.

Visiting and Making the Initial Presentation

For the initial presentation, organize yourself ahead of time and know exactly how much time you have. If it's thirty minutes or forty-five minutes or an hour or two hours, you should know this ahead of time and limit your presentation to these requirements. Also ask your contact how many people will be present. This will help you to plan your presentation and to know how many handouts or brochures to bring. I cover presentations in more detail in Chapter 14; for now you should understand that you must organize ahead of time and take enough brochures and other handouts so that all your potential clients can have a copy.

Maintaining Contact and Gathering Intelligence

Probably the most important part of preproposal marketing is not only to continue to sell at every meeting but also to learn about forthcoming contracts before they are published in the *CBD* and similar publications. Also try to learn the scope of activity and how much money is available for these forthcoming contracts. Tell your potential client the approach you would recommend, and why. In some cases, these approaches will be incorporated into the RFP. This may seem like giving away ideas to competitors, but actually it's not necessarily bad, because you should be better prepared than they to do whatever it was you proposed. At the same time, you should be honest and forthright in selling your ideas and disagreeing (tactfully) with your potential client when information stated is at odds with facts as you know them or if the cost will be more or less than the agency anticipates. In this way, by the time you respond to the proposal, both you and your potential client should understand exactly what is going to be requested, what you are going to propose, and approximately what these services should cost.

Preparing the Proposal

The proposal should contain no surprises. It is a sales document, one that confirms your outstanding ability, not a vehicle for presenting something new that you haven't yet discussed with your potential client. This is true even though you may think of something at the last minute. The reason for this is that no matter how lengthy your sales document (and some proposals are no more than a single-page letter), you do not have sufficient space to explain everything in detail. You will probably not be permitted additional verbal discussions once a proposal has been requested, so you may not be able to explain a new idea sufficiently. Any question that goes unanswered could work to your disadvantage in a competitive review process. Also, no matter how unique and advantageous your new idea might be, time is needed for your potential client to sell the idea to his boss. Remember that any bureaucratic organization, including the U.S. Government, tends to avoid and minimize risk. New ideas that have not been previously sold during the preproposal marketing phase have high risk from the perception of your potential client. Restate what you have already sold, and bid in accordance with the funds and scope of the effort as you uncovered them during your prior contacts.

Negotiating the Contract

Negotiating is a basic skill that is part of your stock-in-trade as a consultant. You will negotiate with clients, subcontractors, members of your client's organization, other consultants, vendors, and many others. So don't assume that negotiating a public service contract is simply a matter of signing a contract for a proposal. It is rare that any proposal is accepted exactly as made. There may be considerable discussion and give-and-take regarding terms, price, delivery, and performance. See Chapter 10 for more help with negotiating.

Some recommended books are:

○ *How to Sell to the United States Government: Marketing Goods and Services to America's Greatest Customer* by Stephen M. Bauer (Citadel Press)

○ *The Entrepreneur's Guide to Doing Business with the Federal Government: A Handbook for Small and Growing Businesses* by Charles R. Bevers, Linda Gail Christie, and Lynn Rollins Price (Prentice Hall)

This chapter completes your preparation for marketing. After applying the methods in the last three chapters, you are ready for your first interview with your prospective client. In the next chapter, we will look at this first interview and how you should manage it.

Notes

1. Bernard L. Ungar, *Government Consultants* GAO-GGD88–99FS (Washington, D.C.: General Accounting Office, 1988), p. 1.

2. *A Citizen's Guide to the Federal Budget: Budget of the United States Government Fiscal Year 2001* (Washington, D.C.: U.S. Government Printing Office, 2000).

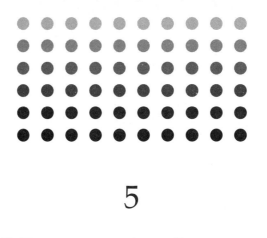

5

MAKING THE INITIAL
INTERVIEW A SUCCESS

In this chapter you are going to learn how to prepare for and conduct the initial interview with your prospective client. Along with general instructions about how to dress and how to act, I will give you the essential questions that you must ask in order to learn all you can about the potential assignment, which will eventually enable you to confirm your understanding of the engagement. In addition, I will point out nonverbal signs to look for and explain what each means, and I'll give you listening techniques that will help you to understand your client's feelings and intentions. Finally, I will show you psychological techniques for building empathy with your prospective client, which leads to a contractual relationship.

Looking and Acting Like a Professional

The first impression you make with your client should be the very best. In some cases, you can never overcome the effects of a questionable image in your client's mind. In large part, this initial image is made up of your appearance and your behavior. You want to look like, and act like, the professional that you are.

Dress is extremely important because it helps you make a good first impression. There are only two rules: Dress as neatly as possible, and try to look as much as possible like your client. For most business consulting, a conservative suit and tie for men and a suit for women are appropriate. However, if after several engagements you observe that in your client's industry a different type of dress is common, follow the second rule and dress like your client. Three good books on the subject are:

- *John T. Molloy's New Dress for Success* by John T. Molloy (Warner Books)
- *New Woman's Dress for Success* by John T. Molloy (Warner Books)
- *Your Executive Image* by Victoria A. Seitz (Adams Media Corp.)

In this first interview, be professional but not pompous. You should always strive to be friendly, understand your potential client, and build empathy. Think back to the different medical doctors you have met over your lifetime. Some are professional and friendly, and you feel a real trust with them. Other doctors, who may be of equal if not greater competence, somehow build a wall between you and them, and you trust them less. The same is true with the business doctor, the consultant. You must maintain a professional attitude, and at the same time you must be tactful, friendly, and empathetic.

Building Empathy with Your Potential Client

Psychologists discovered some time ago that we act more favorably toward those with whom we have rapport. The usual way of gaining rapport is finding some commonality of background, experience, or interest. However, twenty years ago, researchers John Grinder and Richard Bandler discovered a faster, more powerful means. The body of their research they called "neurolinguistic programming." The part we are concerned with, building rapport, they called "mirroring and matching."

Mirroring and matching requires following your client's voice, speech tempo and patterns, word usage, breathing, postures, and movements. You don't mimic in an obvious way. However, you do watch your client. If he speaks in a rapid staccato, you ease slowly into the same speech pattern. If your client speaks more slowly, you do the same. If your client crosses a leg, follow her lead. "Mirror and match." Again, don't mimic them instantaneously. Follow the person you are matching gradually as you continue with the interview. To master this, practice with a friend or spouse until you can do it naturally. Once you are able to do it naturally, you have an amazing tool for developing instant rapport. You will have the feeling that you have known the person you are mirroring for years, and they will have the same feeling about you.

Scientists do not know exactly why mirroring and matching works. They do know that people who already have rapport mirror and match without thinking about it and without any conscious effort. You can verify this yourself by watching two old friends converse. It is as if the brain were saying, "I must like this person because he is exactly like me." And the power of "like," of rapport, is usually more important than any rational, technical argument you can make for getting to agreement.

Asking Seven Essential Questions

During the first interview, there are seven questions that you absolutely must ask. By asking these questions, you will better understand the client's problems and the answers will help you to decide whether to accept the assignment or not.

1. *What problem needs solving?* Whether the client contacted you or vice versa, it is important to find out exactly why the client is seeing you. Something is bothering the client. Some clients will blurt it out immediately; others will say very little, not wanting to reveal the full story until they know more about you. Nevertheless, it is important that you draw them out and understand exactly why they are seeing you.

2. *Exactly what does the client want you to do?* What are the specific objectives of the assignment? Even though your primary purpose is to gain information in this first interview, it is important to have objectives explained explicitly once the reason for the assignment has been determined and you have talked to your potential client at some length about the task. For example, maybe this is a personnel problem; does she wish to decrease employee turnover? Does she wish to increase sales? Is there a problem in new product development, with too many unsuccessful products? Whatever your client's objectives might be, it is important for you to know exactly what they are.

3. *How will you know if the objectives have been met?* At first glance, this might seem obvious. If turnover is bad, the objective will be met when turnover is reduced. If sales are not what they should be, the objective will be met when sales increase, and so forth. However, you can easily see that there is much room for a difference of opinion. Will your client be satisfied if turnover decreases 1, 5, 10, or 25 percent? Or if sales increase 5, 10, or 15 percent? What you're looking for here is an exact figure so that both you and your client will know when the specified objectives have been met.

4. *Are there any particularly sensitive issues that you should watch out for?* Any organization made up of human beings contains political situations of one sort or another. As an outsider attempting to insert yourself into and analyze a particular problem, you may stumble into complicated political situations in the organization. For some types of consulting and for some clients, this will not be very important. For others, however, there will be some very sensitive issues that your client will not want you to disturb. Certain individuals or subjects may be off-limits for interviews. If you are not sensitive to these political issues, you could end up leaving the company in a much worse situation than when you came, even though ostensibly you solved the client's problem. Take pains to ask about and to understand the politically sensitive issues. Pay attention to detail so that you don't stumble around like a bull in a china shop but rather demonstrate the finesse of a real pro.

5. *Who will be your main point of contact?* Usually it's the individual who contacted you first, but this is not always the case. The only way to find out is to ask. Be certain that you have the name, title, and telephone number of this key individual.

6. *Will there be a backup contact?* Even if your main contact plans to be available throughout the assignment, request a backup contact. Your primary contact may have to leave on an unforeseen trip or be absent from the company just when you need her to make an important decision. So you lose time, and you may be forced into making a poor decision that could easily have been avoided. So always ask for the name of someone else in the company with the necessary authority on your project, and get her title and telephone number as well.

7. *What authority does each player have?* This is a key question. A player is anyone who has an impact on your engagement. If you do not take the time and trouble to identify the players, their responsibilities, and their authority, you could find yourself misdirected, either innocently by well-meaning individuals or deliberately by people in the company who do not wish you or the individual who hired you well. Some individuals may give you instructions or even verbal modifications of your contract even though they have no authority. Then you may find yourself in the difficult situation of being unable to bill for work requested by someone who had no authority to do so. Of course, beyond the loss of time and money, misdirection of this type could cause you to lose an important client.

Taking Notes

The only way to remember all you learn during the initial interview is to take notes. For this purpose, I recommend a notebook. I carry mine in my briefcase, and as soon as we start our conversation, I take it out and begin to take notes. If I don't understand a point, I ask the client to repeat what was said. Some consultant students have asked if a tape recorder wouldn't be a better way to record this information accurately, but I don't recommend it. A tape recorder is an intimidating device. Information that you are given as a consultant is frequently confidential; somehow pencil and notebook seem less threatening to a client's confidentiality. I have found that clients open up more if you use a notebook and a pencil.

I want to emphasize that in the very first interview you must find out everything that you possibly can. Never hesitate to ask for such items as the company's annual report or product brochures if you feel they will be useful to you. In fact, even after you have returned to your office, do not be afraid to call and ask for additional information if it will help you consider different ways to attack the client's problem.

Holding Off on Giving Advice

During the first interview, many new consultants are eager to help the potential client and show that they recognize the problem and have the solution. So they immediately begin giving advice. There are reasons you must not do this. One is that you usually don't really know enough about the situation yet to give advice. This is probably true in 95 percent of the cases. However, even in the 5 percent when the answer is obvious to you, do not volunteer anything unless you are already being paid for your time. After you have solved the problem, what reason does the client have to hire you?

I have made this mistake myself, but not anymore. Once a client called me about an exploratory interview and then suggested that I join him and his wife for supper at a nearby restaurant. The net result was that in addition to an hour during which I answered his questions, for the next two hours he and his wife pumped me for information over a delicious steak and drinks. For about a $30 meal, they received several hundred dollars' worth of consulting. On top of that, because I had apparently solved all their problems during our meeting and meal, they did not hire me. Why should they? Their problems appeared to be gone. Maybe the recommendations I made would have been different had I had time to think about them. Maybe I could have served my clients better. So both sides may have lost.

Interpreting Body Language

Psychologists have confirmed by research what salespeople have learned intuitively: What a buyer says may be less important than the message transmitted by the way he holds his body when he communicates with you. A potential client who speaks with arms folded across his chest, eyes avoiding yours, brow wrinkled, and fists clenched is probably feeling threatened by the situation and is not communicating openly with you. You are not getting all the information you could, and the client may not be convinced by what you are saying.

When you observe these physical signs, you should back off and try a different approach—anything to break this attitude and get the client to relax. A sign that you have been successful at this is that the client begins making direct eye contact and leans toward you. If he looks relaxed, with hands not clenched but open or extended, you have gotten through, and he is probably comfortable with the overall situation and is now ready for more open communication. But if he begins to turn his body away from you, avoiding direct eye contact again, you know he either does not want to discuss the issue you brought up or is suspicious of the particular approach you have taken. Again you are not getting through. To be successful, you must try a different approach.

Also watch to see if the client strokes his chin or neck, chews the end of a pencil, or leans back with his hands clasped behind his head. This indicates that what you say is being evaluated; the client is listening, and you are getting through. Continue to observe, and you will know whether you should continue that approach or attempt a new one.

Finally, you may observe a ready, almost eager attitude on the part of the client; he sits on the edge of the chair, leans forward, and catches your every word. Clearly you are making a favorable impression, and the client is demonstrating a readiness to act on your suggestions.

There are many complex issues involved in observing body language, and you need to know much more if you want to become an expert. But if you simply observe your client and think about what his or her body is telling you, you will learn quite a lot.

Three books that will help you understand body language are:

○ *Body Language* by Julius Fast (Pocket Books)
○ *Body Language* by David Lambert (HarperCollins)
○ *How to Read a Person Like a Book* by Gerard I. Nierenberg and Henry H. Calero (Cornerstone Library)

Making Use of Listening Techniques

Certain techniques for listening encourage various responses. You should use them to your advantage to draw the client out and obtain all the information you possibly can. Many of these listening techniques you already know. You learned them naturally, from the time you were are a toddler. However, few of us think about them. Consequently, we fail to use them in some situations when we are distracted by emotion. So reviewing them will help to ensure that you have them at your disposal and can use them consciously when you meet with your client.

If you want to keep the other person talking, neither agree nor disagree with what is being said, but use neutral words in a positive way. "I see" or "How interesting" or even "No kidding" indicates your interest and encourages your client to continue talking.

On the other hand, if you wish to let your potential client know that you understand the information she has been giving you and want her to move to the next point, restate what has been said to you. Say something like "As I understand it . . ." or "In other words . . ." and then summarize.

If you wish to probe for additional information at the same time, you must lead the individual toward that information tactfully. Ask questions such as "Why do you think this is so?" or "Why do you think this happened?"

Finally, at some point you will want to summarize the conversation and the ideas you've had. This is extremely important, because you will play back these ideas when you develop your proposal. You should do this recap when you control the interview. Take your time and use your notes to make certain you have it right. You can say, "Now, if I understand you correctly, these are the main objectives that you wish to cover, for the following reasons."

Identifying Emotions from Facial Expressions

You don't need to be a social scientist to identify happiness or sadness from the expression on a person's face. But other emotions may be more difficult to spot. The fact is, scientists have done considerable research in this area. According to Dr. Ronald E. Riggio, a psychology professor formerly at California State University at Fullerton and now director of the Kraviss Institute of Leadership at Claremont McKenna College, your ability to do this even affects your charisma.

See if you can identify the human emotions on the ten faces shown in Figure 5-1. You may find the exercise more difficult than you thought. (The answers appear on page 84.)

Like body language and listening techniques, your ability to instantly identify facial expressions can help considerably in working with your client and successfully completing the initial interview with a sale.

Figure 5-1. Ten common human emotions.

Ending the Interview

For some short assignments and some special situations, the client may wish to hire you on the spot. When you sense this . . . and you will learn to recognize this with more experience . . . simply ask for the assignment. Tell your potential client how you bill and ask if she would like you to help her with the problem. As I explain in Chapter 8, even though this constitutes a verbal contract, it is very important that you follow up with a letter confirming exactly what you will do and the compensation you will receive.

However, many engagements, especially the larger ones, require a formal proposal and additional analysis on your part to determine the appropriate methodology, the time frame, and the price for your services. Therefore, at the end of the initial interview, you will not be in a position to offer a proposal, only to indicate when you will submit a proposal. If a letter of proposal is satisfactory, always ask if you can call should you have additional questions; if not, ask what form the proposal should take. You should also ascertain whether you are the only consultant being contacted or whether your proposal must compete with others. Most government proposals are competitive. Deciding whether you wish to bid on a competitive contract is up to you. Many consultants refuse to bid on any type of contract and will politely withdraw if there is competition. My own recommendation is to consider all aspects of the situation, including your probability of winning.

Once you have established that a proposal is requested and when it is due, thank your client, make certain you leave your business card, and depart. If there is no specific deadline for your proposal, make sure you submit it as soon as possible. You never know what changes may take place in just a few days that would alter the demand for your services.

o   o   o

To show you the scope of questions that might be useful in an initial interview, I have included as Appendix C a comprehensive checklist of questions, "The Consultant's Questionnaire and Audit." Do not think that you must ask each and every question at each initial interview. Also don't feel that because a question is not included, you may not ask it. In every situation, you should modify this list for the particular client before the interview. During the interview, if additional questions seem appropriate, make sure that you ask them as well.

Identification of Facial Expressions in Figure 5-1

1. Angry
2. Sheepish, embarrassed
3. Happy, contented
4. Puzzled, uncertain
5. Upset, disgusted
6. Surprised
7. Fearful
8. Sly, devious
9. Bored, disinterested
10. Tired, relaxed, relieved

If you got eight or more out of the ten right, you're doing pretty well. Five to seven is fair. Fewer than five says this is something you might want to work on.

In the next chapter, we'll look at what to do after the interview: write a proposal.

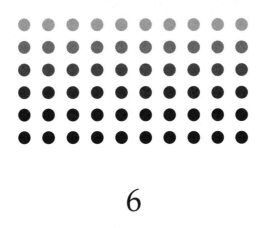

6

How to Write a Proposal

If an agreement is not reached during the initial interview (and often it is not), the prospective client will expect a written proposal. In this chapter, we find out what a proposal must do and why it is necessary. All the essential elements of a proposal are listed and explained, and a proposal structure is provided.

Why a Written Proposal Is Necessary

A written proposal accomplishes five tasks that are important for you in getting on contract and beginning work as a consultant.

1. *The proposal finalizes the agreement.* Sometimes, even after an excellent exploratory interview, you have not yet made the sale. It is not unusual for a potential client to ask for a written proposal even though he is 90 percent certain about hiring your services. The proposal, then, is a sales document that ties together all the loose ends and closes the deal.

2. *The proposal documents what you are going to do.* The services you are going to perform in this consulting engagement should be clearly understood by both you and your client. A proposal does exactly that; it spells out in black and white exactly what you are going to do so that there is a documented basis for understanding.

3. *The proposal documents the time frame of your performance.* Just as what you are going to do is important, so is how long you will take in doing it and the time sequence of each event. Sometimes

the client will want to know partial information before the full project is complete. When the client wants information by a certain period, he may not hire you if he is not certain he will get it by that time. Documenting this time frame helps assure your potential client that he will get what he wants when he wants it.

4. *The proposal documents what you are going to receive for your services.* Unless you are independently wealthy, you aren't in business as a consultant just for fun, even though you may enjoy it immensely. The proposal specifies the compensation that you are going to receive for the services you propose to provide. Documenting this compensation can save you much trouble later on.

5. *The proposal forms the basis for a contract.* As I demonstrate later in the chapter, the proposal can be the basis for a contract. In fact you can actually turn a proposal into a contract by adding a few sentences.

How to Write a Good Proposal

There are four points to remember in writing a good proposal.

1. *Keep the structure clear and logical.* I discuss structure in the next chapter.

2. *Use a professional but friendly style.* When you submit a proposal, just as in a face-to-face meeting, be professional but be friendly. In fact, if you are writing a letter proposal, you can be downright folksy; as long as you avoid stepping over professional bounds, it will only enhance your chances of being hired.

3. *Don't spring surprises in your proposal.* I mentioned this in Chapter 4, and although it sounds very simple, this is one of the hardest things to do. After you return from your initial meeting, you will frequently get new ideas that are different from what you and your client originally visualized. These ideas may be so good that you find it very tempting to include them in the proposal. Resist this temptation, unless you can check with your client first. There may be other reasons you don't know about why the client cannot accept these new ideas. He or she may need time to sell this idea to other employees, even top management in his or her

company. If you surprise your client in the proposal, there may not be sufficient time to do this. Therefore, no matter how good the idea, unless you can clear it with your client before submitting it in the proposal, don't do it yet. You can propose it after you get the contract.

4. *Check before you send.* If at all possible, double-check the main points of the proposal with your client. If it's a short letter proposal, call the client and read it to him or her over the phone. For government contracts and some industrial contracts on a competitive bid, this may not be allowed. However, you should always ask. The worst thing someone can say is no. It is in everyone's best interest that the proposal be on the right track before you send it. Don't assume that changes can be made after your client receives it.

The Structure for a Letter Proposal

Sometimes, especially with large or competitive contracts, the client will specify the structure of the proposal. (This is especially true of the government and large industrial companies.) In this case, follow whatever structure is specified. However, a letter proposal is quite sufficient for most of your consulting engagements. Let's see what one looks like.

Opening

Simply state that you are writing to submit your ideas for the project discussed earlier.

Background

Begin by *restating* the background of the consulting situation. That is, restate your client's assumptions and other general facts in the case. This reassures the client that she has made an astute analysis of the situation. (If the client's assumptions are not correct, then you must convince her of this *before* submitting your proposal. If the customer is determined to use her assumptions, even if you have told her that they are incorrect and why, then you have a choice. You can use the client's assumptions or refuse the assignment. If you refuse, be as tactful as possible. The client will respect your stand and may contact you in the future.)

Objectives

State the objectives of the engagement precisely. Describe exactly what your client will learn or receive as a result of your work. I like to present these objectives in a way that makes them stand out visually—by using bullets, for example:

- Identify at least three secondary retail markets for the new product line.
- Develop sales projections for six months and for twelve months.
- Recommend staffing increases to achieve sales projections.

Study Methods

Describe alternative methodologies for accomplishing the objectives. Discuss the advantages of each alternative and then indicate which method you propose to use, and why. When you describe the methodology, consider your audience. If your client is technical, use technical language; if not, don't confuse things with technical equations or terms. Stating all the alternatives, even those you do not intend to use, is extremely important, especially if you have competition. Competitors may propose alternative methods, and it is important that you show your client why these methods will not work and why the method you have chosen is the best. If you are convincing on this point, your potential client will use your proposal to help swing others to your way of thinking and to adopt your proposed methodology.

Potential Problems

Any project inherently has potential problems that could limit or detract from its achievement. Don't omit or gloss over these potential problems; document them clearly, but also state how you will handle them if they occur. Clients smart enough to hire a consultant are smart enough to realize that potential problems exist. You cannot fool them into thinking that your approach is problem-free. In fact, they will respect you more for anticipating the problems, as long as you have thought through what corrective actions you will take.

Data Flow Charts and Product Development Schedules

One type of a data flow chart is called a PERT chart. PERT (Program Evaluation and Review Technique) was developed for the management of complex multimillion-dollar projects for the government. It shows what tasks you will accomplish and in what order for most efficient management. It is more appropriate for very complex programs, but it can always be included in the proposal. If nothing else, it adds a bit of showmanship to your proposal and demonstrates the control you have over the project. A product development schedule will probably be sufficient for most projects. I discuss how to build both in Chapter 9.

The Finished Product

Your client will want to know what to expect by way of a finished product. Will you be furnishing a report? A staff study? Photographs? How many copies will you provide? This last point can be important, because frequently the client will need to distribute the information to others, perhaps the board of directors or other managers in the company. Specify exactly what you will furnish and what it will contain, the number of copies, drawings, photographs, and other details. Include the date on which you will complete your study and submit your final report.

Cost and Payment Information

For most small contracts, it is not important to break down cost information unless the client requests it. However, the timing of payment is important. The client will want to know not only how much you want but when you want it. For example, do you want 50 percent of your fee up front and 50 percent at completion? One-third at signing of contract, one-third at some intermediate point, and one-third at completion? Work-in-progress billing with monthly invoices, or everything in one lump sum when you submit your report? (The last, by the way, is not recommended.)

Converting a Proposal into a Contract

The last paragraph is a close. *Close* is a sales term meaning that you complete the deal with a prospect. It can, and should, be friendly, but it can also serve as a contract if you combine it with an author-ity to proceed. Here's how to do this in a friendly but professional way. Say something like:

> Please simply sign at the bottom where indicated, for author-ity to proceed under these conditions, and return the original to me. However, if you have any questions or suggestions per-taining to this proposal or the work you would like accom-plished, please do not hesitate to call me at 212-555-1234.

If you decide to use the suggested last paragraph and allow it to be converted into a contract, you may want your attorney to review this information.

An example of a letter proposal is shown in Figure 6-1, and a more extensive proposal is in Appendix D. You can see that both structures are very similar.

Now you know how to go on contract with clients. But how much should you charge for your services? We'll discuss that in Chapter 7.

Figure 6-1. A typical proposal letter.

April 24, 20XX

Mr. Joseph Black
President
Unique Sales Co., Inc.
4571 Plainview Avenue
Pasadena, CA 91107

Dear Mr. Black:

We enjoyed the pleasure of meeting with you on Wednesday, April 18. We were amazed to learn that you had been in the mail order business selling government surplus for over 33 years.

The purpose of this letter is to present our proposal for a research study based on the objectives discussed in our meeting with you. Please keep in mind that this is a proposal and subject to your ideas and suggestions.

A RESEARCH PROPOSAL FOR:

An Investigation of the Seasonal Sales Trend of Unique Sales Co., Inc.

Background

Unique Sales Company is a mail order company that sells to individual consumers as well as to governments of foreign countries. The company originally sold marine equipment but has now expanded its sales to other items, such as aircraft parts, auto parts, and hydraulics.

Unique Sales Company's main objective was to sell government surplus items; however, recently there has been a drastic cut in the availability of government surplus items.

The sales trend of this company has its peak months around the first five to six months of the year; the other months are slow. In the eastern part of the United States, the sales are very much affected by the weather. The more severe the winters are, the higher the sales are, because people stay at home and read the sales catalog.

Objectives

The primary objective of this study would be to gain an insight into the factors causing cyclical variations in sales for the mail order industry and for Unique Sales specifically. Recommendations for Unique Sales' actions will be made upon evaluation of data collected.

(continues)

Figure 6-1. *(continued)*

More specifically, the following areas would be investigated:
  I. Sales trends (cross-section)
      A. Industrial-oriented mail order house
      B. Consumer goods–oriented mail order house
      C. Industrial/consumer-oriented mail order house
 II. Factors affecting sales
      A. Weather
      B. Product line
      C. Target market
      D. Advertising effectiveness

Study Methods

Several market research methods would be incorporated into this study. The first would be an exhaustive search for all readily available secondary market statistics and data. This would be statistical information already published or obtainable at a nominal cost. Possible valuable sources for this information would be U.S. government agencies, trade associations, the National Weather Bureau, and trade periodical publishers, as well as the standard business bibliographies.

In addition, personal telephone calls would be made to selected individuals in this industry, such as those recognized as the most knowledgeable in the industry. From these telephone calls, an attempt would be made to obtain data not uncovered during the search for secondary information.

Potential Problems

In most secondary research studies, the existence of relevant market statistics and data cannot be determined until the actual study is begun. Market statistics do not exist for all industries and, in some cases, exist only in the files of private firms. In these cases, the information is considered proprietary and is not generally released to the business community.

In many instances, the use of personal interviews can compensate for lack of published data and bring to the forefront valuable data otherwise not available.

Overall, even with possible information gaps, the research team is confident we can supply the Unique Sales Company with a viable, well-documented report.

The Report

Our report would consist of a description of the study objective, design, and the findings reported at three levels of detail.

First would be what we see as the major findings or highlights of the study, including our conclusion and recommendations. This section would be followed by a more detailed and documented discussion and analysis of the findings. An appendix would contain brochures and other supplementary materials.

Cost and Timing

The cost of his completed study would be $2,500, one-half payable on authorization to proceed and one-half payable on delivery of final report, two copies of which will be delivered in its final form. The study will be compiled, and the reports delivered, four weeks after authorization to proceed.

We know that you are busy. Therefore, simply sign below for authorization for us to proceed with this work. If you have any questions or suggestions to make regarding this proposal and the proposed study, please feel free to call us at once.

Sincerely yours,

_____

W. W. Smith
Director of Research

_____

Mark Tizon
Principal Consultant

Authorization to Proceed

I agree to the terms in the above proposal and grant authorization to proceed in accordance with these terms.

_____

Joseph Black
President
Unique Sales Co., Inc.

7

PRICING YOUR SERVICES

Pricing is crucial. As well as determining the size of your billings and profits, it has an important effect on your image as a consultant. In this chapter, I will show you how to price your services. I will discuss the three basic price strategies available to you as a new consultant and the different methods of billing for your services.

Established Consultants Can Make a Bundle

We covered part of the potential for compensation in Chapter 1. According to the Ransford Group in Houston, Texas, strategy consultants with major firms earn $41,000 to $58,000 a year. That's on the low side for pre-MBA "associate consultants" with about a year's experience. The high side consists of partners, vice-presidents, and directors who not only have MBAs but on the average have twelve years' experience as consultants. They get $300,000 to $600,000 plus a 40 percent bonus![1] While pay may vary according to consulting specialty, they don't vary much. However, before you rush out to celebrate your new consulting status and start advertising these astronomical rates, you should know that compensation varies considerably depending on the size of the company and that the fees you will be able to charge as an individual will probably be considerably less.

Three Price Strategies

The three basic price strategies available to you are a low-price strategy, a high-price strategy, and a meet-the-competition strategy. Let's look at each one in turn.

A Low-Price Strategy

A low-price strategy is basically penetration pricing. The idea is that you will enter the marketplace with a price lower than your already established competitors; you will attract clients because of your bargain prices. This strategy can work for new consultants, and with it you will be able to attract more business than you could otherwise.

However, there are some serious shortcomings. First, with consulting you are basically selling your time, so you will have to work harder than those established in your profession to make the same amount of money. This also means that your competitors will have additional financial resources to use in countermarketing campaigns if they choose. Second, price has an image connotation. In the minds of many, low price means "cheap," and a low-priced consultant may be viewed as a low-quality consultant. You may be given only the less rewarding, "grubbier" types of assignments and not those that provide high exposure to top-level management. Finally, after choosing a low price, you may find it extremely difficult to raise your price later on as your practice grows.

I have a friend, George W., who is a CPA specializing in tax consulting. When George first started out as an independent consultant, it was part-time and after-hours. To build his practice, he chose a low-price strategy; his billing rate was only 50 percent of the average rate for these services. Some years later, after his part-time practice had grown, George quit his full-time job and bought an established tax consulting practice whose clients were billed at more than twice the rate George had been charging. George now had two different rates for his clients. Because he was now full-time, it seemed to make sense to raise his fees to the higher rate. However, as soon as he did this, every one of his former clients threatened to or actually quit using his services. George needed these clients, so he reversed himself and maintained two different prices. However, he was hardly comfortable with this solution. First, he felt he was cheating his new clients by charging them so much more. But George also felt he was cheating himself, because he clearly was now worth the higher figure even if his older clients wouldn't pay it. When George brought this problem to me for advice, my suggestion was to raise the low rate slowly. George did this, raising his prices from 10 to 15 percent every year. In a couple of years, the amount charged his lower-priced class of customers was close enough to that of the higher-priced class that he could finally accept the loss of the clients who refused to go along with the higher billing rate.

A High-Price Strategy

Another option that any consultant has, whether new or old, is to adopt a high-price strategy. This one is somewhat more risky. You are telling the world that you are worth more money; your image is one of a high-quality consultant. However, your potential clients may not believe you. It goes without saying that you had better be what you advertise. The high-price strategy is, however, a viable one that many new consultants overlook. They do this either because they are afraid they are not worth the money, because they somehow have a nagging feeling they are ripping off their potential client, or because they fear they will get no business if they choose to charge higher prices. The truth is that in many cases, you not only are worth much more than you think but may be worth more than established consultants who are already earning big fees. Before you reject a high-price strategy, consider the following stories; they are all true.

○ My student, Harry S., graduated with an MBA from California State University at Los Angeles and went to work for a major consulting firm. The day after he left the university, the firm that hired him billed Harry's time at $1,000 a day plus $300 overhead, a total of $1,300 a day. This was more than twenty years ago!

○ Some years ago, I got together with two friends. One had been the city manager of a major U.S. city and had retired into consulting; the other was general manager of a division of a major aerospace company. The former city manager said, "Boy, this consulting is great. Do you know that I'm getting $50 an hour?" This friend had more than thirty years' experience as manager of various cities and also had a Ph.D. At the time, I was billing $100 an hour, and I said, "Bob, you are not charging nearly enough. I'm billing at twice what you're billing at. I'm billing at $100 an hour."

The general manager of the aerospace company looked at both of us and smiled. "You're both undercharging," he said. "We pay our consultants $250 an hour, and to my knowledge, none of them are as qualified or as good as either one of you."

○ Several years ago, I received a telephone call from an individual who identified himself as Jerry S., a former student at my university. Jerry said that he had been referred to me, even though he had not been my student, and that he had graduated eight years previously with a bachelor's degree. He explained that he and his partner gave seminars for companies on management styles and had put together a workbook for the seminars. Because I was known as an expert in direct response marketing, he wanted some advice on how they might self-publish this workbook and sell it through the mail. During our talk, I became intrigued with Jerry's frequent mention that his clients were top management, and I finally asked him who his clients were. "Oh," he said, "we give special seminars for small groups of top management in each company. Usually there are no more than five to seven in each group." I asked about his pricing. "Oh, we go high, for image purposes," Jerry replied. "We charge $7,000 a day." I laughed and told him that he understood the marketing of his services very well. Seven thousand dollars a day was far above the average fees charged by many providing similar services who held Ph.D. degrees in those days.

○ A friend of mine, Mary T., was going to start a part-time consulting business doing copyediting for writers. I told her of my concern that people generally charge too little for their services, and I gave her a short talk on not being afraid to use a high-price strategy. At the time of this incident, copyediting services were going for approximately $10 to $15 per hour. But I thought she knew that. A week later, she told me she had her first client. I asked how much she had charged. "Forty dollars an hour," she said. I almost fell over when I found out how much she was receiving, and so did she when I told her that she was receiving three to four times the amount usually charged by experienced copyeditors. And by the way, her client was more than satisfied with her services and employed her again at this rate.

Note that in all cases, these consultants had little difficulty getting the higher fees they charged. In fact, their clients were quite ready to pay them. Again the reason was the image value of the consulting services offered. Therefore, if you are good at what you intend to do as a consultant, do not be afraid to use this pricing strategy. More consultants err by not choosing to use it than by choosing it. It is not a rip-off if you are good at what you do. In some cases, you may find that clients will not even want to engage your services if you charge too low a price. They will feel that either your work is weak or you are too inexperienced. Therefore, even from the standpoint of idealism and wanting to do the greatest amount of good, consider the high-price strategy.

A Meet-the-Competition Price Strategy

This means simply that you choose a price that is approximately the same as your competitors or potential competitors are charging. If you choose this particular strategy, you must offer something else in addition to your regular services. Otherwise, why should anyone deal with you? But if you do offer some differential advantage, and if you promote it to your potential clients, the meet-the-competition price can also be a successful strategy. Differential advantages may include quicker service, specialized additional service not offered by anyone else, around-the-clock availability to answer consulting needs, quicker results, or better results.

If you are going to choose this strategy, spend some time thinking through your differential advantage: What additional service can you offer above and beyond your competition? Or how can you make the consulting service you offer clearly better than anyone else?

Other Considerations

Two other considerations should be taken into account when you are considering your pricing strategy: industry pricing and client price adjustment.

Industry Pricing

Certain industries have accepted prices for certain services. It is very difficult to violate this norm and build a viable practice. For example, employment agencies, on receipt of a job order, send the client several candidates to interview. If one of their candidates is hired, the agency may be paid from 10 to 15 percent of the individual's annual salary. Executive search firms supply three or more candidates for a particular job; if one of their candidates is hired, they get up to 30 percent, or more, of the executive's annual salary. Sometimes they get paid on an hourly or per diem basis whether one of their candidates gets hired or not. They perform essentially the same service, but note the significant difference in pricing. Therefore, when you are developing your fee schedule, it is important to consider the industry you are in. Employment agencies are simply not going to be paid the same as search firms, no matter how good a job they do. Of course, you can deviate from the normal range of pricing in your industry, but if you do, you may find it much more difficult to get and keep clients.

Client Price Adjustment

Some consultants charge different amounts to different clients, depending on who they are or how big they are. For example, sometimes the government (federal, state, or local) has certain restrictions on the amount it can pay consultants, by policy or by law. If you expect to do a lot of government work, this will affect your pricing strategy.

Similarly, small companies generally cannot afford to pay as much as large companies. The examples I gave of the aerospace company that paid consultants $250 per hour and the consulting firm that billed the recent graduate's time at $1,000 a day both had to do with clients that were large companies. Clearly, smaller companies cannot pay these kinds of fees. You are therefore faced with a decision about billing if you deal with both large and small firms. You must either base your billing on the size of the company, have one low price for all, or have one higher price for all. The higher price eliminates a certain segment of your potential market. So may the lower price, because of image. A two-price system may also lead to problems. You must make this decision yourself after considering all the factors in your situation.

Finally . . . You Must Investigate the Marketplace

At this point you probably have a rough idea of what you are going to charge for your services. Before you pick a strategy and finalize your basic price structure, you should investigate your market for a reality check. If you know other consultants in your field, ask them what they charge. You don't have to copy them, but you should at least know how much they're getting, or say they're getting. You can also contact potential clients. If you don't know them personally, attend professional meeting or trade shows, and you'll meet plenty, as well as other consultants you can ask. You can also contact professional associations and the editors of professional journals in your field of expertise. Both keep a close watch on what's going on, and if they don't know the going rates off the tops of their heads, they can tell you where to get this important information.

Your job now is to consolidate all this information: industry pricing, client price adjustment, the marketplace in your geographical area and area of expertise, and the pricing strategy you have decided on. Put it all together, and you have established your price structure. Now let's look at different methods of billing.

Methods of Billing

Basically, there are four different methods of billing: (1) daily or hourly, (2) retainer, (3) performance, (4) and fixed-price. Let's look at each.

Computing Billings Daily or Hourly

Billing on a time basis is fairly common with consultants, but deciding whether to bill on an hourly or a daily rate takes some consideration; as with so many other things, it's a trade-off. Some consultants feel that just getting started on any project will take the better part of a day, so they won't bill at less than a full day's rate. Even if a client wanted just two hours of their time, they would bill their daily rate as a minimum. Other consultants, especially those who work part-time and those who want maximum flexibility in their scheduling, use the hourly rate. Billing hourly lets them work at home or at some other location; they can also work for a couple of hours on one project and a couple of hours on another, and in that way they work with several clients in a single day. Of course you can also bill for fractional hours.

If you are considering a daily or hourly rate, be very certain you don't price yourself so low that you can't make a decent living. Even if you elect to go with a penetration-price strategy, be very careful when you set your fee. Sometimes new consultants get into the field simply because they do not want to work for someone else. They are perfectly willing to work for the same amount that they made at their previous job. At first glance, that seems perfectly logical. However, using your previous salary to set your hourly rate is a trap you should avoid. Let's try out some numbers (pay attention; this is important).

Let's say you are currently making $52,000 a year and your fringe benefits are worth another $5,000; that's a total of $57,000 a year. If you work forty hours a week times fifty weeks (considering that you will have two weeks for vacation), that's two thousand hours a year; $57,000 divided by 2,000 is $28.50 per hour. So should your billing rate be $28.50 an hour? Absolutely not! This figure does not take into consideration the fact that when you are working on your own, you will have overhead to contend with. Even though you'll try to keep this overhead as low as possible, I think you'll be surprised how fast it adds up. For example, let's make the following assumptions about your yearly expenses:

Clerical support	$ 8,000
Office rent	10,000
Telephone	4,400
Automobile	8,000
Insurance, benefits, etc.	7,000
Marketing expenses	20,000
Entertainment	2,000
Professional dues and subscriptions	1,000
Accounting and legal fees	5,000
Miscellaneous	2,600
Total	$68,000

Therefore, to receive $57,000 income a year, the same that you got working for someone else, you must charge $57,000 *plus* the $68,000 overhead, for a total of $125,000 a year. That works out to $62.50 per hour. If you want to tack on a profit for your firm (if it is incorporated) over and above your salary, you must add something to this figure. If you want a profit of 10 percent, you now have a billing rate of $68.75 per hour. That's what you must charge to earn the same salary you were making when you worked for someone else.

Working on Retainer

With a retainer, you receive a constant monthly fee in return for a guarantee that a certain number of your hours will be available to your client. This has advantages for both sides. For you it gives a guaranteed income and cash flow, which can be very advantageous. In fact, most consultants would be willing to take a retainer at a reduced fee in order to ensure that money was coming in every month. For your client, a retainer guarantees that you won't work for a competitor and that the client will get first priority on your time. An additional advantage to you is that if the hours are not used, you get paid anyhow.

Performance Billing

I will discuss performance contracts in Chapter 8. Basically, this means no money without results. You decide on a percentage you will get based on the results attained as a result of your work. For example, for every dollar saved through your recommendations you might get 25 percent.

Industry Week reports that performance-based fee structures, also called value-based or equity-based, are becoming more and more common, with some firms reporting 50 to 70 percent of their fees based on performance.[2]

Keep in mind that:

1. Performance billing is a good marketing tool.
2. It's critical to put all terms in writing.

3. It's a mistake to tie performance to profits, because profits can be manipulated for accounting or tax purposes.

Fixed-Price Billing

A fixed-price contract, which we will talk about in Chapter 8, is one in which you agree to do a certain job and get paid a fixed amount for it. The number of hours you work on the project is entirely up to you; you must put in whatever it takes to get the job done. With a fixed-price contract, you can make more money, but at a greater risk, because you must guarantee accomplishment.

For a fixed-price contract to be profitable, you must be sure to follow these five guidelines:

1. Give yourself a "pad" in your estimations; overestimate a little to allow for miscalculations.
2. Use good estimating techniques, as discussed in Chapter 9.
3. Control your costs closely.
4. Carefully document exactly what you are required to do.
5. Be sure all changes to the contract are in writing.

There are some basic formulas for setting the fee in a fixed-price contract; a typical one is shown in Figure 7-1. In this formula, overhead has been included as 65 percent of direct labor. Obviously, you must cover your overhead some way; this percentage method is an attempt to spread your annual overhead among your various clients. You do this by estimating what you think your yearly overhead expenses will be, converting that into a percentage of your estimated annual income, and then adding that percentage amount onto the labor costs of each contract. In this case, a billing rate of $50 an hour would yield $100,000 annual income; estimated expenses of $65,000 a year works out to 65 percent for overhead. This particular formula incorporates a profit of 10 percent. The profit percentage is somewhat arbitrary, although it may be regulated in government contracts or contracts with companies that limit consultant's profits by policy.

Disclosing the Fee

Sometimes only one of the different ways of presenting the fee to the client is acceptable. Some clients will not accept a daily or

Figure 7-1. A basic formula for a fixed-price contract.

Four elements of the formula are:

1. Direct labor
2. Overhead
3. Direct expenses
4. Profit

Sample Computations

1. Direct labor:

Consultant	12 days @ $600/day =	$7,200.00	
Assistant	4 days @ $120/day =	$480.00	
Secretary	5 days @ $80/day =	$400.00	$8,080.00

2. Overhead (65% of direct labor):   5,252.00

3. Direct expenses:

Air travel	$500.00	
Rental car	$200.00	
Special printing	$100.00	
Travel expenses (hotel, etc.)	$400.00	1,200.00
Subtotal		$14,532.00

4. Profit (10% of subtotal): $ 1,453.20

   TOTAL PRICE $15,985.20

hourly rate; they prefer a fixed-price contract. Therefore, it is a good idea to calculate your fee using all the various methods. If one way is unacceptable to your client, try another. However, in disclosing the fee, it is generally best to provide the minimum amount of financial data that is required. Therefore, for a fixed-price contract, if possible indicate only the bottom-line price. In the example in Figure 7-1, indicate the price as $10,918.60. If you are billing on a daily rate, give just that rate—$400 a day plus expenses, for example.

Some clients, especially the government, require full disclosure. In such cases, you have to make a full presentation, such as that in Figure 7-1, showing exactly how your figures are arrived at. The average client probably doesn't care about your overhead.

Certainly there is no value to you in divulging your overhead so that potential competitors could discover it as well. Simply include it within your daily or hourly rate or within the fixed price if your fee is stated in this fashion.

Now you have your pricing structure and you know the various methods of billing. Let's see how we will use this information in the next chapter to develop consulting contracts.

Notes

1. The Ransford Group, from *National Business Employment Weekly* on the Internet at public.wsj.com/careers/resources/documents/19980529-stratconsult-tab.htm
2. Glenn Hasek, "Sharing the Risk," *Industry Week* (May 4, 1998).

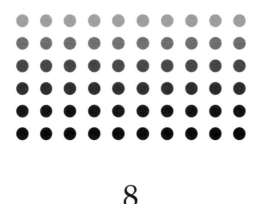

8

WHAT YOU MUST KNOW ABOUT CONSULTING CONTRACTS

In this chapter, I show you why consulting contracts are necessary and how you can develop your own. I will also discuss the different methods of incurring a contractual obligation, the different types of contracts, and the major elements of any contract. Finally, I will include a sample contract to help you develop your own.

Why a Contract Is Necessary

You may think a handshake should do it among people of goodwill. And it might. In fact, a handshake may be contractually binding. But the kind of contract we're talking about does more. It is written. A good written consulting contract:

○ Ensures that you and your client both understand fully the services you are to perform. For your part, this will prevent wasted time, wasted resources, and wasted effort. It will also help ensure that you have a happy client at the end of the engagement. And a happy client will give you more work in the future and good referrals to others.

○ Will help you to get paid. Always keep in mind that even though you really enjoy your work, you must get paid in order to survive. Consulting may be a lot of fun, but without getting paid you won't be around to enjoy it. Having a written contract that documents your compensation will help you to gently remind your client of the financial obligations. If all goes sour and you must sue to get paid (this rarely happens, but it could), a signed contract is almost a necessity.

Developing Your Own Contract

It is most definitely possible to develop your own standard consulting contract and to use it in every situation with only minor changes regarding the particular client, services, compensation, time period of engagement, and other factors. I will talk more about this later on in this chapter under "A Sample Contract," but note now that you should have your attorney assist you with this. Do not, however, dump the whole project on your attorney; it will cost you excessively. A better procedure is to develop each element yourself, using the information in this chapter, and rough out the contract the way you would like it. Use the sample contract shown in Figure 8-1 as a guide. Once your rough contract has been formulated, have your attorney review it and put it in final form.

If Your Client Has a Standard Contract

Sometimes your client will be a large corporation that has a standard contract. You may be asked to use this contract rather than yours. Naturally, the final decision is always up to you. You should have your attorney review it, but usually these contracts are not unfair, and you may find them entirely acceptable.

Methods of Incurring a Contractual Obligation

There are five basic ways that a consultant can enter into a contractual obligation: (1) formal contracts; (2) letter contracts; (3) order agreements; (4) purchase orders; and (5) verbal contracts.

Let's look at each of these in turn.

Figure 8-1. Sample consulting contract form.

_____, 20___

CONSULTANT AGREEMENT

AGREEMENT made _____, between _____,
                              date   name of client
with principal offices at _____ hereinafter called
                                         client's address
"Client" and _____ of _____
                    name of consultant   consultant's address
hereinafter called "Consultant."

1. Services. Consultant, as an independent contractor, agrees to perform, during
the term of this Agreement, the following services: _____
_____
_____
_____

under the terms and conditions hereinafter set forth.

2. Products. The term "Products" shall mean the client's line of _____
_____

3. Compensation.
(a) Client shall pay Consultant at the rate of ____ per hour for each hour that
Consultant shall perform services during the term of this Agreement; provided that the
number of hours does not exceed _____ without the written consent of Client.
(b) In addition to the hourly compensation provided herein, Client agrees to
pay Consultant $_____ under the following conditions: _____
_____

4. Term. The initial term of this Agreement shall commence on the _____
day of _____, 20___, and end on the last day of _____, 20___, provided however that either party may terminate this Agreement at any time during the
initial term of any extension term by giving the other party _____ days' notice in
writing.
This Agreement may be extended beyond the initial term or any extension term
only by the written agreement of both parties prior to the expiration of the initial term
or any extension.

5. Designation of Duties. Consultant shall receive his requests for services to be
performed from _____, _____,
                        client's name   title
_____.
                 company and address

6. Restrictive Covenant. During the term of this Agreement, Consultant shall not
make his services available to any competitor of Client in the specific field in which he
is performing services for Client.

7. Indemnity and Insurance. Consultant shall indemnify and hold harmless Client, its officers, and employees against all losses, claims, liabilities, damages, and expenses of any nature directly or indirectly arising out of or as a result of any act of
omission by Consultant, its employees, agents, or subcontractors in the performance
of this Agreement.
If Consultant uses, or intends to use, a personal automobile in the perform-

ance of this Agreement, Consultant shall maintain throughout the term of this Agreement automobile liability insurance in accordance with the law of the State of _____ and not less than _____.

8. Patent Rights. Consultant agrees during the term of this Agreement and for a period of 12 months after the termination of this Agreement, to assign to Client, its successors, assignees, or nominees all right, title, and interest in and to all inventions, improvements, copyrightable material, techniques, and designs made or conceived by him solely or jointly with others, relating to Products, in the performance of this Agreement, together with all United States and foreign patents and copyrights which may have been obtained thereon, and at Client's request and expense, will execute and deliver all proper assignments thereof.

9. Confidentiality. Consultant shall not disclose, publish, or authorize others to publish design data, drawings, specifications, reports, or other information pertaining to the work assigned to him by Client without the prior written approval of Client. Upon the expiration or sooner termination of this Agreement, Consultant agrees to return to Client all drawings, specifications, data, and other material obtained by Consultant from Client, or developed by Consultant, in connection with the performance of this Agreement.

10. Reimbursable Expenses. The following expenses will be billed in addition to compensation:

(a) Travel expenses necessary in order to perform services required by the Agreement. Use of personal automobile will be billed at __¢ per mile.

(b) Telephone, telegraph, and telex charges

(c) Computer charges

(d) Printing and reproduction

(e) Other expenses resulting directly from performance of services in the Agreement.

11. Warranty. Consultant services will be performed in accordance with generally and currently accepted consulting principles and practices. This warranty is in lieu of all other warranties either expressed or implied.

12. Limitation of Consultant Liability. Client agrees to limit any and all liability or claim for damages, cost of defense, or expenses against Consultant to a sum not to exceed \$_____, or the total amount of compensation, whichever is less, on account of any error, omission, or negligence.

13. Payment Terms. Terms of payment are as follows: \$_____ due on the signing of Agreement and \$_____ due _____, 20____. \$_____ due on delivery of _____. A _____% per month charge will be added to all delinquent accounts. In the event Consultant shall be successful in any suit for nonpayment, Consultant shall be entitled to recover reasonable legal costs and expenses for bringing and maintaining this suit as a part of damages.

IN WITNESS WHEREOF, the parties have signed this Agreement.

_____

Consultant

_____

Client

Formal Contracts

The formal contract is a written document describing the obligations of both parties. For most assignments, I would recommend that you formalize your engagement in this way. It will save you many problems, heartaches, lost fees, and misunderstandings later on. I used the sample contract shown in Figure 8-1 as the basis of a contract with a major multibillion-dollar corporation.

Letter Contracts

A letter contract can be evolved from a proposal. It is in written form, but it is much simpler than a formal contract. However, it contains the basic elements of the contract, and though it may look like a letter, it qualifies as a contract.

Order Agreements

Order agreements have the force of contracts. They are typically used for the purchase of consulting services to be accomplished over a period of time. They commit both you and your client to contractual terms before work is authorized. For example, an order agreement may commit you to so many hours of consulting over, say, a year's period; it also specifies how much you will be paid. However, your client decides when to initiate the agreement. In other words, an order agreement ties both you and your client to terms, but not necessarily to a start date. In some cases, the order agreement will be combined with an option that gives the client flexibility on whether or not to actually use these services. But if the services are used, the terms are as set forth in the order agreement.

Purchase Orders

A purchase order is an internal form authorizing you to do work and to bill for it. It is generally used by larger companies to acquire relatively low-cost products or services. Consulting services may be "ordered" on a purchase order rather than a formal contract because your client can do this quickly and simply, as compared with going through the formal contractual process, which could involve your client's legal staff and some time delay. Usually purchase orders have a limit specified by company management, say, $25,000 or less.

Verbal Contracts

Always remember that a verbal contract is still a contract. Verbal contracts are very common in consulting, but they are not always desirable. They are definitely not recommended in two situations: with new clients and for large projects. If the nature of the consulting situation with a new client is such that a more formal written contract is not possible, try to get a significant part of the payment up front before you start work. Also be very clear with your client: Spell out your objectives, what you are going to do, and how and when you are going to do it.

Types of Contracts

There are four basic types of contracts in consulting, each with variations. These are: (1) fixed-price contracts; (2) cost contracts; (3) performance contracts; and (4) incentive contracts.

There is no one best contract for all situations but rather a one best contract for a particular situation. Therefore, it is important to know the advantages and disadvantages of each one of these contracts.

The Fixed-Price Contract

A fixed-price contract is one in which you agree to do a certain job for a predetermined amount. With few exceptions, no price adjustment is made after the award of the contract, regardless of your actual cost in performing it. As the consultant, you assume all the cost risk. If your estimate is poor, you could actually lose money on a fixed-price contract. On the other hand, if you can reduce the cost below the original estimate, you have the potential for making increased profit. Therefore, the more certain you are of your cost and your potential for reducing it, the more willing you should be to take a fixed-price contract. Conversely, the more difficult it is to estimate a particular job, the more risk you assume and the less willing you should be to accept such a contract. With all types of contracts, it is important to have an accurate estimate, but with the fixed-price contract, it is crucial.

The Cost Contract

In a cost contract, you are paid on your actual cost of performing the services: that is, your time plus related expenses such as the cost of reproducing your reports. As long as you put the time in, you are paid.

Obviously this type of contract involves a very low risk to you as a consultant. However, some clients will not accept cost contracts; they want to ensure that the project is actually completed within a certain budget. Thus, even when costs are difficult to estimate, you may have to choose between a fixed-price contract and no contract at all. One solution may be to break the overall task into subtasks. Those subtasks that you can cost out with minimum risk can be taken under a fixed-price contract; others, under a cost or a performance-type contract (performance contracts are described in the next section). Another solution may be to insert a "not-to-exceed" clause in the contract, so that you are paid for the work you actually do, but the client is guaranteed that your fee will not be higher than an agreed-upon amount.

The cost contract has several variations, two of which—cost plus fixed fee and cost plus incentive—are frequently used by the government for research and development projects. With the fixed-fee type of cost contract, the consultant is paid the total of the cost plus a fixed amount agreed to by both parties prior to performance. With the incentive-fee type, the consultant is paid the cost plus a variable incentive fee tied to different levels of performance agreed to in the contract. The incentive type of performance contract is discussed in more detail in the next section.

The Performance Contract

In the past, pure performance contracts were rare. Now more firms are using them. The Thomas Group, Inc., of Irving, Texas, has used this model successfully for some years. James E. Dykes, executive vice-president for corporate development, says that in some cases up to 50 percent of the company's fees are based on quantifiable results. These may include various cycle or time reductions, inventory reduction, margin enhancements, profit improvements, or revenue increases.[1] More commonly, performance contracts may be made a part of a modified-cost or fixed-price contract, wherein increased performance may earn a higher fee or reduced performance a lower one.

With a pure performance contract, your payment is based solely on actual performance. Executive recruiters who work on contingency—that is, they receive a fee only if one of the candidates they recruited is hired by their client—are actually working with a performance contract. Performance contracts can also be based on an increase in sales, a decrease in turnover, or other measurable factors. One cautionary note here: Do not accept a performance contract based on profits. Profits have too many definitions and are too easy to adjust upward or downward for accounting and taxation purposes. Although you may have done a great deal to increase performance, that work may not show up in accounting profits at the end of a year. (In my opinion, even a performance contract based on profit improvements, such as taken by the Thomas Group above, is excessively risky if taken on a routine basis.)

However, by themselves, performance contracts are useful in closing a deal. Here's how to use a proposed performance contract to help you come to terms with your potential client. Let's say you have been negotiating with a prospective client and, while he seems satisfied about most aspects of the project, he is not quite ready to finalize and sign a contract with you. Perhaps you have been thinking along the lines of a fixed-price contract, which you have costed out at $5,000. To close the deal, you could say something like this:

> Look, Mr. Smith, I am absolutely convinced that I can do this job for you and do it within the time period and at the price I indicated. However, I can see that you are hesitating, so let me make an offer that I don't think you can refuse. Let me design this marketing campaign for you, and if it doesn't increase

your sales by at least 25 percent, you pay me nothing. However, if your sales increase by 25 percent or more, and I have every confidence that it will be more, then you will pay me the $5,000.

You can see how the performance contract works. Either you perform or you receive nothing. That's why it's such a great close during negotiations. Your prospective client thinks, *Well, now, if this individual is ready to take a performance contract, what have I got to lose? He must be convinced.* Sometimes your client will agree to *your original terns* rather than the performance terms.

Incentive Contracts

Incentive contracts are also tied to performance. An incentive may also be combined with a fixed-price or cost contract based on achieving certain preset objectives or goals. When setting these goals, you must help your client; be certain that the incentive-fee structure is not unrealistic on either side. Remember that you are trying to build a long-term relationship, and terms that are unreasonable to you or your client, even if agreed to at the time, could lose you business in the future.

A client once asked me to help him increase attendance at his seminars. In return I would receive, in addition to a fee, an additional $20 for every seminar attendee above an agreed minimum (which was his maximum the previous year). I was to receive this $20 bonus not for just this one seminar, or even for all similar seminars in a single year, but for life. That is, as long as attendance was higher than the previous year's high attendance, with no increase in costs, I was to receive $20 for each and every attendee above that number, whether or not I performed any additional services for his company. In my opinion, these terms were unreasonable and unfair to my client. We finally restructured the compensation, retaining an incentive contract in which I would be reimbursed with a fixed amount up front and then an amount for each seminar attendee over the minimum; however, I would get this for three years, not for the rest of my life.

Elements of a Contract

There are five basic elements that should go in any contract:

1. *Who?* Who is the consultant, who is the client, and who are any other parties that are in any way involved in the project?
2. *What?* What services are to be provided to the client?
3. *Where?* Where are these services to be provided? What is the address of the client, what is the address of the consultant, and are there special locations involved in the consulting?
4. *When?* When are the services to be performed, and when is compensation to be paid?
5. *How much?* How much does the consultant receive for his services?

In addition to these five basic elements, other important conditions of the engagement should also be covered. These include:

- Competitive restrictions
- Patent rights
- Insurance coverages
- Confidentiality

A Sample Contract

Look again at the sample contract in Figure 8-1. Note how the contractual elements fit in. You can use this sample as a basis for developing your own contract. But don't forget to have your attorney go through it to ensure that everything applying to your situation has been taken care of and that your rights are fully protected.

In the next chapter, you will see how to plan and schedule the consulting project. This will impact your costing of the project and your ability to take on and complete several projects simultaneously. The information from your planning and scheduling will also go into your proposal and may well impact on the type of contract you decide to accept.

Note

1. Glenn Hasek, "Sharing the Risk," *Industry Week* (May 4, 1998), www.industryweek.com/currentarticles/asp/articles.asp?articleid=222

9

PLANNING AND SCHEDULING THE CONSULTING PROJECT

Planning and scheduling all but the simplest of consulting engagements are absolutely essential. Not only are these steps necessary for preparing the proposal, but once you are on contract, having a firm and good schedule in hand will save you time and money and will increase the quality of your performance as a consultant. Every organization that I ever worked with that had problems with project management had one outstanding thing in common—a failure to properly plan and schedule their projects before they began the work. Proper scheduling is not difficult. In this short chapter, I will give you a special form that will help you do this.

The Project Development Schedule

Refer to the project development schedule in Figure 9-1. Start with the column headed "Task." Your first job is to list every task associated with the consulting project that you intend to undertake. Next, figure out how long each task will take to complete in days, weeks, or months (in Figure 9-1 the numbers at the tops of the columns represent whichever time period you choose). The hours each task takes will be put in later numerically. Measurements of task length (days, weeks, or months) and task time (hours) are not

Figure 9-1. Project development schedule form.

TASK	1	2	3	4	5	6	7	8	9	10	11	12
TOTALS												

identical. A market research survey may require eighty hours of labor, which would be two weeks of eight-hour days, or four weeks if only four hours per day were spent on the project. An organizational audit that requires interviews with twenty different company executives may take four calendar weeks to complete (because of the difficulty of scheduling executive time), but only forty hours of your time.

You also need to decide who will accomplish each task. If you are doing all the work yourself, this is easy. But in some cases, you will have other consultants or even other organizations working for you.

Figure 9-2 shows a project development schedule in which the tasks have been determined. After you write each task down on the schedule, draw a double horizontal line, starting at the place where the task will begin and continuing to the right until the task is complete. Consider each horizontal row as being either days, weeks, or months after the authority to proceed. (Note that in the example in Figure 9-2, the time period being used is months.) Later, when you get the contract, you can write in the actual days, weeks, or months and use this schedule to manage the project. Convert the hours into dollar expenses for each period and total both hours and costs. Use a diamond figure like this ◇ to indicate critical date and times when something of great importance to the project must occur, such as the date a report is due. (Later, when the critical task is complete, you will color the diamond).

Once you are on contract and have the authority to proceed, you can use the schedule as indicated in Figure 9-3. On a new form, substitute the actual dates for the estimated time periods. (On Figure 9-3, note that, e.g., month 1 is replaced by June, month 2 by July.) Copy onto your new form the double horizontal lines that show when each task will begin and end. As you proceed to carry out the contract, shade in portions of the rectangular block formed by the double line to show the percentage of the task completed. At the end of each month, fill in actual hours worked on each task and compare with hours forecast. If you know that a task must be delayed for some reason, adjust your schedule by the use of a triangle and a series of dashed lines as shown in the horizontal area to the right of "Interviewing" in the figure.

Figure 9-2. Proposed project development schedule, showing tasks and hour and cost estimates.

TASK	$50/hr 1 Hrs/$	2 Hrs/$	3 Hrs/$	4 Hrs/$	5 Hrs/$	6 Hrs/$	7 Hrs/$	8 Hrs/$	9 Hrs/$	10 Hrs/$	11 Hrs/$	12 Hrs/$
Development of Research Tool	20/1000											
Secondary Data Collection	10/500											
Interviewing		20/1000	20/1000	20/1000	20/1000	20/1000	20/1000					
Data Recording		2/100		5/250	5/250	5/250	5/250	3/150				
Data Analysis and Computations			5/250	5/250	5/250	5/250	5/250	10/500				
Follow-Up Interviews			2/100	3/150	2/100	1/50	1/50	5/250				
Final Report Preparation									40/2000			
TOTALS 269/$13,450	30/1500	22/1100	32/1600	33/1650	32/1600	31/1550	31/1550	18/900	40/2000			

MONTHS AFTER AWARD OF CONTRACT

Report due end of ninth month after award of contract

Figure 9-3. Project development schedule after project initiation.

TASK	Hours F/A* June	Hours F/A* July	Hours F/A* Aug.	Hours F/A* Sept.	Hours F/A* Oct.	Hours F/A* Nov.	Hours F/A* Dec.	Hours F/A* Jan.	Hours F/A* Feb.	Hours F/A* Mar.	Hours F/A* Apr.	Hours F/A* May
Development of Research Tool	20/18											
Secondary Data Collection	10/13											
Interviewing		20/16	20/21	20/16	20/	20/	20/					
Data Recording		2/3	5/6	5/5	5/	5/	5/	3/				
Data Analysis and Computations			5/4	5/4	5/	5/	5/	10/				
Follow-Up Interviews			2/3	3/3	2/	1/	1/	5/				
Final Report Preparation												
TOTALS	30/33	22/19	32/34	33/28	32/	31/	31/	18/	40/			

New estimated completion date

Report due March 1

*Forecast/Actual

A PERT Chart

The Program Evaluation and Review Technique (PERT) was developed by the U.S. Navy Special Projects Office working with the management consulting firm of Booz, Allen, and Hamilton in 1958.

As you might have suspected when I mentioned the U.S. Navy, PERT was designed for use with big contracts and projects. But that doesn't stop you from using it with a small consulting proposal. Not only will it help you when you go to implement the project, it's quite impressive to your prospective client as a part of your proposal. It really shows that you've thought things through!

When you use PERT, you receive a lot of benefits. Delays, interruptions, and conflicts in developing, coordinating, and synchronizing the various parts of the overall project and in expediting completion are minimized.

PERT depends on just two elements: events and activities. An *event* is a specific task accomplishment that occurs at a recognizable point in time. An *activity* is the work required to complete an event.

Want an example? The publication of an advertisement is an event. Writing the copy, getting the artwork, preparing the layout, and submitting the advertisement for publication are all activities. As you can see, events take no time themselves. However, they do mark the beginnings and ends of the activities needed to complete the events.

Look at the graphic depiction of a PERT network shown in Figure 9-4. Events are represented by circles, and activities by arrows joining the circles. Remember, every event represents a specific point in time, and the arrow or activity connecting events represents the actual work done and the time needed to plan and do the work.

With PERT, time is usually calculated in calendar weeks. A *calendar week* is the number of working days required divided by the number of working days per week. The expected time for any activity, also known as the *expected lapse time,* is calculated by the following equation:

$$T = \frac{a + 4b + c}{6}$$

Where T = expected lapse time, a = the most optimistic time, b = the most likely time, and c = the most pessimistic time.

If a = 1 week, b = 2 weeks, and c = 3 weeks, then:

$$T = \frac{1 + (4)2 + 3}{6} = \frac{12}{6} = 2 \text{ weeks}$$

Figure 9-4. Simple PERT network with four events and four activities.

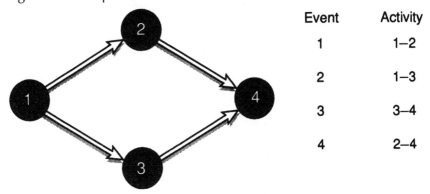

Event	Activity
1	1–2
2	1–3
3	3–4
4	2–4

Earliest Expected Date

The earliest expected date is represented by the letters TE. It is the earliest possible date that a particular task can be completed. In Figure 9-5, you can see that there are two paths through the net-

Figure 9-5. Simple PERT network showing significance of TE.

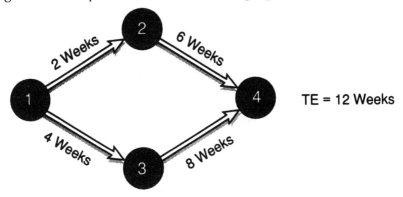

TE = 12 Weeks

work: One path is represented by the numbers 1, 2, 4; the second, by 1, 3, 4. Path 1, 2, 4 takes eight weeks (2 + 6); path 1, 3, 4 requires twelve weeks. Since all events have to occur before the project is completed, you must wait four additional weeks after completing path 1, 2, 4 before you can complete event 4. So the earliest expected date for the network shown in Figure 9-5 is twelve weeks.

Latest Allowable Date

Latest allowable date is represented by the letters TL; it is the latest allowable date that an event can take place and still not interfere with the scheduled date of the entire network.

Take a look at Figure 9-6. In this network, the TE of event 6 is sixteen weeks. This is through path 1, 3, 5, 6, the longest of the three paths through the network. Path 1, 3, 5, 6 is therefore the critical path. So if any progress is to be made in reducing the time necessary to complete this project, you must reduce the activities on this path. It makes no difference whether or not you reduce the

Figure 9-6. Simple PERT network showing earliest possible dates at each event.

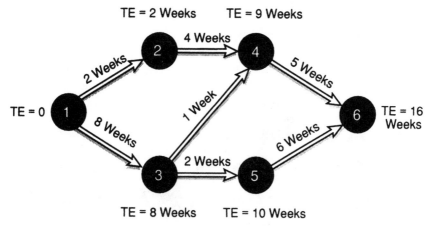

Adapted from Richard I. Levin and Charles A. Kirkpatrick, *Quantitative Approaches to Management*, 3rd ed. (New York: McGraw-Hill, 1975).

time of the activity on path 1, 2; path 1, 2 is not critical in this sense. Even if you reduce the activity on path 1, 2 to zero, the TE remains sixteen weeks. To reduce the TE of event 6, you must reduce the activities on path 1, 3, 5, 6.

The earliest expected dates for the six various events are shown in Figure 9-6. You would expect to complete event 4 nine weeks after initiation due to the critical path 1, 3, 4. If activity begins immediately thereafter, you might expect to complete event 6 in a total of fourteen weeks after the project was initiated.

But a closer look tells you that the time is actually sixteen weeks because of other required activities. This should also tell you that event 4 really doesn't need to be completed in nine weeks; it could actually be completed in eleven weeks (11 + 5 = 16) after the project was begun and still not interfere with the scheduled network time of sixteen weeks at event 6.

That is the significance of the latest allowable date. For event 4, it is eleven weeks after the project begins. This is because at that time you still have five weeks' work to complete activity 4, 6 and exactly five weeks in which to do it.

Slack

Slack is the difference between the latest allowable date and the earliest expected date. At event 4 in Figure 9-7, slack time is eleven weeks minus nine weeks, or two weeks.

You can see how a complex consulting project can be controlled fairly easily by using PERT. It shows you where you can save time and let the schedule slip and where it is critical to get a particular event done exactly on time. It shows you where to concentrate or to switch resources from noncritical paths to critical paths to effect time savings. PERT also shows you how to save money by avoiding putting resources where they will be less effective in impacting on critical dates.

The project development schedule or PERT will demonstrate to your potential client that you know what you are doing and that you have carefully thought through the entire consulting project. It will give you a much better chance of having your proposal accepted. Once you are under contract, these management tools will

Figure 9-7. Simple PERT network with the latest allowable dates and slack time added.

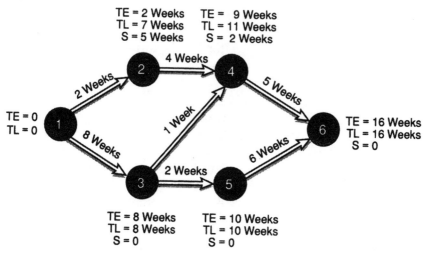

Adapted from Richard I. Levin and Charles Kirkpatrick, *Quantitative Approaches to Management,* 3rd ed. (New York: McGraw-Hill, 1975).

assist you in controlling and avoiding slippages and cost overruns. You will have more happy customers and fewer worries and ulcers.

Now you are ready to go to work to negotiate everything you've prepared with your client. We'll learn how to do that in Chapter 10.

10

NEGOTIATING WITH YOUR CLIENT

Whether a consulting engagement is profitable or unprofitable has much to do with your ability to negotiate with your client. Why is this? Because even if you perform flawlessly, if you negotiate a contract that is sufficiently unfavorable, you may lose money, reputation, or both.

Robert Ringer describes an amazing negotiating incident in his best-seller, *Winning Through Intimidation*. Ringer had been observing a difficult negotiation in which a businessperson he knew had ruthlessly demanded and received outrageously advantageous terms. The other party had agreed to these terms because he was clearly desperate to get the contract. Further, there were heavy penalties for failure to comply with all of the terms of the contract. On the way out, Ringer commented to this businessperson that it would be very difficult for the other party to live up to the terms. The businessperson smiled and said, "If you look at the contract carefully, you will see that he is already technically in violation of the contract."[1]

Unfortunately, many consultants become so desperate for a contract that they also negotiate extremely unfavorable terms for themselves. Don't let this happen to you. Plan the negotiation of the contract before you begin.

Six Steps in Contract Negotiation as Seen by Uncle Sam

The U.S. Government negotiates billions of dollars in contracts every year. Sometimes we read about the screwups in the newspaper: the $650 toilet seats and so forth. But considering the fact that more than a million contracts are negotiated every year, government negotiators do a pretty good job.

The government breaks down the process leading to final contract negotiation into six steps:

1. Evaluation and ranking of offers (if there are more than one), considering evaluation criteria in the Request for Proposal
2. Identification of those proposals that are determined to be within a competitive range
3. Identification and elimination of unacceptable proposals due to major problems with price or technical merit
4. Written or oral discussions with those competitors remaining, permitting revision of proposals to correct isolated deficiencies
5. Notification of a cutoff date for receipt of a best and final offer
6. Selection for award or for final negotiations if appropriate

If you are bidding a contract against competitors, whether dealing with the government or not, you can assume that your prospective client will use a similar process. Note that there may be several steps to the negotiating process, but that even in the last step, final negotiations may be necessary. It is in these final negotiations that some consultants "give away the store" and get into trouble.

Goals and Objectives of the Party with Whom You Are Negotiating

In a general way, your prospective client is simply trying to close the deal and make the final arrangements so that you can begin work. But you may never understand the full situation, including limitations and pressures that affect the way he or she negotiates. You may be definitely interested in a win-win outcome, but there are very broad definitions of what a win-win negotiation is.

When I teach negotiation, one of the simulations I use is negotiation for the purchase of a computer. The computer sellers are given the following confidential instructions:

> You are the vice-president of sales of a company that designs computer systems for business. Yesterday you received an emergency notice from top management. This message told you that you must withdraw and junk one of your older models, the XC-1000 computer, immediately. This is due to the implementation of a government regulation requiring additional features to prevent tampering, which this model does not have.
>
> Unfortunately you cannot modify the XC-1000, as it was built to "last forever." You can't even use it for parts. By law you must sell or get rid of all computer systems such as the XC-1000 by April 3 (this is April 2). After that date, you cannot offer it on the market at any price. You can't even give it away.
>
> Fortunately you have only one of the XC-1000s left in inventory. In fact you haven't sold any of these models in several years. This morning your assistant contacted the Acme Junk Company. It agreed to pick up your XC-1000 and melt it down to sell for scrap, at no charge to you.
>
> Before you can make final arrangements, you receive a call from Consolidated Unlimited. Its director of Management Information Systems (MIS) would like to meet with you tomorrow about the possible immediate purchase of an XC-1000. You tell him there is one left and that the price is negotiable. You delay your arrangements with Acme and begin to prepare for your meeting with Consolidated.
>
> Do not reveal any of this information to any person not on your team. You will have thirty minutes to complete the answers to the following questions:
>
> 1. For what price do you expect to sell the XC-1000, and why?
> 2. What is the lowest price you will accept, and why?
> 3. What is your strategy for your meeting tomorrow?

Now, as the computer seller, the student feels the pressure of having to sell to this potential buyer or getting nothing for the computer at all. Furthermore, being in the business of manufacturing computers, the seller probably knows all about the state of the art of competitive systems. From this person's viewpoint, they are desperate to sell, yet they don't have much of a product. They are probably wondering why in the world Consolidated Unlimited wants such a system.

I designate another group as buyers. They also receive confidential instructions. If you knew what these instructions were, you would know that Consolidated Unlimited was desperate to buy your product and would probably be willing to pay quite a bit more for it than you might expect. The instructions to the buyers are:

> Several years ago, you became director of MIS for Consolidated Unlimited, a small company manufacturing copper tubing. One of your first actions was to buy an XC-1000 computer. One of this computer's most attractive features was its lack of need of maintenance. In fact, when you bought the computer, it came with a three-year money-back guarantee if the computer didn't perform in any way. For three years and one month, the computer performed beautifully, but this morning your XC-1000 failed completely.
>
> One of the first things you did was have your assistant look for a newer replacement model that would perform the same functions. Unfortunately, as your company grew, all functions were built around your XC-1000, so you have very limited options. As a matter of fact, the lowest-priced replacement computer other than an XC-1000 is $50,000.
>
> You made some tentative calls around the country to other companies that you knew had bought XC-1000s. You discovered that most companies had replaced them long ago. You were also a little concerned about buying a used model, because none were less than three years old and the guarantees had expired.
>
> You called the president to apprise her of the problem, but her response was, "Get another new XC-1000." You called the manufacturer of the XC-1000 and arranged a meeting with the vice-president of sales tomorrow for an immediate purchase of an XC-1000. When you asked her the price, she told you

there was one left and the price was negotiable. You began to prepare for your meeting.

Do not reveal this information to individuals not on your team. You have thirty minutes to complete the answers to the following questions:

1. What price do you expect to pay for the XC-1000, and why?
2. What is the highest price you will pay, and why?
3. What is your strategy for your meeting tomorrow?

Now you can see that both parties to this situation have a serious problem. If the sellers do not sell the computer, they get absolutely nothing. If the buyers do not buy the computer, they must pay $50,000 to get another system elsewhere. And of course, the president of the buyer's company has ordered that one of these computers be purchased. So you see, at any price other than zero or $50,000, both sellers and buyers gain. It is a win-win situation as long as they come to an agreement within these limits.

However, if we were calculating a fair price, we would probably agree that it would be the midpoint between zero and $50,000— that is, $25,000.

But remember, neither side has the information that the other has. Both know only of their own problem and not the main problem putting pressure on the other party.

What results do I get? Interestingly, the prices vary widely between zero and $50,000 among different groups of buyers and sellers negotiating on the same day. Yet conditions are the same for all.

The last time I gave this exercise, it was to four groups of graduate students. The prices for which the computer was sold were $2,500, $12,500, $27,300, and $45,000.

This should tell you that in any situation in which you are negotiating with a client, you do not know the client's side of the story, and he or she does not know yours. Therefore, even if poor cash flow or some other situation causes you to be hungry for a job, you still want to negotiate for what you are worth.

How can you best do this? The key is preparation.

Preparation: The Key to All Contract Negotiations

For all but the simplest of contracts, you can assume that your prospective client is going to get all of the needed data together. He or she is going to do the homework, check the facts, prepare a case, anticipate your arguments, and develop responses to them. Most important, he or she will develop specific negotiation objectives related to your price, performance, or timing. To be prepared, you must do the same.

Do more than review your facts. Know the areas in which you can afford to be flexible and where you must stand fast. Know the price for your services below which you cannot go. Know the areas in which you can speed things up and complete your tasks earlier and where you cannot. Understand where you can increase or decrease the level of performance and what this will cost or save. And most important, write down your specific negotiating objectives.

What if your client fails to do his preparation, or doesn't do as good a job preparing as you? In that case, you have the advantage in the negotiation. I know you want to treat everyone fairly, and you do not want to take advantage of your client. However, you should keep two things in mind. First, not everyone feels as you. Some potential clients feel the same as the businessman that Robert Ringer described. These individuals will try to take every advantage they can from the situation. Second, if you are in control of the situation, you will be better able to negotiate an engagement that works to your client's benefit as well.

Telephone Negotiations (Be Wary)

Telephone negotiations may or may not be good for you depending on your preparation. But you should always be wary. If you are prepared and ready to negotiate the deal, a telephone negotiation can be a quick way to close and get authority from your client to begin work. On the other hand, if you are not prepared, a telephone negotiation can be a disaster.

The problem is that unless the telephone negotiation is set up ahead of time, you may have other things on your mind. You can't think of two things at once, and trying to negotiate under these circumstances is impossible.

One day I was engaged in "fire fighting" some emergency or another. I received a call to finalize the price on an assignment I had been asked about several days earlier. I hadn't really had an opportunity to work out the pricing (in those days, I used a formula to price this type of work). Still half-thinking about the emergency, I attempted to use the formula and negotiate the price. I ended up negotiating a price only 30 percent of what I usually charge. This didn't happen because of hard negotiating tactics by my prospective client. It was due entirely to the distraction of the emergency and my own screwup.

Don't make the same mistake. After submitting a proposal, be ready for a telephone call to finalize the contract. Keep your material close to the telephone. If you get an unexpected call, as I did, ask if you can call back. Complete the project you are working on, clear your mind, review your material, and then call to negotiate the contract.

Negotiation Plan

To reach your objectives successfully, prepare a negotiation plan. The negotiation plan should include an overall objective and a target price. Write down your limitations. As I mentioned earlier, know your bottom-line price, below which you cannot go without losing money. Then work out a strategy to achieve your objectives.

Your strategy in reaching your planned price objective might be simply to restate the price in your proposal. If this is questioned, you might show how your pricing is similar to or lower than pricing on other jobs that you or others have done. You might compare this price against the benefits that will be achieved as a result of your work. Finally, if price is still an issue, you might have a few fallback positions to show what you can accomplish for lower prices.

At every step, you should anticipate questions or objections, work out answers to the other party's questions, and counter his or her tactics to overcome objections.

Negotiation Gamesmanship

Even when both parties try to look out for each other's interests, a great deal of gamesmanship goes on in any negotiation. Some tactics are no worse than beginning at a higher price than you actually want because you know that your client always wants to negotiate you down to a lower price. However, some prospective clients see any negotiation as a competition that must be won at all costs. Such individuals may use a wide variety of tactics against you, some of which may be highly unethical.

Some people believe that lying in a negotiation is perfectly acceptable. A friend of mine who teaches negotiating says, "A lie is not a lie when the truth is not expected." He points out that when labor and management are negotiating, one or the other will make a statement something like this: "We will never, never agree to these terms. Never, never!" The next day, the contract is signed under the very terms they claimed they would "never, never" agree to. Was the statement that they would never agree a lie? You must make your own judgment about this. Regardless, you should be ready in case a prospective client uses negotiating tactics against you.

Here are some of the more common ploys used:

○ *Making the other party appear unreasonable.* A prospective client may point out that other consultants charge such and such or have agreed to certain terms that you won't agree to. The implication is that something is wrong with you and the way you do business—that you are being unreasonable.

Your defense against this tactic is to point out how this situation is different from the others. Of course you can always add what I consider the ultimate response: *"I am a lot better consultant than those you have mentioned."*

○ *Placing the other party on the defensive.* A prospective client may ask a question for which you are unprepared—another good reason to make certain that you are as prepared as you can be.

Maybe the party you are negotiating with has a dollar limit to his or her negotiating authority, which you both know is $100,000. During the negotiation, you agreed not to go above this amount. Just as you think you have a deal, your prospective client asks a question like this: "You aren't going to embarrass me by making your price so close to $100,000 that my supervisors will suspect what we are doing?" Being on the defensive, you could end up dropping your price several thousand dollars to protect the other party's "vanity." You may still be profitable several thousands of dollars lower, but if that is below your standard price, it is less than you are worth, and the difference comes out of your pocket. Chances are that your negotiating partner gets his or her bonuses this way.

If you are prepared for this ploy, you can say something like, "I'm sorry. I've been negotiating in good faith. This is my best offer."

o *Blaming a third party.* Here your prospective client attempts to shift the blame for unwillingness to give in on a negotiating point to someone or something over which he or she has no control: "I agree with what you are saying, but it's the policy of the company. It won't allow me to do it."

This is a difficult problem to overcome. It may mean that your prospective client absolutely will not give in on this point. If you feel strongly enough about the issue, you can test it by refusing to give in and suggesting that the negotiations be suspended while the other party checks out the situation with "the boss." Or you can explore how you might achieve the results you want while not violating this "company policy." For example, if you want money up front but company policy is not to pay until work is done, you can suggest a progress payment shortly after an early contract milestone.

o *The good guy–bad guy technique.* The good guy–bad guy technique began with the interrogation of prisoners. One interrogator, the "bad guy," would yell and scream and even beat the prisoner. If he didn't get the information he wanted, he would leave the room. Then the "good guy" would enter. The "good guy" would offer the prisoner a cigarette and commiserate with him on what a monster the other interrogator was. He might even embellish his partner's performance by describing how another prisoner had died under the "bad guy's" interrogation. The "good guy" would suggest that the prisoner give part of the information or make a reduced confession just to appease the "bad guy."

This works because of the contrast between the two interrogators. Someone under the extreme pressure applied by the "bad guy" is in need of support, which the "good guy" provides. The "good guy's" demands seem so slight in comparison with those of the "bad guy" that the prisoner is likely to go along with them.

The same technique is sometimes used when you are negotiating with more than one member of the prospective client company. The "bad guy" continually puts pressure on you and rudely presses every point. While you won't get slapped around, the "bad guy" may actually yell and scream. The "good guy" says something like, "Gee, I think it's terrible the way he is behaving. Maybe if you can give him just a little of what he wants, he'll be satisfied. If you can do this, I'll try to help."

When you see this kind of performance, just remember that it is probably exactly that—a performance. When negotiating with someone else, the two may actually switch roles! Just remember that both are on the other side of the negotiation, and look out for your own interests.

○ *Straw issues.* Straw issues are nonissues. They really aren't important to your prospective client at all. However, they may be strongly introduced as a negotiating point so that they can be given up later in exchange for a real concession from you.

The Soviets, who were quite good at negotiating, did this all the time when we would negotiate with them on various arms control issues prior to the breakup of the Soviet Union. They would sometimes introduce positions that were completely unreasonable. They would allow themselves to be negotiated out of these positions in exchange for major concessions on the other party's part. As a result, right up until the end, some of the treaties negotiated with the Soviets were quite lopsided in their favor. Yet when asked how it could have possibly agreed to such terms, our negotiating team would respond, "But you should have seen the position they started with!"

When your prospective client is unreasonable or introduces straw issues, offer little or nothing in exchange for dropping them.

○ *The walkout.* The walkout ploy is used infrequently because it may be difficult to get negotiations going again if the ploy fails. Your prospective clients say something like, "We can't pay any more and that's it." Then they prepare to leave. This is a supreme test, and you can either attempt to move toward their position or call their bluff and let them go. Many times, even if they leave, you can call them later and reopen negotiations. Sometimes they will even call *you* to reopen negotiations. But occasionally they are not bluffing. I am biased in favor of letting them go, unless you really have been unreasonable previously; otherwise, they're going to think you're desperate and take advantage of you even more.

○ *The recess.* This is almost always a good tactic because it does not break off negotiations. It allows the air to cool and may offer an opportunity for either side to rethink its position. If your prospective client calls for a recess, don't panic. It may be called simply to put pressure on you while you ask yourself why it was called. Sometimes a prospective client calls a recess when you are in a hurry, as when you must catch a plane. In that case, you can show your resolve by refusing to accept the pressure: Reschedule your flight. If necessary, stay an extra day.

○ *The time squeeze.* Time is money. You know this, and so does your prospective client. Your prospective client may try to put pressure on you to come to an agreement on his or her points by using delaying tactics. The recess is one way of doing this, but there are many others. For example, your prospective employer may say, "We can't continue to negotiate past three o'clock because we have some people flying in for an important meeting."

What can you do? Tell your prospective client, "I understand, but I want to be certain that the engagement gets started right. Then we won't have problems later. If you aren't available after three o'clock, let's set a time when we can complete our negotiations."

More Negotiation Tactics

My friend Dr. Don Hendon at the University of North Alabama teaches negotiating in a seminar. Here are a few of his favorite from more than two hundred tactics he has documented:

○ Big Pot: Make big demands at the beginning. This gives you more room to negotiate. Also, after making concessions, you'll still end up with more than if you started too low.

- Whipsaw/Auction: Let several competitors know you're negotiating with them at the same time.
- Divide and Conquer: Sell one member of the other side's negotiating team on your ideas. Get him on your side to sell the others.
- Be Patient: If you can afford to outwait your opponent if he or she needs something that only you have, you can win big.
- Trial Balloon: Leak your possible proposal to a third party before the decision is made and test the reaction before you make the proposal.

Some General Negotiating Hints

Here are some general hints for negotiating that will help you to negotiate fairly, yet competently:

1. When things get tense, try humor.
2. Don't ridicule or insult anyone. Don't be rude. Be courteous and considerate.
3. Don't try to make anyone look bad.
4. Be reasonable (unless you are using being unreasonable as a tactic).
5. Try to find the best for both parties.
6. Negotiating means both talking and listening. Remember to do both.
7. Don't accept any statement made by the other party as 100 percent accurate. Remember, the person may be honest and trustworthy, but he or she may be "just negotiating."
8. You can give in on small points, but fight hard for the issues that are important to you.
9. Price may be only one aspect of the negotiation process. Remember that you can also manipulate time and performance. Sometimes your prospective client will give in on these to get a lower price.
10. Don't forget the computer negotiation example mentioned earlier in this chapter. You don't know your prospective client's situation. Chances are you are in at least as good a position as your prospective client.

11. If you see a good offer, take it. Don't feel that you must always knock something off a deal that is offered you.
12. Don't discuss an issue you aren't prepared for. If something comes up for which you aren't prepared, defer the issue until you are.
13. Don't assume that the other side completely understands all the advantages you are offering. Take the time to spell them out.
14. Don't make big changes in your offer; give in very slowly and give in very small bits.
15. Never tell anyone how you outsmarted someone in negotiations. It could come back to haunt you. Several years ago, Donald Trump sold Merv Griffin a casino for hundreds of millions of dollars. Trump even went on national television saying how he had "taken" Griffin to the cleaners. Not too long afterward, Trump went bankrupt. Did one have anything to do with the other? I don't know, but if Merv Griffin had an opportunity to return the favor and "renegotiate the deal" through his influence in another situation, you can bet he would have done so.

When you are eager to begin work, you may have a tendency to rush into negotiations ill-prepared and eager to get them over with. Negotiations are an important part of the overall consulting process. Take the time to do them right. This will pay dividends during the engagement and will do much to enhance the profitability and reputation of your practice.

You've completed phase one and have one or more contracts. Now what? We'll look at ways you can solve some of your client's problems next.

Note

1. Robert J. Ringer, *Winning through Intimidation* (New York: Fawcett Books, 1979).

11

HOW TO SOLVE YOUR CLIENT'S PROBLEMS EASILY

In this chapter, I will show you a logical, step-by-step approach to problem solving as well as some important psychological problem-solving techniques. The step-by-step methodology does more than help solve problems; it also organizes your thinking process and provides an outline for presenting your analysis, conclusions, and recommendations to your client, both as a written report and as a formal, in-person presentation. I cover every step in detail and then show you a sample problem that you can work yourself, including forms to assist you. Then I go over the solution to this problem and analyze the results.

The Harvard Case Study Method of Problem Solving

The technique I'm going to show you is commonly known as the Harvard Case Study Method of Problem Solving; it is also known in the military as the Staff Study Method. It is used by the legal profession to analyze cases and by the psychological profession in helping to diagnose and treat patients. It is a structured, step-by-step process of considering and analyzing the various alternatives available to solve a problem and honing in on the best solution. Let's take a look at the six steps of this method:

1. Defining the central problem
2. Listing relevant factors

3. Listing alternative courses of action or solutions, with advantages and disadvantages of each
4. Discussing and analyzing alternatives
5. Listing conclusions
6. Making recommendations

Defining the Central Problem

Defining the central problem in a particular situation is the single most difficult, and most important, task in consulting problem solving. If you correctly identify the main problem in a situation, you can find many different approaches to solving it. But if the wrong problem is identified, even a brilliant solution will not correct the situation. You are well-advised to take all the time necessary; be sure you are indeed looking at the central problem.

One of the major errors that new consultants make in defining the central problem is confusing the symptoms with the problem. For example, low profits are not a central problem but a symptom of something else that is the central problem. Frequently a case has many different problems; in fact, there usually is more than one. The object then is to locate the *main* problem in the situation, the one that is more important than any other and is therefore "central." If you find more than one major problem in a particular situation, you should handle each one separately.

Once you have identified the central problem, write an initial draft explaining what the problem is. Try to keep this statement as simple as possible by making it as short as you can—a one-sentence central problem is usually best. Be aware, however, that even if you have spent some time in both identifying the problem and wording it as concisely as possible, in many cases you will have to go back and modify it as you proceed through the analysis.

Also be careful not to word the problem as if it were the solution, by assuming one particular course of action is correct before you analyze it. Remember, too, that your goal is to develop as many different courses of action as possible. Try not to word your statement so that only two alternatives are possible. For example, don't ask the question, "Should a new product be introduced?" That allows for only two alternatives: yes or no. Occasionally there are some situations where only two alternatives need be analyzed.

Usually, however, you can reword the problem statement in a way that opens it up to more than two courses of action.

In your statement, include important specifics about the problem. "What should be done about the possibility of introducing a new product?" is not the best problem statement. It allows for more than two alternatives, but it omits specifics about the problem that may be important to readers of your report who are not as familiar with the problem as you or the individual who hired you.

Be careful about making your problem statement too long by incorporating various additional factors. Even if these factors are relevant, they will make the problem statement unwieldy, awkward, and difficult for any reader to understand.

With these cautionary notes in mind, begin formulating your problem statement. Phrase it as a question, beginning with *who, what, when, where, how,* or *why.* Or you may start with an infinitive, as in "To determine the best source for borrowing $10,000, . . ."

Listing Relevant Factors

Note that this section of the structure speaks of "relevant factors." Both words are important. *Relevant* is critical because even though there will be many different factors in any situation you are to determine and list only those that are relevant to the central problem you have decided on.

In this task, you will be listing factors, not just facts. You may include estimates, computations, assumptions, and even educated guesses in addition to facts. Naturally, if one of your relevant factors is not a fact, label it accurately as an assumption, an estimate, or whatever so that you won't mislead anyone.

Listing Alternatives

In this section, you list every solution or course of action that could possibly solve the central problem. Then list the advantages and the disadvantages of each one. It is frequently at this point that you must go back and modify your central problem statement. You may think of a solution that is excellent, but not a solution to the central problem as you originally wrote it. To include this course of action, you must restate your central problem so that it fits with this alternative. This is important: Each solution or course of action listed must potentially solve the central problem as you have stated it.

Although theoretically it is possible to have an alternative with all advantages and no disadvantages, this is highly unlikely. If this were the case, the solution would be self-evident, and this problem-solving procedure would be superfluous.

Discussing and Analyzing the Alternatives

In this fourth section, you analyze and discuss the alternatives thoroughly in light of the relevant factors you have listed. As you proceed, additional relevant factors may come to light. If so, go back and add them to your list. However, the focus of this section should always be to compare, and discuss in detail, the relative importance of the advantages and disadvantages of each course of action. For example, the disadvantages of one course of action may be unimportant when measured against the relevant factors. Or an alternative could have advantages that are very important.

At the end of this discussion and analysis section, and even as you are doing the analysis, certain conclusions start to become obvious. Don't state these conclusions in the discussion and analysis section, however, save them for the next section. In fact, here is an accurate test of the clarity of your thinking so far: Show the entire analysis up to this point to someone who is not particularly familiar with the problem. Have him or her read your central problem, the relevant factors that you have identified, the alternative courses of action with the advantages and disadvantages, and finally your discussion and analysis. Then ask what his or her conclusions are. If they are identical to yours, you have correctly worded your discussion and analysis. If the conclusions are different, you have made an error either in the wording of the discussion and analysis or in the logic of your conclusions.

Listing Conclusions

In this section, you list the conclusions arrived at as a result of your discussion and analysis. Do not add any explanations; they belong in the previous section. Also don't list conclusions based on information extraneous to your analysis: Your conclusions are based solely on your discussion and analysis. Another common error here is to restate relevant factors as conclusions.

Making Recommendations

In this section, you explicitly state the results of your analysis and your recommendations on what your client should do to solve the central problem you have identified and defined. As with your conclusions, do not include extraneous information or explanations; all such explanations go in the discussion and analysis section. If you are presenting this orally, your client can always ask additional questions; if this is a written report, your client can always contact you for additional information. However, if you have done the analysis correctly, there will be no need to explain your recommendations; your reasons will be obvious from your discussion and analysis.

Many consultants first learning this methodology ask about the difference between conclusions and recommendations. With a recommendation, you put your reputation on the line. You make it clear and unequivocal what you want your client to do. You are accepting full responsibility for the recommendations you make. A conclusion is written in the passive tense: "Marketing research should be done." Recommendations are written in the imperative: "Initiate marketing research." If a conclusion on your list reads, "A new accountant should be hired," the recommendation would be, "Hire a new accountant."

The Charles Benson Problem: A Case Study

Now we're going to work on a problem using the methodology just discussed. Assume that the chief engineer of the Zeus Engineering Company has come to you for consulting advice. You are to analyze the chief engineer's problem, define it explicitly, and, using the methodology just described, make recommendations to him. The problem situation, forms that will help you use the problem-solving structure to arrive at the solution, the solution, and a step-by-step critique follow. Do not read the critique until you work the problem in detail. Time spent now in learning to use and apply this problem-solving methodology will pay dividends later on.

A Description of the Charles Benson Problem

Charles Benson, age thirty-five, had been employed as a design engineer for the Zeus Engineering Company for seven years.[1] He was a reliable employee as well as a skillful and inventive engineer. Seeking to earn additional money, he decided to pursue his own business evenings and weekends. His products were similar to those made and sold by Zeus Engineering. Benson's supervisor found out about Benson's business but took no action for several months, believing that the business probably would not amount to much and that eventually Benson would drop it. However, one afternoon Benson's supervisor found him using company time and a company telephone to order materials for his business. The supervisor reprimanded Benson on the spot and warned him that such practices would not be tolerated. He also said that the incident would be reported to the chief engineer. A few days later Benson received written notice from the chief engineer that he must divest himself of the business within the month or resign from the company.

A month later, Benson's supervisor asked him directly for his decision. Benson stated that he had thought it over and talked with friends as well as officers of his union, and he had decided that he would not give up the business, nor would he resign. He argued that he was a good employee and that his outside company did not interfere with his work for Zeus Engineering. The small amount of business that he did could not hurt the company, and he was neither using company resources nor soliciting its accounts. Therefore, what he did with his own time was of no concern to the company. Benson's supervisor reported the conversation to the chief engineer.

You are the chief engineer. What action should you take?

Form to Use in Solving the Charles Benson Problem

Central Problem

_____
_____
_____
_____
_____

Relevant Factors [*List*]

1. _____
2. _____

3. _____
4. _____
5. _____
6. _____
7. _____
8. _____
9. _____
10. _____
11. _____
12. _____
13. _____
14. _____
15. _____

Alternative Courses of Action

1. _____
_____

Advantages

A. _____
B. _____
C. _____

Disadvantages

A. _____
B. _____
C. _____

2. _____
_____

Advantages

A. _____
B. _____
C. _____

Disadvantages

A. _____
B. _____
C. _____

3. _____
   _____

Advantages

A. _____
B. _____
C. _____

Disadvantages

A. _____
B. _____
C. _____

4. _____
   _____

Advantages

A. _____
B. _____
C. _____

Disadvantages

A. _____
B. _____
C. _____

5. _____
   _____

Advantages

A. _____
B. _____
C. _____

Disadvantages

A. _____
B. _____
C. _____

Discussion/Analysis

_____
_____
_____
_____
_____
_____
_____
_____
_____
_____
_____
_____
_____
_____
_____
_____
_____
_____
_____
_____
_____
_____

Conclusions [*List*]

1. _____
2. _____
3. _____
4. _____
5. _____
6. _____
7. _____
8. _____
9. _____
10. _____

Recommendations [*List*]

1. _____
2. _____

3. _____
4. _____
5. _____
6. _____
7. _____
8. _____
9. _____
10. _____

Solution to the Charles Benson Problem

Central Problem

Begin by zeroing in on the central problem; this may require several attempts. Here are some alternative central problems along with criticisms of each:

1. *Should Charles Benson be retained as an employee of the Zeus Engineering Company or fired?* This way of stating the problem limits the solutions to two courses of action—retaining or firing.

2. *What should be done about Charles Benson?* This statement lacks specifics about the problem that are important if the analysis is to be presented to someone else.

3. *What policy should Zeus Engineering set regarding employees establishing outside businesses?* This may be a problem that needs to be worked on, but its solution disregards specifics of Benson's case, including the earlier warning.

4. *What should be done about Charles Benson's outside business considering the fact that he was warned, that the union may take action, and that he has been a good employee and a superior engineer?* This one tries to incorporate all the relevant factors, resulting in an unwieldy and awkward statement of the central problem.

5. *How to keep Charles Benson with Zeus Engineering?* This statement assumes one alternative course of action as the solution before the analysis is done.

6. *What action should be taken regarding Charles Benson's outside business activities?* This is a simple, concise statement of the central problem, and probably the best. In any case, we will use it to proceed with our analysis.

Relevant Factors

Facts

1. Charles Benson has been a superior engineer and a reliable employee prior to the problem.
2. Benson has been with the company seven years.
3. The products that Benson makes are similar to the products made by Zeus Engineering.
4. Benson's supervisor knew about the business but took no action for several months.
5. Benson's supervisor observed him doing business on company time and using a company telephone.
6. The chief engineer ordered Benson, in writing, to drop the business or resign from the company.
7. Benson states that he will not give up the business or resign from the company.

Assumptions

1. Benson has stated that he has contacted union officers and that they support his position. This is presumed to be true.
2. Benson states that he is not soliciting company accounts. This is presumed to be true.
3. Benson's current level of business will probably not hurt the company in the sense of his being a competitor, nor will his present product line directly compete with Zeus Engineering's product line.
4. It is assumed that Benson's business activities are no longer done on company time and that his outside work does not currently interfere with his work at Zeus.
5. Current company policies do not specifically forbid an outside business, although conflict of interest laws, secrecy clauses, and the company's ownership of ideas resulting from company work have an impact on the legal aspects of the problem.
6. Benson is not a key employee, in the sense that his leaving the company will not of itself have a major negative impact on the company.

Alternative Courses of Action

Alternative 1. Discharge Benson

Advantages

1. Will enforce discipline, since Benson was warned that he must give up the business or resign.

2. Will discourage employees in the future from starting outside businesses.
3. Will solve any problem of conflict of interest arising from the nature of Benson's business.

Disadvantages

1. May lead to union problems, considering their current support of his position.
2. May lead to a morale problem if it is believed by other employees that the company has acted unfairly.
3. Will lose a superior engineer and an otherwise reliable employee.

Alternative 2. Retain Benson

Advantages

1. Will avoid any problem with the union.
2. Will retain a superior engineer and an otherwise reliable employee.
3. Will avoid any feeling among other employees that Benson is being treated unfairly.

Disadvantages

1. May result in a discipline problem, because Benson was ordered to give up the business or resign.
2. May eventually result in a direct conflict of interest due to the nature of the products and the customers.
3. Will effectively establish a company policy on this matter that may not be desired.
4. Will encourage other employees to start outside businesses.

Alternative 3. Discharge Benson as an employee but retain him as a consultant. (The mechanism for the discharge should be Benson's resignation.)

Advantages

1. May avoid any problem with the union.
2. Will reward Benson for past performance as a superior engineer and otherwise reliable employee.
3. Will maintain discipline, because Benson was warned that he must give up the business or resign.

4. Will solve any problem of conflict of interest arising from the nature of Benson's business.
5. Will avoid setting policy or precedent regarding employee businesses.

Disadvantages

1. May encourage other employees to become consultants rather than employees with the company.
2. May set policy of a different kind: that employees who start their own businesses will be retained as consultants.
3. May not solve the problem if Benson refuses to resign to accept a consultancy.

Discussion/Analysis

1. Several important issues bear on this problem:
    A. The disciplinary issue and the fact that Benson was told to resign or to divest himself of his business.
    B. The importance of fair treatment and its potential effect on other employees. Benson has been a "superior engineer and otherwise reliable employee." There is currently no conflict of interest, and no further misuse of company time is anticipated.
    C. The policy issue. If Benson is retained, this will tend to set policy and may encourage other employees to similarly start businesses on their own.
    D. Potential union involvement and a legal suit.
2. All of these issues are important and must be considered in the decision. Therefore:
    A. Discharging Benson should be avoided beause it has considerable potential for affecting the morale of other employees (who may consider it unfair treatment of a superior and otherwise reliable employee who made one "mistake") and because it could lead to problems with the union and a legal suit.
    B. Retaining Benson should also be avoided because of its potential effect on discipline and its tendency to set policy and encourage other employees to start their own businesses.
    C. Discharging Benson as an employee but retaining him as a consultant is the only solution that is not negatively affected by the main issues.
3. If Benson fails to accept the solution of resigning to become a consultant, then he should be discharged. Under these circumstances, there is less chance of his treatment being perceived as unfair. While the

company still risks union problems and a lawsuit, discipline will be maintained, no policy on outside businesses will be set, and other employees will not be encouraged to follow in Benson's footsteps.

Conclusions

1. Discharging Benson as an employee but retaining him as a consultant is the best solution considering the major issues involved.
2. If Benson fails to resign to accept a consultancy, he should be discharged.
3. The consultancy solution must be presented to Benson as the only all-around fair solution, and not as punishment, in order to maximize his accepting it; however, it must be presented in such a fashion that other employees recognize that resigning or discharged employees are not automatically hired as consultants.
4. A policy on outside employee business should be established and publicized as soon as possible.

Recommendations

1. Discharge Benson as an employee and hire him as a consultant.
2. If Benson fails to accept this solution, discharge him immediately.
3. Establish and publicize a policy on outside employee businesses as soon as possible.

Psychological Techniques for Problem Solving

The logical, step-by-step technique to problem solving is very effective, but it is based primarily on using only the left half of the brain. Because the human brain has two halves, it makes sense to use the right brain for problem solving as well, especially because the right half of your brain is the creative half. Also, the step-by-step approach uses only your conscious mind, but you can use your unconscious mind as well.

Some consultants avoid psychological techniques like the plague. They think psychological approaches are too uncertain and smack of a "touchy-feely" orientation. These same consultants would be surprised to learn that they have already used some of these techniques without realizing it. Have you ever awakened in the morning with the solution to a problem that had been bothering you? When your conscious mind was unsuccessful at arriving at a solution, your subconscious mind took over while you were asleep. When you woke up, it turned the solution over to your conscious mind.

Many famous and successful people use the subconscious mind to solve important problems and help in their decision making. When Thomas Edison had a problem that his conscious mind was unable to handle, he went into a darkened room and laid down. He refused to be disturbed until the solution came to him.

Builder and wheeler-dealer Donald Trump tells of an instance in which his subconscious mind worked on a problem even after his conscious mind had come to what proved to be the wrong decision. "The papers were being drawn up, and then one morning I woke up and it didn't feel right." So, listening to the conclusions of his subconscious mind, Trump changed his mind. He didn't invest in a project that many experts, and his conscious mind, said was a sound investment. Several months later, the company about which Trump made his decision went bankrupt. The investors lost all of their money.[2]

After your conscious mind has collected and analyzed all the relevant factors in a situation, your subconscious mind sometimes comes to a better decision than your conscious mind. Why is this so?

1. *No pressure.* Your conscious mind may be under the pressures of time, a demanding client, or deadlines. Your subconscious mind doesn't recognize these pressures.

2. *Distractions.* Your conscious mind may be distracted by family or business problems, noise, or even a lack of sleep. Not so your subconscious mind.

3. *Limited time.* Most consultants don't have the time to work on a single problem all day on a continuous basis. But your subconscious mind has all night, and it will work effortlessly on a problem that needs solving.

4. *False knowledge.* For a variety of reasons, your conscious mind may be influenced by false assumptions or inaccurate facts. Your subconscious mind may know better.

How to Help Your Subconscious Solve Your Consulting Problems

If you want to use your subconscious mind to help you solve a problem, first learn all you can about the problem. As when you use the Harvard Case Study, or Staff Study Method, gather all the relevant factors and spend a great deal of time arriving at the central issue in the case. You can also mull over the alternatives, talk to other people and get their opinions, and do additional research. Do this until you feel slightly overloaded.

Before you go to sleep, set aside a half-hour to an hour to do nothing but think about the problem, analyze the data, and think about potential solutions.

Go to sleep in the normal way. Don't try to force a solution to your problem. Although the solution is usually ready for you sometime the next morning, it could come in the middle of the night. If it does, be ready for it by having pencil and paper nearby to quickly scribble down the solution and any other insights.

Sometimes answers come in indirect and strange ways. In 1846, when Elias Howe was struggling to invent the sewing machine, he was stumped. Howe had invented a machine that could push and extract a needle into and out of cloth. The problem was the thread. Because the thread went through an eye in the needle at the end opposite the point, the entire needle had to go through the material and back again in order to make a stitch. That was impossible. Howe was at an impasse. Then, for several nights in a row, Howe had identical dreams; Howe's subconscious mind was trying to tell him something. In the dreams, Howe found himself on a South Pacific island where natives armed with spears danced around him. But the spears were very strange. Each spearhead had a conspicuous hole. Only after several days did Howe realize the solution to his problem: to construct sewing needles with eyes for the thread near the point rather than at the opposite end.

If you want outstanding solutions to your client's problems, use both the right and left sides of your brain and your conscious as well as your subconscious mind.

Here are some books that can help you:

○ *The Confident Decision Maker: How to Make the Right Business and Personal Decisions Every Time* by Roger Dawson (Quill)

○ *Decision Traps: Ten Barriers to Brilliant Decision-Making and How to Overcome Them* by J. Edward Russo and Paul J. H. Schoemaker (Fireside Press)

○ *101 Creative Problem Solving Techniques: The Handbook of New Ideas for Business* by James M. Higgins (New Management Publishing Company)

In the next chapter, we'll see how to do the research that is necessary for any problem-solving activity.

Notes

1. Adapted from "Theodore Thorburn Turner," a case in *Principles* of *Management*, 4th ed., by George R. Terry (Homewood, Ill.: Richard D. Irwin, 1964), p. 222.

2. Donald J. Trump and Tony Schwartz, *The Art of the* Deal (New York: Warner Books, 1987), pp. 27–28.

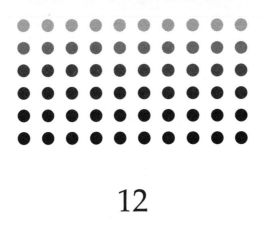

12

HOW TO RESEARCH A CONSULTING PROJECT

Research is an important part of many types of consulting. Whether you are finding the demand for a product or services, discovering what the consumer wants or does not want, or looking for sources of raw materials, products, or capital, research is required. In this chapter we will look at how you can do this research easily, and for the most part, at low cost. Knowing how to do research is like anything else. Until you know how, it is a mystery. It seems not only complicated, but almost impossible to master, like flying a jet airliner or performing surgery. But to a pilot or surgeon, who have been trained to perform these complex tasks, they become almost routine. Research is similar. If you haven't done it before, research may appear forbidding. But once you know how to do it, you will find that most research that you need for consulting is very simple. Usually only if you need to use some of the more sophisticated statistical techniques do you have to learn something a little out of the ordinary . . . and even these techniques can be learned from a night school course or a book.

Two Basic Kinds of Research

All research can be categorized into two basic types: primary research and secondary research. *Primary research* is research in which you gather the information firsthand. *Secondary research* is information that someone else has researched and published. All you need to do is to find it.

For example, let's say you want to research a company. Always go to secondary sources first. If it's a public company, look it up in *Standard & Poor's* and *Moody's* at your library. Get a copy of the company's annual stockholders' report. If the company is fairly large, they may have a public relations department. Call and ask for information about the company, its catalogs, product information, and so forth. Check the company's Web site. This is all secondary research. If you talked to the company's customers, suppliers, or members of the company itself, it would be primary research.

You may have heard of entrepreneur Joe Cossman. Joe is the fellow who sold over a million ant farms and various other products. After investing a great deal of time and money in his first deal, exporting laundry soap, he found that his supplier had "disappeared." He went to the New York City Public Library and consulted a series of books, which are still in print, called *The Thomas Register of Manufacturers*. In it he found listed more than seventy soap manufacturers throughout the United States. That's secondary research. Then he called each and every manufacturer on the list until he found one that manufactured, and had available, laundry soap. That's primary research. This not only illustrates the difference between the two types of research, but it also demonstrates that you should do secondary research first. There are two reasons for doing research in this order:

1. Secondary research is far less expensive because someone else has already done it. You might find your answer during your secondary research and not need to do any primary research. For example, if Joe had been able to find a source that identified which soap manufacturers made laundry soap (and had it available), he would have been able to make a single call to order the soap, not the more than fifty calls he actually made.
2. For more complex primary research, it makes sense to find all you can about the subject before you begin to invest your valuable time and resources.

Therefore, I'll start the chapter with information about secondary research before an in-depth look at primary research.

Sources of Secondary Research

1. *Chamber of Commerce.* Chambers of commerce have all sorts of demographic information in which you may be interested, such as household income levels, educational facilities, and businesses, including their size and sales volume for their geographical area.

2. *Trade associations.* Trade associations have information regarding the background of their members as well as information abut their industries.

3. *Trade magazines and journals.* Trade magazines and journals contain articles that describe competitive companies, products, strategies, and markets; they also frequently survey their readers about various issues.

4. *The Small Business Administration (SBA).* The U.S. SBA was set up to help small businesses. The studies sponsored by the SBA can be extremely valuable to anyone doing research for the situational analysis of a marketing plan. Other published aids supplied include listings of statistics, maps, national market analyses, national directories for use in marketing, basic library reference sources, information on various types of business (including industry average investments and cost), and factors to consider in locating a shopping center.

5. *Databases.* Databases are electronic collections of relevant data based on trade journals, newspapers, and many other public or private sources of information. They are accessed by computer; you purchase "computer time" to search the databases companies have available, although some databases allow access. *The Federal Database Finder*, 5th ed., by Matthew Lesko (Gale Research) is a directory of both free and fee-based databases available from the federal government.

6. *Earlier studies.* Earlier marketing studies are sometimes made available to interested companies or individuals. These studies may have cost $40,000 or more when done as primary research. As a consequence, their results are not sold cheaply—although in

effect you are sharing the cost with other companies that purchase the results with you. Several thousand dollars for a short report is not atypical. Nevertheless, if the alternative is to do the entire primary research project yourself, it may be less expensive to purchase it.

7. *The U.S. Industrial Outlook.* Every year the U.S. Government publishes a document known as the *U.S. Industrial Outlook* that contains detailed information on the prospects of more than 350 manufacturing and service industries.

8. *The Statistical Abstract of the United States.* This abstract is also an annual publication of the U.S. Government. It contains a wealth of detailed statistical data having to do with everything from health to food consumption, population, public school finances, individual income tax returns, mortgage debt, science and engineering, and motor vehicle travel. It is published by the U.S. Department of Commerce, Bureau of the Census.

9. *The U.S. Department of Commerce.* If you are interested in export, the U.S. Department of Commerce has numerous sources of information, including amounts exported to foreign countries in the preceding year, major consumers of certain items, and detailed information on doing business in countries around the world. You can find the local office listed under the U.S. Government in the telephone book.

10. *The U.S. Government.* The U.S. Government has so many sources of information that it is impossible to list them all here. But there is a lot of information available, and so much of it is free, that you would be well advised to see what can be obtained from federal government sources. *Information U.S.A.,* rev. ed., by Matthew Lesko (Penguin) is a good source for locating this information.

11. *The Internet.* This relatively new source of secondary research will be covered in Chapter 16.

The Library

Your local library is still your best starting point for most types of secondary research. First, tell the librarian what you need. Frequently, librarians can assist you, either sending you directly to the documents you need or giving you likely sources to check.

Then look at some general sources, such as an encyclopedia; you can find general information about your topic and also additional sources, such as lists of books related to the topic. Often, another source will not only provide additional information but more sources. So, there is a "pyramid" effect, which builds as your research progresses.

Simple Primary Research Projects: How to Do Them

The kind of research you do is limited only by your imagination. Some research can be done, even primary, at very little cost except for your time. Here are some examples of simple marketing research done by or for small businesses.[1]

1. *License plate analysis.* In many states, license plates give you information about where car owners live. Therefore, simply by taking down the numbers of cars parked in your location and contacting the appropriate state agency, you can estimate the area from which you draw business. Knowing where your customers live can help you in your advertising or in targeting your approach to promoting your products or services. By the same method, you can find out who your competitors' customers are.

2. *Telephone number analysis.* Telephone numbers can also tell you the areas in which people live. You can obtain customers' telephone numbers from sales slips, credit card slips, or checks. Again, knowing where they live will give you excellent information about their lifestyles.

3. *Coded coupons.* The effectiveness of your advertising vehicle can easily be checked by coding coupons that can be used for discounts or inquiries about products. You can find out the areas that your customers come from, as well as which vehicle brought them your message.

4. *People watching.* Simply looking at your customers can tell you a great deal about them. How are they dressed? How old are they? Are they married or single? Do they have children or not?

Many owners use this method intuitively to get a feel about their customers. However, a little sophistication, such as a tally sheet, for a week can provide much more accurate information simply, easily, and without cost. It may confirm what you've known all along, or it may completely change your opinion about your typical customer.

More Complex Research Projects: How to Do Them

Some of the primary research you may need to do can be done only in a more complex project. The four basic methods of doing this research are surveys: personal, mail, telephone, and electronic. Usually, these surveys have to do with marketing research, but the methodologies work for all types of research.

Now let's look at the advantages and disadvantages of each method. Every technology has sampling challenges, but regardless of the technology, some sampling basics remain. Samples that depend solely on voluntary response will almost always be subject to significant biases. Samples that start with the total population of who you want sampled and attempt to obtain cooperation from each prospective respondent will yield more reliable results.

Personal Interview Surveys

The personal interview survey is one of the most frequently used methods in marketing and other types of primary research. This is primarily due to its flexibility. Of the three most popular survey methods—mail, telephone, and personal interview—it is personal interview surveys that collect the best feedback from voice, facial expressions, and body language. Many different aids can be used in the survey, including pictures, problems, diagrams, and advertising copy. In addition, the selection of respondents can be far more precise. A marketing research study of brand preference for beer eliminated individuals who were intoxicated at the time of the testing. Accurate elimination due to intoxication would have been more difficult to determine without face-to-face, personal interface.

Furthermore, because of the rapport that can be developed face-to-face, and the reluctance of many potential respondents to reject a face-to-face request, the number of refused responses is much less when compared to other survey methods.

However, face-to-face interviews do have drawbacks. The primary disadvantage is the cost. The personal interview survey is the most expensive method. Even though cost can be minimized by keeping the researcher at one location or by using a limited number of respondents for exploratory research, you can expect to pay more for research done by this method than the other survey methods.

Mail Surveys

With the mail survey method, a single questionnaire is prepared, duplicated, and sent to a list of potential respondents. This method requires minimal time for gathering the research, and for this reason, it is potentially very economical. In exchange for the costs of printing the questionnaire, mailing it, and providing return postage, a completed interview is accomplished. Despite this major advantage, there are drawbacks to mail surveys. First is the response rate. The response rate from the general public is generally very low, sometimes less than 15 percent.

However, to get the maximum response rate, make it as easy as possible for the respondent to respond. This means a relatively short, easy-to-answer questionnaire, as well as the use of a self-addressed, stamped envelope so that the respondent only needs to put the answered questionnaire in the envelope to return it. It was once thought that personalization, such as hand-addressed envelopes, would add to the response rate. However, it has been found that computer labels can be used without a significant loss.

Other factors that increase the response to mail surveys include the length of the interview, subject matter, use of mail and/or phone reminders, and the use of incentives. Reminders can have a tremendous effect, in some cases doubling or tripling mail survey response rates. Incentives can be given after you receive the completed questionnaire or can be included right in the envelope along with it.

A typical incentive is money. A very successful survey from

one researcher included a questionnaire that was accompanied by a brand-new one-dollar bill. In the cover letter, the one-dollar bill was described as a small gift in appreciation for the time spent in filling out the survey. The one-dollar bill was extremely effective in increasing respondents' results because of its psychological impact. On the one hand, it is very difficult, if not impossible, to throw the "gift" away. On the other, it is equally difficult to pocket the money without a feeling of guilt if the survey is not completed.

However, if you are going to include something of value to increase response, you may need to advertise this fact on the outside envelope. A textbook publisher wanted to use this technique to increase response in a survey of professors. A one-dollar bill was included in every envelope. The envelope was also marked with the publisher's logo. Unfortunately, the publisher had been using a similar envelope for its advertising literature. The marketing researcher won no kudos when it was discovered that most of the envelopes had been thrown away unopened. (The results may also say something about this company's advertising material.)

For special populations in which good lists are available and high cooperation is possible because of the intrinsic interest of the topic, mail surveys can be highly successful.

Telephone Surveys

Telephone surveys combine some of the advantages and disadvantages of both mail and personal interview surveys. As does the mail survey, telephone surveys avoid interview travel expenses, and they are useful for research over wide geographical areas. They are more flexible than mail surveys because, based on verbal feedback, interviewers can ask more detailed questions or encourage respondents to answer questions when respondents hesitate. However, it is more difficult to obtain the same rapport that is possible through face-to-face personal interview surveys, because the researcher loses the advantage of what he or she can see. Additional problems with telephone interviews are that respondents must be limited to those with telephones and with listed numbers and that there is a nonresponse bias due to busy signals, no answers, and refusals, which are more common than with personal interview surveys.

Since World War II, the most widely used method for obtaining market research and other survey data has been by telephone. There were two major reasons for the switch to telephone surveys:

- The percentage of households with telephones increased from less than half before World War II to more than 90 percent by the 1960s to a current level of about 95 percent.
- The steep increase in the costs of door-to-door surveys due to the reduced availability of respondents (the rapid rise in the percentage of working women means that it is time-consuming and costly to find people at home, even if interviewing is done on evenings or weekends) translated into large interviewer travel expenditures; telephone surveys cut interviewing costs roughly in half.

Electronic Surveys

Widespread computer ownership created a new way to reach the general population and administer surveys—just as rising telephone ownership once did. Given the potentially favorable costs of electronic surveys, the interesting capabilities of computer-based data collection, and the declining effectiveness of telephone surveys, it seems likely that electronic surveys will displace telephone surveys as the survey method of choice within the next quarter-century.

It is tempting to simply put a questionnaire on a Web site and to obtain information from whomever responds, but this is simply a more technologically sophisticated version of a volunteer survey with potentially large biases. Unless the site attracts the population you want to survey, this is not a good way to proceed.

There are two ways you can capture reasonably good samples for electronic surveys:

1. *E-mail directories.* Many companies that sell to businesses have e-mail directories of their customers. This allows them to e-mail questionnaires to a particular sample or to post the questionnaire on a Web site and use e-mail to ask customers to visit the site and complete the questionnaire. As with mail surveys, multi-

ple follow-ups will increase response. You can also "rent" e-mail lists of this type from e-mail list brokers.

2. *Sample visitors to a Web site.* Visitors can be asked to register when they visit the site, and these registrations generate a list for later sampling purposes. Visitors also can be taken immediately to a questionnaire.

You Can Research Anything

Research is a very broad topic. There are consultants whose entire practice consists of nothing but research. These include marketing research firms, political pollsters, television (e.g., Nielsen) and even "finders." The latter make their money from finding everything from venture capital to a buyer for several tons of scrap plastic or reclaimed railroad track. Obviously, we can research anything and find the answer somewhere if we ask enough people or look in enough places. Here are some books that will help you:

- *Business Information: How to Find It, How to Use It,* 2nd ed. by Michael R. Lavin (Oryx Press)
- *Find It Fast: How to Uncover Expert Information on Any Subject* by Robert I. Berkman (HarperCollins)

Now we are ready to look at one of the most important consulting topics: ethics, in Chapter 13.

Note

1. Many of these ideas were suggested by J. Ford Laumer, Jr., James R. Hams, and Hugh J. Guffey, Jr., professors of marketing at Auburn University of Auburn, Alabama, in their booklet "Learning about Your Market," published by the U.S. Small Business Administration.

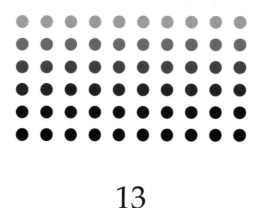

13

THE IMPORTANCE OF ETHICS IN CONSULTING

Not too long ago I completed an in-depth study of leadership. Later I published the results in a book.[1] After surveying more than two hundred combat leaders, including sixty generals and admirals, eight principles showed up time after time. They did not appear, even by frequency, in any particular order. That is, except for one. This principle was clearly so important that many of the individuals I surveyed wrote me notes or letters to explain their feelings. This first principle, or "universal law of leadership" as I term it, was to maintain absolute integrity. The complete list is:

1. Maintain absolute integrity.
2. Know your stuff.
3. Declare your expectations.
4. Show uncommon commitment.
5. Expect positive results.
6. Take care of your people.
7. Put duty before self.
8. Get out in front.

When you are performing as a consultant, you are in a leadership role. You are helping, coaching, and influencing someone else to reach a better state. You are a leader. Therefore, ethics, closely aligned with integrity, must be a primary consideration.

Ethics has a strong impact on everything we are involved with as consultants. This chapter explains why the application of ethics to a consulting practice is so important and provides some thoughts on how to practice consultancy ethically. As we will see, ethics is not simply a matter of obeying the law, and ethical problems are not always simple.

Business Ethics: Not Clear-Cut

If ethical questions could be expressed in clear terms of black or white, decisions regarding corporate conduct would be easy. But that is seldom the case. Let me tell you about a few situations in which decisions of business ethics may not be all that straightforward.

Ethics vs. Jobs: The Lockheed Case

Some years ago, Lockheed executives were found to be bribing Japanese officials to secure contracts for their aircraft in Japan. Today it is noted as one of the most infamous examples of corporate lawbreaking and lack of corporate ethics.

Without commenting on the legal aspects of this case, what would be the motivation of those Lockheed executives who made the decision for these payoffs? After all, it was not simply a case of payoffs for personal profit alone. These were senior executives. Certainly pride and the competitive drive probably entered into this decision. Maybe there were bonuses if the contracts were obtained. Still, it's a safe bet that these executives were already pretty well off financially.

If the contacts had been lost, thousands of jobs would have been lost—not the jobs of the executives concerned, but those of the workers and managers at lower levels. I do not suggest that saving jobs was necessarily the motivation for the payoffs, but it probably wasn't personal profit either. If ethics is defined as a set of moral principles for the greater good, then the "bad" of the payoff must be weighed against any good that results. If this were done, one could make an argument that the payoffs were justified.

The Ethics of Marketing Research

Marketing research can be completely honest and aboveboard. However, marketing research is frequently competitive research, and that presents an opportunity for questionable practices. Let me tell you about my own introduction into this field.

As a newly promoted manager of research and development, I studied the possible solution to one of the problems my company faced. Because the business was heavily government-oriented, our production was a continual series of peaks and valleys. The government orders all came during one part of the year, and then we would become extremely busy, producing like mad to fulfill our contracts. Other parts of the year, we had practically no business at all, and our workers were idle. The choices in such circumstances are usually pretty limited. We could either try to manufacture our products for someone else, retain our workers and pay them for essentially doing nothing, or fire our workforce every year. None of these solutions were very attractive.

Obviously, if we could find some other product to make that would fill the valleys when no government work was under contract, this would solve the problem. Our company was involved in fiberglass protective products such as pilot helmets. One additional fiberglass product that we considered was personal protective body armor for the military and police, but we knew very little about this market. To learn more, we decided to hire a marketing research firm, in other words, an independent consultant. Bids were requested from several of the leading firms in our area. The firm that won the opportunity to undertake this task had a fine proposal and a good reputation.

One aspect of the research bothered me. Because the information we required involved the total size of the market along with competing products, sales, and other proprietary information, I wondered how such information could be obtained. As I recall, I even commented to one of the executives of the research firm that I didn't know how they were going to get this information, because obviously they couldn't just call up a competitive company and ask for it.

Two months after the contract had been initiated, I was given a final report of several hundred pages, along with a personal presentation by a representative from the marketing research firm. The information it provided was exact, precise, and explicit. It had all the information about our potential competitors, the size of the market, the sales, and even, in some cases, strategies that the competition intended to follow in the coming years. I was amazed at the detail. Innocently, I asked where such information could be obtained. I was told that the gathering had been done in a very straightforward fashion. The researcher had simply called the president of every company in the business and misidentified himself as a student doing a report on the unusual product of body armor. In almost every case, this researcher had gotten complete information that was highly competitive and proprietary.

How do you rate that research technique on an ethics scale? How would most marketing research professionals? Let's find out.

Washington Researchers is a well-known consulting firm that does competitive research on companies, products, and strategies. It also conducts seminars around the country on how to accomplish various types of competitive research. Several years ago I had the good fortune to attend one of these seminars. As a part of the seminar, all attendees participated in a survey of company information–gathering techniques. This survey was developed originally because participants had asked Washington Researchers for judgments about the ethics of various means of company information gathering. Washington Researchers decided that the issues were too complex to allow for easy answers. So they decided to conduct this survey as a simple measurement of individual and company practices.

This questionnaire asks the respondent's opinion about several research techniques or strategies that might be used in obtaining marketing research. Results from more than five hundred professional marketing, planning, and business researchers who took the survey at seminars around the country are summarized in Figure 13-1. But before you look at the results (on page 173), let's answer the questions in the survey ourselves.

Washington Researchers Survey of Company Information Techniques

During past seminars, participants have asked Washington Researchers for judgments regarding the ethics of company information gathering.

There are too many complex issues involved to allow easy answers, but we have decided to attempt a simple measurement of individual and company practices. For the purposes of this questionnaire, *assume that you are asked to find out everything you can about the finances, products, marketing strategies, etc. of your company's closest competitor.* Several research techniques or strategies are listed below. Please respond to each by indicating the following:

1. Would your company encourage or condone the use of the technique?

2. Aside from your company's policies, would you (personally) feel comfortable using the technique?

3. Do you believe that other companies in your industry would use the technique in trying to find information about your company?

Note: If unemployed, answer question 1 in each series about a company you would like to work for.

Research Strategy Alternatives

A. Researcher poses as graduate student working on thesis. Researcher tells source that dorm phones are very busy, so researcher will call back rather than having phone calls returned. In this way, researcher's real identity is protected.

1. Would your company use this technique?   Yes _____ No _____
2. Would you personally use this technique?   Yes _____ No _____
3. Do other companies use this technique?   Yes _____ No _____

B. Researcher calls the V.P. while s/he is at lunch, hoping to find the secretary who may have some information but is likely to be less suspicious about researcher's motives.

1. Would your company use this technique?   Yes _____ No _____
2. Would you personally use this technique?   Yes _____ No _____
3. Do other companies use this technique?   Yes _____ No _____

C. Researcher calls competitor's suppliers and distributors, pretending to do a study of the entire industry. Researcher poses as a representative of a private research firm and works at home during the project so that the company's identity is protected.

    1. Would your company use this technique?   Yes _____ No _____
    2. Would you personally use this technique? Yes _____ No _____
    3. Do other companies use this technique?   Yes _____ No _____

D. The competitor's representative is coming to a local college to recruit employees. Researcher poses as a student job-seeker in order to learn recruiting practices and some other general information about the competitor.

    1. Would your company use this technique?   Yes _____ No _____
    2. Would you personally use this technique? Yes _____ No _____
    3. Do other companies use this technique?   Yes _____ No _____

E. The researcher is asked to verify rumors that the competitor is planning to open a new plant in a small southern town. The researcher poses as an agent from a manufacturer looking for a site similar to the one that the competitor supposedly would need. Researcher uses this cover to become friendly with local representatives of the Chamber of Commerce, newspapers, realtors, etc.

    1. Would your company use this technique?   Yes _____ No _____
    2. Would you personally use this technique? Yes _____ No _____
    3. Do other companies use this technique?   Yes _____ No _____

F. Researcher corners a competitor's employee at a national conference, such as the one sponsored by the American Marketing Association, and offers to buy drinks at the hotel bar. Several drinks later, the researcher asks the hard questions.

    1. Would your company use this technique?   Yes _____ No _____
    2. Would you personally use this technique? Yes _____ No _____
    3. Do other companies use this technique?   Yes _____ No _____

G. Researcher finds an individual who works for the competitor to serve as informant to researcher's company.

    1. Would your company use this technique? Yes _____ No _____
    2. Would you personally use this technique? Yes _____ No _____
    3. Do other companies use this technique?   Yes _____ No _____

Figure 13-1. Washington Researchers survey: typical results.

Percentage of "Yes" Responses					
Question A	1.	39%	Question E	1.	36%
	2.	46%		2.	36%
	3.	86%		3.	80%
Question B	1.	63%	Question F	1.	63%
	2.	65%		2.	60%
	3.	86%		3.	91%
Question C	1.	41%	Question G	1.	35%
	2.	47%		2.	36%
	3.	88%		3.	80%
Question D	1.	33%			
	2.	38%			
	3.	71%			

Used with permission of Washington Researchers, Ltd., Washington, D.C.

An Executive Recruiting Story

Along the same lines, I would like to tell you this story about executive recruiting. The neophyte executive recruiter (headhunter) has two tasks. One is to cold-call companies, as described in Chapter 2, in order to obtain what are known as job orders—the authority to do a search. The other task is to identify candidates with the qualities specified by companies and to recruit them for the position. Both components of this task are challenging.

    This particular neophyte headhunter was told to cold-call a list of potential clients and get as many job orders as he could and then to start recruiting candidates for these jobs. Naturally, not all the companies called were in need of a headhunter's services, and some of the contacts were not particularly polite. One of the companies this neophyte called was the "Dynamic Petroleum

Company," whose vice-president of engineering gave a most memorable response. He began to yell and shout and curse at the headhunter. He said that he never dealt with headhunters, that no one in his company was permitted to talk to headhunters, that he would fire any of his engineers or even his secretary for talking to headhunters, and that, furthermore, if he was ever called again, he would institute legal action; with that he hung up. This unnerved the neophyte, who was observed by the president of the search firm. The president of the search firm said, "Let me show you how to handle this. A guy like this isn't a client; he is the source of our product. These are the people that we recruit from."

The president immediately phoned that same vice-president at Dynamic Petroleum. He said that he was a college student whose professor had told him to contact one of the petroleum engineers at Dynamic, that he had forgotten this engineer's name, and that he was afraid to call his professor back. Over the next half-hour, the vice-president of engineering proceeded to read off the names of over 150 different petroleum engineers in his organization, describing them by specialty, background, years of experience, and personal appearance. He gave away an immense amount of intelligence, which was ultimately used by the headhunter who was calling for recruiting purposes.

I once told this story to a group of approximately fifty managers. Several commented on the lack of ethics of the search firm president. But one individual present was himself president of a search firm. He protested, "But that's the business. That's how it's done. You can't be a headhunter if you don't operate in this way."

Again, I don't want you to draw any conclusions about my personal feelings regarding these matters one way or the other. I want you merely to consider that at least some headhunters consider this practice common, if not ethical.

A Japanese View of Duty

When I was his student, Peter Drucker told me the story of a large Japanese company that wanted to open an American plant. After an investigation of many locations in several different states, a suitable site was located. So important was this operation that a special ceremony was scheduled that included the governor, many senior state officials, and the CEO from Japan.

The Japanese CEO spoke fairly good English; however, to ensure that everything he said would be understood despite his accent, the company hired an American of Japanese descent to translate his speech into English.

With dignity and measured tones, the Japanese CEO began to speak, noting the great honor it was for his company to be able to locate in this particular state in the United States with mutual benefits to his company and the states' citizens. He also discussed the benefits to the local economy and to Japanese-American friendship. Then, nodding in the direction of the governor and other state officials, he said: "Furthermore, Mr. Governor and senior officials, please understand that we know our duty. When the time comes that you retire from your honored positions, my corporation will not forget and will repay you for the efforts which you have expended in our behalf in giving us this opportunity."

The Japanese-American translator was horrified. Instantly she made a decision to omit these remarks in her English translation. The Japanese CEO, who understood enough English to realize what she had done, but not why, continued his speech as if nothing had happened. Later, when the two were alone, the executive asked the translator, "How could you exclude my reassurances to the governor and officials? Why did you leave this important part out of my speech?" Only then could it be explained to his amazement that what is ethical, even a duty, in Japan is considered unethical and corrupt in the United States.

Ethics and the Law Are Not the Same Thing

Some years ago, when jet turbine engines were first being developed, General Electric, Westinghouse, and Allis-Chalmers formed what would technically be considered a cartel. Cartels, of course, are illegal under the antitrust laws of this country, and this one was declared illegal and abandoned. But here's my point. The net result was that when the cartel broke up, prices went up, with a resulting drop in demand, bringing a considerable loss of jobs and the eventual bankruptcy of Allis-Chalmers. Again, a question here:

I don't recommend either breaking the law or establishing cartels, but which was the more ethical conduct?

An even more glaring example might be that of Nazi Germany. Under Nazi law, Jews were persecuted. They could not practice in the professions, they could not own land, they could not be employed by non-Jews, and they could not attend universities. Later, they were rounded up, sent to concentration camps, forced to work as slave labors, starved, and killed. It was against German law to help Jews. If you helped Jews, you had to disobey the law. You were sent to jail, or worse. Were those who disobeyed the law and sent to jail unethical?

Typical Problems Relating to Ethics in Consulting

In the practice of consulting, you will eventually be involved in numerous ethical questions. Fortunately, some of them can be anticipated. Consider the following example from my own seminars and courses on consulting. Usually there is no simple solution, although some issues are easier to resolve than others.

1. *Client already knows the solution that he or she wants to a problem.* This typically occurs when a client requires an outsider to confirm information that he or she already knows. For example, you may run into a situation such as the one I described in Chapter 1. Suppose a division of a company has already done a very thorough internal study that suggests the division get into the such and such business. However, because this study was done by the division itself, it is suspect. Top management may wish to have an independent study by a consultant. You may be engaged by that division of the company, and yet the client makes it very clear to you what answer is expected. Do you accept such a consulting engagement or not?

Some consultants say it doesn't make any difference. You're getting paid to do the study even if the answer is known. If the client makes it very clear at the beginning that what he expects is a yes answer, that's what he's paying for and that's what he'll get. Other consultants take the position that they will do the job and provide whatever answer results from their analysis. If the client insists upon having a yes answer and nothing else (usually this insistence is not stated explicitly but is very subtle), they will refuse to undertake the study.

There are many different issues to consider. It will be difficult to escape your need for cash and possible additional business from this client later. But there is no right answer. You have to consider it yourself, and my only advice is to think about the alternatives now, because you will almost certainly encounter this situation sooner or later.

2. *Client wants you to omit information from your written report.* This generally occurs when you have included information in your report that your client feels will hurt her with others, either inside or outside her company. After reviewing your report in draft form, she may ask you to delete certain information. Some consultants take the position that they will decide how to handle this based on relevance to the central issue. If the information is not relevant, they will exclude it. Otherwise they will refuse. However, other consultants feel that because the client is paying and because "the customer is always right," if the customer wants this information left out, it will be left out. Still others stand on their professionalism and refuse to change so much as a comma. You pay your money and take your chance.

3. *Client wants proprietary information that you learned while employed with someone else.* This situation usually arises when you first become a consultant. A former competitor immediately contacts you about a potential engagement. It soon becomes clear, however, that he is hiring you not for what you can do but rather for what you know about your former employer. This situation can also come up when a potential client realizes that you have completed a consulting job for a competitor.

If it becomes clear that all the potential client wants is proprietary information, most consultants will refuse to get involved. Unless you are a professional industrial spy—which, by the way, is illegal aside from the ethics issue—a client who hires you for information that you learned while working for a competitor will suspect that you will betray his proprietary information to some future client. As a result, he will probably not hire you for any other purpose.

If a competitor wants to hire you for a job similar to one you did as a consultant for another company, it may be completely acceptable. "I heard about the great job that you did with the ABC Company; we'd like you to do the same thing for us," he may say. One fully ethical approach is to tell your potential client something like this: "I'd be happy to do this for you if I can get permission from the ABC Company. I don't think that I would be giving away any of their secrets if I did the same job for you. However, because you two are competitors, I would rather have their concurrence. Is that okay with you?"

A question that sometimes comes up is: Who owns proprietary data or information that you develop as a consultant? Usually this is more of a legal question than an ethical one. Many companies, as well as the U.S. Government, are well aware of this issue. Your contract may specify that your client owns all data developed unless you negotiate the contract otherwise. Anything that you develop as part of a consulting engagement but consider your own might possibly be challenged in a court of law in the future. Therefore, if you think something that comes out of an engagement may be useful to you in the future, it's better to agree what will belong to whom up front. For some types of information, this may not be a problem. It's just too difficult to prove that techniques or methodologies that you developed came out of one specific assignment, or out of many. However, some results from marketing research done for a company, or information about a company, clearly belong to the company for which you developed it. But in all cases, it's better to make it contractual. Then you'll know where you stand from the start. Most companies could care less about who owns consulting methods or techniques. But they rightfully feel that the information developed from these techniques, which they pay for, belongs to them.

4. *Client wants you to lie to her boss.* This usually involves a lower-level manager who wants you to lie to a manager at a higher level, or it could be the president of a company who wants you to lie to her board of directors or someone else outside the company. Some consultants have stated that it depends on the lie. They might go along with a harmless "white lie" to protect someone's feelings. Others would not. Let's say that you are on assignment for the

vice-president of a company that is owned by the president, and as a part of this job, you have to analyze the efficiency and effectiveness of all managers working for this vice-president, one of whom happens to be the president's son. You rate the son as a very poor executive. When the vice-president sees this report, she says something like this: "Look, the president of our company has a heart condition. If you report that her son is a very poor executive, it could easily upset her and may actually bring on a heart attack. How about toning this down a bit and saying that this executive is unsuited to his present position?" Many consultants would consider this a "white lie" and would go along with this request. Other consultants might take the position that this executive was very poor and that this is what they intended to put in their report, heart attack or not.

Other lies are far more questionable in both their motives and the net result on the company officials, the company's well-being, or even the general public. Some would say that agreeing to lie would depend on the effect that the lie would cause. Others say simply that they would refuse to lie under any circumstances.

5. *You are a headhunter, and a member of a client's company wants you to recruit him.* This situation again demonstrates that what might be ethical under some circumstances is totally unethical under others. To honor this request is unethical for any headhunter. Under no conditions can a headhunter recruit from his client's company, and no ethical headhunter would even consider it. If a member of a client's organization wants you to recruit him, you should first seek approval from this individual's boss. Alternatively, you can refer the individual to another headhunter.

One question that comes up, however, is: For how long a period after you complete a search for a company is the firm still considered a client? Few would still term a company a client after five years with no new assignments. For a lesser period, you have to make your own decisions. Many headhunters indicate that clientage lasts something less than three years after a search is completed.

6. *Client wants you to bill for more or for less than the actual amount.* This can involve the law as well as ethics. And you can be certain that the IRS would take a very dim view of this suggestion.

But, aside from its possible legal connotations, it is also a lie. Would you do it or would you not?

All these are typical problems, and you will see many more in your practice. In all cases, only you can decide on the action to take. Some otherwise unethical practices are often considered ethical because of the nature of the work accomplished. These would probably include the marketing research and headhunting situations noted earlier that are acceptable in their professions but certainly considered unethical for anyone else. The only analogy that I can think of is spying in war. The professional soldier is prohibited from spying. Spying is illegal. A person caught spying may be hanged. Yet for a spy, spying would probably be considered ethical behavior.

More than twenty years ago, a young U.S. Air Force lieutenant was ordered by a superior officer to falsify a report in order to make a score from a simulated aircraft attack appear better than it actually was. This lieutenant faced a serious moral and ethical dilemma; it appeared that his future career in the air force hinged on an outright lie. Despite considerable pressure, the lieutenant resisted and refused to lie. The threat of punitive action was never carried out, and he had an outstanding career right up until the time he left the air force. Today this lieutenant has major responsibilities outside of the government that have little to do with flying. He rates his success in entirely different activities in no small part to this instance when he decided who he was and how he would live his life.

Ethical questions are rarely simple and rarely easy to resolve. Frequently it's a question not of lying, cheating, or stealing but of doing either the greater good or the lesser evil. Whatever you do, you must be able to respect yourself in the future. Otherwise, you will be useless to your clients and to yourself.

The Institute of Management Consultants Code of Ethics

The Institute of Management (IMC) is a not-for-profit national professional association founded in 1968 to set standards of professionalism for the management consulting profession. You can find IMC's address in Appendix E. You may be interested in the IMC code of ethics. IMC members pledge *in writing* to abide by the Institute's code of ethics. The members' adherence to the code signifies voluntary assumption of self-discipline above and beyond the requirements of law. Key provisions of the code require that IMC members, and their Certified Management Consultants (CMCs), to:[2]

- o Safeguard confidential information.
- o Render impartial, independent advice.
- o Accept only those client engagements they are qualified to perform.
- o Agree with the client in advance on the basis for professional charges.
- o Develop realistic and practical solutions to client problems.

The code also includes provisions regarding clients, engagements, and the consulting profession.

Clients

- o We will serve our clients with integrity, competence, and objectivity.
- o We will keep client information and records of client engagements confidential and will use proprietary client information only with the client's permission.
- o We will not take advantage of confidential client information for ourselves or our firms.
- o We will not allow conflicts of interest which provide a competitive advantage to one client through our use of confidential information from another client who is a direct competitor without that competitor's permission.

Engagements

- o We will accept only engagements for which we are qualified by our experience and competence.
- o We will assign staff to client engagements in accord with their experience, knowledge, and expertise.

○ We will immediately acknowledge any influences on our objectivity to our clients and will offer to withdraw from a consulting engagement when our objectivity or integrity may be impaired.

Fees

○ We will agree independently and in advance on the basis for our fees and expenses that are reasonable, legitimate, and commensurate with the services we deliver and the responsibility we accept.
○ We will disclose to our clients in advance any fees or commissions that we will receive for equipment, supplies, or services we recommend to our clients.

Profession

○ We will respect the intellectual property rights of our clients, other consulting firms, and sole practitioners and will not use proprietary information or methodologies without permission.
○ We will not advertise our services in a deceptive manner and will not misrepresent the consulting profession, consulting firms, or sole practitioners.
○ We will report violations of this Code of Ethics.

Performing your work with high ethical standards is tough. But it's worth it. When you respect yourself, others will respect you as well. Not only are high ethical standards and integrity the right principles to maintain, but you will find that their maintenance is good business.

Notes

1. William A. Cohen, *The Stuff of Heroes: The Eight Universal Laws of Leadership* (Marietta, Ga.: Longstreet Press, 1998).
2. From the Institute of Management Consultants Web site, www.imcusa.org, July 30, 1999.

14

MAKING PROFESSIONAL PRESENTATIONS

The success of a consultant engagement is based not only on actually doing the assignment professionally, but on your ability to present the results of your work to your client. Presenting is crucial. Yet one survey of company presidents showed that more were afraid of public speaking and presenting than of dying. In this chapter I cover the important skills and techniques of presentations and show you the five keys to presentation success.

Objectives of Presentations

With a presentation, you want to inform your client of the results of the assignment, make recommendations that will benefit your client, and confirm that you have done a good job so that you will be retained in the future. Each of these objectives is, in its own way, important.

If you don't take the time to build a case for your recommendations, explaining what has happened during the engagement, your client is less likely to accept your recommendations. Your client wants to know how you arrived at the conclusions that led to these recommendations, and why you used one methodology over others. If you've run into problems, your client also wants to know what these problems were and how you handled them. Did you have to make assumptions because you could not obtain certain information? It is important to tell your client what these assumptions were. If there were changes to the original contract, even though prior approval has already been given, you should restate them, both to remind your client of these changes and to inform others.

The quality of your work, the information you provide, and the usefulness of recommendations you make for action are the bottom line of the consulting engagement. You get paid for results. Without them the engagement, although it might make an interesting case study, would be of no benefit to your client.

Confirming that you have done a good job so that you will be retained in the future is also important. If you've done a good job, you deserve recognition for it. You can do this only by convincing your client through your presentation. If you do it properly, your client will come away from the consulting engagement looking good, and you will be retained again; furthermore, you will get referrals to additional clients who would like you to duplicate your success for them.

Five Keys to a Successful Presentation

Every successful presentation has five essential components. These are: (1) professionalism; (2) enthusiasm; (3) organization; (4) practice; and (5) visual aids.

Let's look at each in turn.

Professionalism

The quality of professionalism must be evident throughout your presentation. It is demonstrated by your dress and personal appearance, the quality of the visual aids you use, your demeanor, your preparation, and your delivery.

If you show up for a presentation wearing a suit that needs pressing or clothes that are not appropriate for the occasion, you will not be perceived as a professional.

If there are typographical or grammatical mistakes in your visual aids, or if the lettering is sloppy, this also will not be perceived as professional.

If the way you handle yourself during the presentation indicates that you are unsure of yourself or defensive, or that you do not know what you are talking about, you will not be perceived as a professional.

If things go wrong during your presentation because of an obvious lack of preparation, again, you will not be perceived as a professional.

But if your presentation is clear and well organized, if it goes off like clockwork and you are prepared to answer all questions asked, if your appearance matches your performance—then your professionalism will be obvious.

Enthusiasm

Enthusiasm is absolutely crucial. If you do nothing else, be enthusiastic. If you are not enthusiastic about what you did, I guarantee you that your client will not be enthusiastic either. In my opinion, enthusiasm is the most important secret of making a good presentation.

What should you do if you really are not enthusiastic? First of all, it is very difficult for me to believe that you could ever become a good consultant and *not* be enthusiastic about what you are doing. But if, for whatever reason, you really are not enthusiastic about a particular assignment, there is only one thing you can do: *Pretend.* Whenever I speak about the absolute necessity of enthusiasm in presenting, I always tell the story of General George S. Patton, Jr., one of the most successful generals of World War II. He won battles *and* saved the lives of his men by motivating them to do their very best. And he did this by becoming a consummate actor.

I have read Patton's published diaries, which go back as far as the turn of the century, when Patton was a cadet at West Point. During World War I, while still in his twenties, he was a colonel in command of the U.S. Army's first tank corps. Patton wrote his wife, Bea, regularly. These letters were published with the diaries. In one letter, Patton says, "Every day I practice in front of a mirror looking mean." Patton called that his "war face." Can you imagine that? A hard-boiled colonel of the U.S. Army practicing looking mean in front of a mirror? But Patton did this for a reason. He knew that his ability to motivate his men—sometimes by joking, sometimes by intimidation—would win battles and save lives. So he made himself become a great actor.

If Patton could act to save lives and win battles, then you and I can act, and act enthusiastically, to make a successful consultant presentation. Remember, you must do this. It is not an option. To repeat: *It is the most important secret of success in presenting.* You must be enthusiastic, and you must show this enthusiasm to your client audience. I promise you that the enthusiasm, even though self-generated, will come through, and it will help make your presentation successful.

Organization

You can't just stand up and speak without having thought ahead of time about what you are going to say. Even a terrific off-the-cuff speaker would get into trouble making consultant presentations that way. If you try it, invariably certain facts will be left out, and then your presentation will not be as clear and logical as it must be. If you are questioned because of this lack of clarity, the pressure on you will increase, and your difficulties will become even greater.

Proper organization of your presentation ahead of time will prevent many problems once you are face-to-face in a formal presentation setting with your client. Fortunately, you already have the ingredients of your presentation from the work you did in earlier chapters, including material from the contract, the proposal, and even your initial interview. So you can organize the facts of the engagement and present them to the client in a clear and logical manner using this outline:

1. Background of the consulting assignment and the problem to be solved
2. Statement of the project objectives
3. Methodologies used to do the assignment, along with alternative methodologies and reasons why they were rejected
4. Problems encountered during the engagement and how each was handled
5. The results or conclusions stemming from this engagement
6. Specific recommendations to the client on what he or she

should do as a result of the work you have done, not ex-
cluding additional work that you or someone else must do
in the future

Frequently you can incorporate the problem-solving methodology explained in Chapter 11. This is especially useful in presenting your analysis of alternative solutions to a problem, which will
lead logically to your recommendations.

Practice

Practice does not mean that you must read your report aloud or
that you must memorize anything. In fact the contrary is true.
Reading will make the presentation boring and stilted. It is not
natural. The same is true of memorization. Even if you have the
ability to memorize quickly, I do not recommend using it in a consulting presentation. First, the time spent in memorization can be
better used in getting your presentation together. Second, there is
always a chance that, under the pressures of the situation, your
timing and memory may be thrown off by a question asked out of
turn or a discussion initiated by your client.

I learned this lesson the hard way. As a young air force officer
flying B-52s out of Altus, Oklahoma, I was extremely interested in
navigation. On one occasion, the Association of Texas Math and
Science Teachers contacted my wing commander to ask if there
was someone who could travel to its annual meeting in Wichita
Falls, Texas, and speak for about an hour on a subject of interest to
the members. The wing commander asked me, and since I had
been waiting for a chance to do research on space navigation, I
jumped at the chance. Using notes collected over several months, I
wrote a terrific one-hour presentation (at least I thought it was
terrific, and it must have been reasonably good, because a national
magazine later published it). I was also given the opportunity to
have excellent artwork prepared as 35mm slides. I felt that I had
the very best support possible. Unfortunately, I made one mistake:
I memorized every single word in that one-hour presentation. I
even knew where to pause for the commas!

When the time came, I drove down to Wichita Falls, Texas,
and in full uniform, looked out at nearly three hundred math and

science teachers. I had been a junior high school student in that very same city, and seeing so many teachers looking at me immediately had its effect. I forgot parts of my presentation, became flustered, and eventually had to read it word for word. What a failure! But it taught me a valuable lesson, and I haven't memorized anything since then, even though I am frequently a guest speaker for many different organizations. Do not repeat my mistake. Do not memorize, and do not read anything.

If you don't read and you don't memorize, how are you supposed to make your presentation? It's easy. Once you have your material organized, you can use either 3- by 5-inch file cards or visual aids to help you discuss each point. You might have one card that says "background of the consulting assignment and the problem." You would then simply look up at your audience and talk to them about this background. If there are any important statistics that you do not wish to leave out, you would put them on other cards sequentially. Other main ideas are also on sequential cards. But you should write no more than one sentence on each card. The idea is not to read what is written on each card but rather to talk about that one sentence. If you are using visual aids, they could display the key sentence or statistics to remind you of what you are going to talk about at that particular time.

Controlling Time

It is extremely important as a part of your practice to control the time available for your presentation. If your client wants a one-hour presentation, make it a one-hour presentation. If your client wants thirty minutes, make it that. Do not under any circumstances extend your presentation unless requested to do so. To do so is disaster. Let me tell you three stories to prove my point.

I was once associated with a major aerospace company that was bidding on a multibillion-dollar contract for the government. On one of the final reviews, representatives of the government visited our organization for a four-hour briefing by our engineers. These engineers lost control of the time and went well over the limit requested by the customer. Despite frantic signals from company employees, they completed their presentation more than an hour and a half late. The customers remained the extra hour and a half without complaint, but many of them missed their return flights. And while I would not say this was the only reason that the large contract was lost, there is no doubt that irritating the customer at this critical time didn't help.

Some years ago, I was on a search committee to find a new professor for our department at the university. The procedure in academia is somewhat different than in industry, and in many cases the professor must be voted on and accepted by the entire department before the university can make an offer. Usually a candidate for faculty membership must not only interview with many department members but also make a formal presentation to the department members as a group.

On this occasion, the candidate, who had only recently obtained his Ph.D., was asked to make a twenty-minute presentation on the research for his dissertation. The time limit was necessary because many faculty members had other meetings to attend. The candidate had graduated from an excellent university, and prior to his visit most of the department members had made their minds up to vote for his hiring based solely on his background and experience.

During the visit, the individual interviews seemed to be going fairly well. The presentation was the final obstacle before the department voted on his hiring. He began his presentation. Five minutes passed. Ten minutes passed. Fifteen minutes passed. Twenty minutes came and went. The presentation continued on and on. The entire department became restless; all of us were late for other meetings. Individuals slipped out, one after the other. Finally, after forty-five minutes, the candidate concluded. By then the once-receptive faculty was no longer so receptive. The faculty did eventually vote to hire, but only for a one-year appointment. In fact it was two years before this individual was finally granted the permanent position that he all but had even before his visit. It is no exaggeration to say that failure to control time—the twenty-five additional minutes—cost two years of promotion, pay, and other benefits.

While attending the Industrial College of the Armed Forces in 1989, I saw an otherwise excellent course go awry because the professor failed to have the students control the time of their required presentations. The result was lack of attention and problems with car pools, and the professor himself received a poor course evaluation.

Never think that time control is a small item: It is very important.

The Practice Sequence

Here's the practice sequence I use: First, I note the time available and outline the presentation using the organization structure indicated earlier in this chapter. I write this information on 3- by 5-inch file cards. I then go through the presentation once, using the cards. In this run-through, I change the cards, add facts if required, and delete or change others if they don't seem to fit. I watch my time closely as I make this presentation to myself, and I make adjustments, through insertion or deletion of material, so that my presentation is several minutes less than the time I have been allotted. This is important, as frequently your presentation will not go exactly as planned. So a little bit of pad never hurts.

If there are several presenters, I insist that we practice together. Some consultants simply divide the available time and develop separate presentations, but I have found that such a presentation doesn't quite fit together when done before the client. Further, frequently one or more of the presenters will exceed the amount of time allotted, and the total presentation runs much longer than anticipated.

I practice at first very informally—perhaps in a room by myself, perhaps sitting around a table with the other presenters. I do this several times until I am confident of the overall structure and the time. Now I also know what visual aids I will need, and I can have them made.

The Formal Practice Presentation

The formal practice presentation is done as if it were real. In fact, I insist on doing it in front of someone who can give me feedback. Usually this is my wife, but it has also been a colleague or someone else who was not involved in the presentation itself. You must present it to an outsider who is not part of the consultant presentation team.

The Live Demonstration

If there is some demonstration to be done as a part of the presentation, I insist on a practice demonstration. This is essential to make sure that it fits into the time and that the results of the demonstration are as anticipated. You will find that in actual presentations everything that can go wrong will go wrong. Therefore, you must anticipate and eliminate potential problems before they actually happen.

Let me give you an example of how important this can be. Once, I attended an annual meeting of the Survival and Flight Equipment Association, an organization of industrial, military, and civilian airline personnel who develop and manufacture life-support equipment for people who fly. A project manager from the navy made a very interesting presentation on a very important piece of equipment he had developed.

A navy flier has special problems because he flies over the sea. If she must eject from the aircraft, she eventually enters the water. She must climb into a small life raft while weighted down with equipment such as survival gear, boots, and helmet. This is difficult enough even on a calm sea, but it is almost impossible if the parachute is still attached to the pilot's body, because even the slightest wind can cause problems. If the open chute fills with water, it can drag the aviator straight to the bottom. So the approved procedure is to use a quick-release, attached to the harness, to get rid of the parachute just as the aviator's boots touch the water. The problem with this procedure is that it is very difficult to judge height over a flat surface like the ocean, and it's even more difficult in the dark and under the pressure of emergency conditions. As a result, some aviators who think they are just about to touch the water are actually 100 feet or more in the air. Jettisoning the chute at that height is clearly not recommended. The navy's solution was highly innovative as well as effective. A small explosive charge called a squib in the parachute harness separates the chute from the harness on contact with water; the water completes an electrical contact. Thus, when the aviator enters the water, the parachute is blown away from her automatically.

Now you may be thinking, "That's just fine for the ocean water, but what if a pilot must eject through a rain shower? Does this mean the apparatus will become wet and the aviator will be dropped thousands of feet?" The navy anticipated this problem. The device worked only in seawater, which has a high salt content.

The navy project manager explained all this in a most interesting fashion and finally came to the most dramatic point of the presentation. He donned a parachute. While he could not submerge his whole body, he had two live wires leading to the squib and had a glass of seawater on a table before him. He then described in vivid terms exactly what would happen. He would take the two wires and thrust them into the seawater. We would see a flash and hear a loud bang, he said, and the parachute would be separated from the harness instantly.

The entire audience waited in great anticipation; several people stuck their fingers in their ears. Knowing that he had everyone's attention, the presenter, with the parachute strapped tightly to his body, took the two wires and jammed them into the seawater. Nothing happened. At first there were smirks; then scattered laughter spread throughout the room. This presenter—who had otherwise made a perfect presentation—took the harness off and discovered that someone had failed to replace the electrical batteries in the harness.

Now sure, we realized that under flight conditions, this would have been checked several times by maintenance personnel and by the pilot himself during preflight. But the drama of the presenter's conclusion was ruined by the mishap.

Let this teach you the lesson that it taught me: Always prepare for any live demonstrations by actually doing them ahead of time. Don't assume that something will work as planned. Actually do the demonstration as part of your practice.

Visual Aids

Visual aids are also essential to a good presentation. In general, you have six options for good visual aids: (1) flip charts; (2) overhead transparencies; (3) 35mm slides; (4) handouts; (5) blackboards; and (6) computer presentations.

Flip Charts

Flip charts are large charts connected at the top that are flipped over as each one is used. The main advantage of flip charts is that they don't require any type of projector. However, since they are large, they are sometimes difficult to transport. And depending on the size of your audience, you may not be able to make the lettering large enough to be seen by everyone in the room.

Overhead Transparencies

Overhead transparencies require the use of an overhead projector. Transparencies themselves usually have a viewing area of approximately $8^1/_2$ by 11 inches. Today you can make transparencies instantly on your computer's printer or a copier. Even if you own neither, many office-supply stores, printers, and sometimes hotels have facilities where you can do these yourself. This is really wonderful, because in the old pre-high-technology age a graphic artist made your transparencies. You always had to allow sufficient time to correct typographical errors, which invariably occurred. Moreover, these overhead transparencies were very expensive. Nowadays, making these are a piece of cake, and they are much less expensive.

Transparencies themselves are fairly easy to carry around. They are not as small as 35mm slides, but they are easier to use than slides and much easier to transport than flip charts. I put each of mine in a clear transparent plastic covering. The covers have holes for a loose-leaf binder. This protects your transparency during both transportation and use. This is important because transparencies can still cost you a couple dollars each.

35mm Slides

Slides are very easy to transport. They do require the use of a slide projector, however, and they can be expensive. As is sometimes the case with transparencies, slides require additional lead time, usually a week or so. For some types of presentations and multimedia presentations in which high-quality photographs are to be used, this method is the only one that makes any sense. I try to avoid them, however. Somehow gremlins always manage to get at least a couple of your slides turned the wrong way in the tray, and getting them put back in right side up and inside out while your audience is waiting is always a real pain.

Handouts

Handouts can be typed on a piece of paper and reproduced through one of the many photographic reproduction processes at a few cents per page. They can be used for either small or large groups, and the expense depends on the number that must be reproduced. You can make the handouts yourself, and they can be prepared at the last minute without a long lead time, both important factors.

For smaller groups, it is fairly easy to carry around the handouts with you. However, for a large group and a lengthy handout, this visual aid becomes cumbersome and expensive. Fortunately, if the group you are presenting to is fairly large, they will frequently offer to reproduce the handout for you. Recently, a client asked for my handout on a computer disc. I'm wasn't the only consultant, and the intent was to reproduce all of the handouts on a CD-ROM, which will be given to participants.

One additional disadvantage of a printed handout is that your audience may tend to read ahead of you; if you have some dramatic point to make, it could be spoiled by your audience's getting there first.

Blackboards

I use blackboards, but the boards may be green or some other color. Also, there are smooth white boards on which you can write in washable colors. I like the latter: no more scratching sound as you write, and no more chalk dust on your hands and clothes.

Still, the advantages and disadvantages of all types of boards on which you write for group consulting presentations are the same. One advantage is flexibility. Until you actually touch chalk to board, you are not committed to revealing anything. Even after you use the board, changes are easy to make on the spot. Along with flexibility is the timing of what you display. You don't write anything down until you need it. Cost is another advantage. There is no cost in preparing for a chalk presentation as long as you don't have to buy a board. Also, as long as you have something to write with and some means of erasure, there isn't much that can go wrong as with electronic gadgetry.

Disadvantages? You can't reproduce a chalk presentation the way you can with overhead or 35mm transparencies. Also, if you have a lot to write down, what is your audience doing while you are writing?

I once started a presentation while my partner tried to write extensive material on a blackboard. Talk about distractions! I don't recommend it. Also, if you can't print clearly, the professionalism of your presentation will suffer.

Computer Presentations

Computer presentations with multimedia sound, movement, and a wide assortment of bells and whistles are available and affordable. Probably the most popular one on the market is Microsoft's PowerPoint, although there are others. If your client has the computer and projector, in theory, all you need to do is carry around a computer disc. Moreover, because you don't need to make transparencies, you save a lot of money. And you can generate handouts using the computer program. Sound too good to be true? Well, as with all methods, there are drawbacks.

The biggest problem I've run into is depending on someone else's computer and programming working with your disc. I've discovered that 50 percent of time, on average, something is not compatible, and your disc won't work. I won't go into the reasons; they are many and varied. I'm just telling you this has been my experience.

A couple years ago I was a major general in the Air Force Reserve working on a project directly for the Chief of Staff of the Air Force. Part of my job was to fly around the country and make an extensive presentation having to do with the navigator career field and retention. I was assigned two of the sharpest majors in the active duty air force to help me: Major Craig Smyser and Major Dorilynn Gimondo. Together we developed one heck of a presentation, which they put on PowerPoint. Based on my 50 percent failure rate experience, we backed it up with overhead transparencies. We visited four different bases around the country. The disc worked in two out of the four.

A friend overcomes this problem by running around the country with her own computer and her own projector. To me, that's a lot of trouble. She didn't make transparency backups. In fact, she accused me of being a Neanderthal because I lean so heavily toward their use. Then a couple months ago, her equipment got misdirected while on a trip. Guess who was busy making shadow images with her hands? I don't know whether she still takes all her equipment, but I do know she now makes transparency backups.

The other drawback to this system is getting seduced by all the neat noises and motions you can do in your presentation. This tends to become a demonstration of systems capability and such a neat light and sound show that it distracts from the information you're trying to convey.

The bottom line? Computer presentations are wonderful, but don't think they solve all your problems, because they don't.

Whatever option you select for visual aids, make sure you keep these points in mind:

1. *Use large type.* The print must be large enough to be visible. If your visual aids cannot be read, you may as well not use them.

2. *Keep it simple.* Don't put too much information on a single slide, transparency, chart, or page of a handout. The information should only be keys to remind you of your major points and to reinforce these major points with your audience. Entire explanations, facts, figures, and so forth can be included as an appendix to your written report. If you put too much information on a single visual, you will only confuse your audience.

3. *Allow lots of lead time.* While handouts can be changed fairly easily, flip charts, transparencies, and slides sometimes take longer. Plan to have them completed a couple of days before the presentation itself. Typographical errors are common, and they must be corrected before the presentation. Even a simple spelling error leaves the thought in your client's mind: *If this consultant has made this error and allowed it to pass, what else is screwed up?*

Overcoming Stage Fright

Every great presenter is a little apprehensive about making a presentation. If you weren't apprehensive, you would be indifferent, and the presentation would be boring. So a little bit of stage fright is fine. On the other hand, you do not want to be so apprehensive that you cannot make a smooth, forceful, and motivating presentation.

In order to overcome stage fright, I do two things: First, as I discussed earlier, I accomplish at least two formal rehearsals before people not familiar with the presentation so that I can receive feedback and criticism on what I say. This criticism often uncovers rough points I never thought about and allows me to polish my presentation.

The second thing I do is something called *creative visualization.* Somehow I stumbled into this technique, and because it is a little strange, for many years I didn't tell too many people about it. Then, almost twenty years ago, in the *Wall Street Journal,* I read an article about it. A performance psychologist, Charles Garfield, had found one reason why some people were superior performers. It was the trick of mental rehearsal, something top athletes had done for a long time. Top chief executives would visualize every aspect of what it would be like to have a successful presentation—sort of a deliberate daydreaming. In contrast, Garfield said run-of-the-mill executives would organize their facts but not their psyches. Thus, my creative visualization got official blessing from a performance psychologist and the *Wall Street Journal.*

Believe me when I tell you the technique is simple. I like to do it the night before I make the presentation, just before I go to sleep. I'm lying there with nothing else to do; I go through my entire presentation, not memorizing it but going through it in my mind from start to finish, from the time I first enter the room until my conclusion. I visualize everything that happens, including standing up and shaking hands and describing the background of the assignment, the objectives of the project, the methods I used and why I chose them, the problems and how they were handled, the resulting conclusions, and the recommendations to my client. I even visualize questions that are asked and my answering them forcefully and correctly. I visualize smiles all the way around, knowing that I have made an excellent presentation and that everyone, including and especially the client who hired me, is happy with the excellent job I have done. I don't stop at doing this once; I repeat the visualization episode over and over again. This doesn't take a lot of effort, because you can visualize an entire hour presentation in a few seconds.

To my way of thinking, this creative visualization technique offers several outstanding features. First, when you actually go to make the presentation, it doesn't feel new. You've done it dozens of times before. This takes the sting out of stage fright. Second, I believe that visualizing my presentation in a positive fashion, as a success, makes me feel that I am going to be successful. I believe that my presentation will be successful, and therefore it is. I sense that my audience will be friendly to me, and therefore it is. I have confidence in my ability to answer questions because I have already seen myself doing these things.

In my years of using this creative visualization technique, it has never failed me. I strongly recommend that you try it too. The results will amaze you.

One variation I have heard about is called the *split focus technique,* where you visualize the presentation while you physically do something else, such as working in the garden or taking a shower.

Answering Questions

Many presenters fear answering questions more than anything else; yet research has shown that 85 percent of the questions asked during a presentation can actually be anticipated. Therefore, when I prepare myself for a presentation, I sit down and try to anticipate questions that members of my client's company are likely to ask me. I actually write them down. Some of the questions bring up items I feel should be included in my presentation, so I modify it accordingly. Others I just think I should be ready for, so I simply think them through and write out the answers. If additional statistics or information is necessary to give a complete answer, I make sure I have this information available. In some cases, I even go so far as to make up a special visual aid with the information, which I hold in readiness to use only if I am asked this question.

When I am actually asked a question, I always repeat it. This gives me additional time to think about the answer, and at the same time it ensures that other members of the audience hear the question too. After repeating the question, I first state my answer, and then explain why my answer is what it is, giving supporting facts. I try never to be defensive about a question, even if it is asked in a belligerent tone of voice. In fact, remembering that the customer is always right, I try never to get into an argument with a client. This does not mean I agree that the client is right if that's not the case. It simply means that I state the facts as I know them, and if the client insists on arguing, I explain my position as tactfully as possible and move on to something else.

One important key to answering questions, and for your whole presentation, is to view members of the audience as friends, not adversaries. Do this even if the climate is political and some members of the audience can be expected to snipe at you. You can at least treat them as friendly snipers, not as enemies out to demolish you.

The other point to watch out for is not to give long-winded answers. Try to make your answers short and to the point. Long-winded answers only fuzz up the issue and may lead to more probing than you want to get into in a public format.

If you follow this advice, you cannot fail to have an outstanding presentation. Not only will you receive accolades for it, but your advice will be respected and followed and will lead to further consulting assignments.

Technology has developed so much that I want to take the next two chapters to talk about some useful, no let me say indispensable, tools for any consultant: the computer and the Internet.

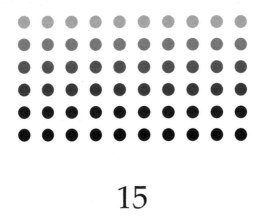

15

What a Computer Can Do for You in Consulting

Computers suitable for consultants didn't exist when I first "hung up my shingle." Today a computer can do more to raise your consulting productivity than any other single tool I can think of. This is so true that it is hard for me to imagine a consultant doing business without a computer, even though it is possible to do so, and I know of a few consultants that don't use them. But I find it hard to believe in this day and age.

How I Got My First Computer . . . Late

It took me a long time to become fully aware of all the things a computer could accomplish. For several years after computers became available, I could think of no reason to buy one. What could I do with a computer that I couldn't do with pencil, paper, or typewriter?

Friends told me I should get a computer to use in writing my books. I told them that if I got a computer to write with, it would probably cause my productivity to decline. This was because I dictated much of my books onto an audiotape. My typist would type out a draft from the tape, and I would correct it and return it to my typist. I couldn't see how I could beat that method unless computers that would type as I spoke became available. (As we will see later, there are now programs that will do that.) But I was wrong about computers.

How the Computer Revolutionized My Writing and Consulting Practice

It was my wife, Nurit, who got me to use a computer. Nurit was working on her doctoral dissertation in psychology and insisted that a computer could save her lots of time. As I had completed my own doctoral dissertation some years earlier without a computer, I wasn't really convinced. Whenever I needed computing done for research, I had it done on the big mainframe at the university. True, each draft of my dissertation had to be more or less completely retyped. That cost me a bundle. But when you are that close to completing your doctorate, you tend not to worry about the cost of typing.

Anyway, Nurit made her case and got one of the IBM PC "clones." The clone was completely compatible with the IBM PC and could do everything an IBM PC could do. However, it cost a good deal less.

I was amazed by how easily Nurit mastered the computer. The advantages of using it were obvious. She could quickly revise entire chapters of her dissertation without having to retype them. When I reviewed her work, I was also surprised at the lack of typographical errors and the neatness of the printout. Unlike many typewritten pages, the right side of the page was as even as the left (this process is as easy as the stroke of a key and is called justification). Further, the entire document could be stored on a floppy disk. Anytime she wanted to work on it, she simply put the disk in the computer. That made it a space saver.

It wasn't long before I got her to teach me how to use the word processing program for my correspondence. The time I saved was just incredible. If I misspelled a word, it was easy to correct before I printed the letter. I no longer faced the terrible choice between a messy erasure or correction fluid and retyping an entire letter; there were no more typos. There was a spelling program on another disk. I just loaded that and my spelling mistakes disappeared. If I had to write a similar letter to someone else, it was easy just to modify the old letter on the disk.

Not too long afterward, I went on contract for a college text-book. A textbook is different from a regular book in that you write the basic text, but your publisher also usually wants ancillary ma-terials. In my case, I had to furnish a three-hundred-page instruc-tor's manual and another manual with twenty-one hundred multiple-choice and true-or-false questions. Further, this publisher wanted these additional materials as "camera-ready copy." This means that instead of typesetting, the publisher simply took a pic-ture of each page that I furnished and reproduced it. Conse-quently, my manuscript had to be letter-perfect and error-free, because it was not reset in type later.

I made an audiotape that I sent to my typist. Instead of send-ing me a corrected manuscript, my typist worked with her com-puter, using the same word processing program I used. She sent me a disk that I put in my computer. I made the corrections I wanted, and I printed the final "camera-ready copy" myself. Now that was fast!

How the Computer Can Double or Triple Your Productivity

Word processing by itself allowed me to double the work I turned out in a given amount of time, and the quality of work was better too. But I soon discovered that my computer could do other things that saved me time and money and made my consulting operations more efficient.

Proposals and Desktop Publishing

In the "bad old days," I used to pay a graphic artist to do my layout and typesetting for proposals, brochures, flyers, or other booklets. This typically cost a minimum of $100 or more per job and took at least a week before I even had the material to proofread. Now, using a software program costing less than $100, I do everything myself. I have a choice of hundreds of different typefaces (fonts) and sizes of type. As a bonus, I don't have to wait. Except for my own time constraints, or the time constraints of people I hire to help me out from time to time, I get the work done exactly when I want it.

I don't mean that I never use a graphic artist, but much of the routine work I can do myself because I can buy thousands of images, photographs, and so forth that I need on CD-ROM that are copyright-free. Or I can sometimes find copyright-free images that I can get from the Internet. As a result, I can do the work better and faster. Moreover, there are inexpensive programs available to help me design my own stationery, business cards, and brochures. I can design them, and using my own printer, print just what I need in a few minutes.

I used to have a minimum of three hundred brochures printed. Less than that was uneconomical. I'd probably use less than half before something would change and I'd need to update the material. Then I'd just have to throw out the old brochures and start over. Now, I never print more than ten at a time. And I update my brochures every time I print them.

About a year ago, I received twenty-four hours' warning that a delegation from a foreign country would unexpectedly visit an institute that I directed at my university. I needed a special brochure for these visitors describing the capabilities of my institute. Even the university printers couldn't help me out. The graphics people required a job order, and with a rush priority, could design and do the job in a week.

I bought a brochure design software program and a package of blank brochures for less than $20 at my local office-supply store. By "cutting and pasting" information I had on file in my computer, I had professional-looking brochures in a couple of hours.

"The Stuff of Heroes" brochure in Appendix B, which promotes my seminars, workshops, and consulting, was done easily on my computer with the help of a word processing program. The only artwork is the Greek figure holding the torch with the shield bearing the words "The Stuff of Heroes," drawn by nationally acclaimed and award-winning artist Cynthia Ing, who took a course on salesmanship I taught at the university. Among Cynthia's national awards is one for the best poster commemorating the five hundredth anniversary of the discovery of America.

Need Overhead Transparencies? No Problem!

The same is true of overhead transparencies, which I use for consulting presentations or seminars. It once took at least a week to have these done. Further, as I mentioned in Chapter 14, there were always typographical errors, some of which I caught too late to have corrected. With my word processing and graphics programs, none of these problems occur. I do all my own "stuff," with incredible savings in time and cost.

Another bonus is that l am able to save all of my material so that if I ever want it again, or want it with minor changes, it's easy to make the changes and print out the new material. All of this material is filed on the hard drive of my computer and backed up on separate computer disks. The material is together where I want it, takes up little space, and is easily retrieved.

Managing Your Practice

If you are concerned with managing the financial side of your practice, or if finances have been a drag in the past, worry no more. There are hundreds of programs around to help you with your financial decision making and record keeping. There are programs that track your income, accounts receivable, payroll, or inventory. Programs can help you make loan decisions and decide whether to make or buy equipment. There are complex accounting programs, and there are very simple ones.

There are even programs that help you prepare your own state and federal income tax forms. They are fantastic and will cut the time for tax preparation (if you do your own) by 50 percent or more. They save you time even if you use an accountant.

Direct Marketing

Certain programs allow you to merge a list of current or potential clients with one of your sales letters. This means that every letter is personalized to that individual customer. What once was a tedious project that you sent to someone else, you can now do at home. This is especially valuable for relatively small mailings that aren't cost-effective to have someone else do. You can do these mailings almost on a moment's notice. If the list is already available, it is actually possible to mail an advertisement or announcement to thousands of people the same day you make the decision to do it.

Correcting Your Writing

In addition to programs that correct your spelling, there are also programs that will correct your grammar, give you choices of the words you may want to use (a thesaurus program), and help you make your writing more readable, interesting, and so forth. A computer software program probably can't turn you into an instant professional writer, but it certainly can turn you instantly into a more competent one. If you want help with writing for your ads, there are programs for this also. There are programs that automatically create headlines, theme lines, slogans, and jingles.

Naming Products and Services

Other programs can help you select names for products or services. Many consultants work with their clients on the crucial decision of naming new products or product lines. These programs analyze the statistical properties of letter combinations while using special filters for rejecting poor name formations. They even check names for hidden or embedded profanities in several different languages and have the "smarts" to review a trillion permutations of a fifteen-letter word. Try doing that for a client over the weekend without a computer.

Making Forecasts and Plans

One of the most common computer uses for business is that of the spreadsheet. A spreadsheet program can be used to do sophisticated calculations, provide data for graphs, do forecasts, view results by changing various "what if" variables, estimate costs, and so forth. Basically, a spreadsheet is simply a chart with rows and columns filled with numbers. But the beauty of this type of program is that you can do the formula calculations to fill in these rows and columns with hundreds of accurate numerical results almost instantly. You just plug in the basic numbers that the formula calls for.

There are also software programs around to assist you in developing plans of all types incorporating the spreadsheet concept. Let's say you are developing a marketing plan for a client. Can you imagine the time you'll save when all you have to do is plug in numbers? From those numbers, the program develops charts, alternative strategies, financial ratios, balance sheets, cash flow analyses, income statements, sales projections, and a lot more for you simply by your pressing a few basic keys.

Evaluating Potential Employees

Big companies pay big fees to consultants to obtain complete psychological evaluations of potential key employees. Even this has been computerized: You can obtain programs in which you input data based on questions answered by the candidate. The output can tell you how the individual is likely to behave in different situations. Or the information can be used for vocational counseling. In Europe, especially, handwriting analysis is popular for prehiring evaluation of executives. Handwriting analysis computer programs are also available.

Simplifying Marketing Research

There are probably hundreds of marketing research programs. They not only help you to design your research tool but analyze your data and interpret the results; therefore, much of the time-consuming drudgery of manipulating the results from research is eliminated. The computer prints all the backup analysis for you, as well as the bottom-line results you need for your client.

Voice-Activated Word Processing

Remember that before I bought my first computer I erroneously said that the only way I could improve my productivity was if the computer typed out what I said aloud? Well, that time has arrived. There have been voice recognition programs around for several years. I have one, but to tell the truth, I haven't tried it out yet. A friend of mine who has one is very pleased. He says he saves the time and expense of having a secretary by simply dictating to his computer his reports, e-mail, presentations, spreadsheets, or whatever.

Gaining Access to Information the World Over from Your Office

Modems, which are simple devices that attach to your computer, can gain you access to immense databases and a lot more, all through your telephone lines and more recently through cable or even remote access. The potential of this device for multiplying your effectiveness and efficiency in consulting is almost unbelievable. For example, you can exchange messages quickly with clients and other consultants through an electronic mail system (e-mail). In fact, you can send an entire report to a client this way in a few seconds, and it will cost you only pennies for the transmission time. When he or she receives the report, it can either be viewed on a computer or printed out using a word processing program. In seconds, you can call up product ratings from consumer reports or access key articles in leading magazines. You can research just about any topic you want; you can even do comparative shopping and make travel arrangements.

Here's one example of how you can make your operation more efficient through the use of a modem. Let's say that you need census tract data, demographics, and market potential for a client. Normally, you might need to go to a specialized business library and the chamber of commerce or consult various other sources, which may take you hours or even days. Through use of a modem, you can reach hundreds of databases and complete the job in minutes.

For several years, electronic publishers have been selling information via e-mail, or by print-on-demand, all possible due to the modem. As I write these lines, a major publisher is allowing customers to purchase a book this way, before the release date of their hardcover printed copy. You can see that this technology, and its use, is advancing by leaps and bounds. We'll look at more of this in the next chapter on the Internet.

I hope I've said enough to show you what a computer may be able to do for you. Your local computer software store can show you most of the programs I've described and a lot more (hundreds of new programs are being developed every day). If you live in a town that doesn't have a software store, get a copy of one of the many computer magazines that are now being published. Not only will you see many programs advertised and described right in the magazine, but you can obtain catalogs from companies that publish hundreds of other programs to help you run and build your business.

What You Need to Know about Computers

Before I begin, let me say that you really don't need to know much. But if you are unfamiliar with computers, the topic may seem confusing. I'm going to clear up that confusion right now. When you buy a computer, you need a keyboard; the "computer proper," with one or more disk drives; a visual indicator (called a monitor), and a "mouse." The mouse is simply a hand controller that is electronically connected to a mark on your video screen. You "point and click" with the mouse, and your computer performs various functions. As a consultant, you are also going to need a printer. Nowadays, most computers incorporate a CD-ROM drive as one of the disk drives supplied integral to your computer. A CD-ROM is simply a disc that has the capacity to store many times the information that can be stored on a regular disk. If you can use a typewriter, you can run a computer. In fact, you don't even need to know how to type to use a computer. I can tell you this because I never learned how to type, and I'm doing just fine. You do not have to learn a special computer language. You do not need to learn how to "program." All that has been done for you by a programmer. All you need to do is turn the computer on. Just start up the program and follow the directions in the manual that comes with the program. Frankly, once you get a little experience with various programs, you can usually figure out most of the functions even without the manual.

The keyboard attaches to the computer and is very similar to the one on a typewriter. It has a few more keys than most typewriters but nothing overly complicated. The instructions that come with any program you buy tell you what keys to press or where to put the mouse indicator on the screen and then click (depress a lever on your mouse) to get the computer to perform some function. Through the keyboard and the mouse, you tell the computer what you want it to do. What is called *typing* on a typewriter is called *word processing* on a computer. Each time you push a key, you're telling the computer to make a letter on the screen of your monitor. Today, most are color monitors, and most programs either require or work best in color.

The disk drives work like a record player. You play your computer programs on them. The programs themselves are on disks and are known as *software.* The old standard was the $5^1/_4$-inch disk that held 360,000 bits of data, however, it's pretty much passé. The industry standard today is the $3^1/_2$-inch disk that holds 1.44 million bits of data, read as 1.44 megabytes or 1.44MB. However, there are other disk drives available today that hold many more times this amount. For example, recordable CD-ROMs hold an astounding 650MB. That is enough for five hundred or more full-length books. There are also special disk drives that will compress your information, allowing you to store many times the information on your $3^1/_2$-inch disks. Then there are disk drives for LS-120 diskettes that have 120MB of storage space. These latter disks are great for individual use. However, if you are going to send a disk to a client with some information on it, better make it a $3^1/_2$-inch 1.44MB diskette.

In addition to containing software programs that you may want to run, disks are also used for storing data such as your advertising brochure, customer lists, and sales letters. Even the standard 1.44MB disk allows you to store several hundred typewritten pages.

Now I know that this sounds like a lot, but you will soon discover that it's not. The beauty of a hard disk, which is a permanent part of your computer, is that it will store up to several gigabytes of data, depending on its size. Most people put the programs and data they use frequently, say word processing and desktop publishing, on their hard disks, and they back up their data on floppy disks. Accessing data from a hard disk is much faster and more convenient than retrieving them from a floppy disk.

What Kind of Computer Should You Buy?

The two most popular personal computers on the market today are the IBM, and IBM-compatibles, and Apple's Macintosh. The biggest advantage of the IBM and its clones is the amount of software available; everybody and his brother develops software for the IBM. The advantage of the Macintosh is its ease of use. At one time, the Macintosh was far superior technologically to the IBM, and far easier to use. However, with the advent of Microsoft's Windows, this advantage has largely disappeared.

RAM stands for random access memory; the more you have the better: Your computer will operate faster, and you'll be able to handle more applications. The same with your processor, the higher the megahertz (MHZ), the faster your computer will run.

Nowadays, most computers will come "ready to go" with multimedia, that is, with a sound card and speakers. This is important because many programs come with sound and you'll need this capability. Other standards are the CD-ROM disk drive running at 24X or better and a modem.

You may want a scanner. That allows you to scan typewritten pages, pictures, and so forth and to import them into your computer to work on, change, save, or incorporate into another document. They are pretty handy but not required. Color scanners are much more expensive than black and white, but if you get one, color is my recommendation.

Technology is changing so fast that you should talk to a dealer to get the best value for your money.

Desktop, Laptop, or Palmtop?

Today, you have a choice. Do you want a large computer with maximum capability that sits atop your desk or on a specially built computer cabinet? Then you want a desktop. If you do a lot of traveling and frequently work at client locations where you need a computer, then that argues for a laptop. Laptops have most, if not all, of the capabilities of desktops. However, they are not as convenient to work with. If you need to have a computer with you occasionally when you travel, but don't like lugging around a laptop, which weighs about five pounds with ancillary materials, you need a palmtop—they usually fit in your palm and weigh a pound or so. Palmtops are less expensive than laptops. However, whereas a consultant can probably make do with just a laptop, a palmtop is strictly an auxiliary computer. It can't match the other two types in power, speed, or features. If you own a palmtop, you're going to need one of the others as well. Palmtops are handy, however, and interface with your other computer, so any work you do on one you can upload on the other.

There was a time when I didn't recommend buying a computer by mail, but sometimes you can find real bargains that way. Today, the state of the art is such that it is far easier to set things up and get started without problems. There are telephone numbers you can call for technical assistance, and many mail purchases include in-home servicing. As a result, I buy most of my computers and computer equipment through the mail or over the Internet. If nothing else, in many cases you will save the sales tax, which where I live runs 8.25 percent.

What Kind of Printer Should You Buy?

Your major decisions when buying a printer have to do with quality, speed, black-and-white versus color, and internal memory. You'll find many color printers that cost less than black-and-white printers, usually because some are inkjet printers versus laser printers. I suggest getting a laser printer because quality becomes an issue if you are printing graphics other than line drawings.

With computer printers, what we see as the letter A is actually made up of hundreds of little black dots. Now if you are printing words or line drawings, 600 dots per inch (dpi) is just fine. But if you want to print photographs and use your printer for desktop publishing, you should look for a printer that has the capability of twice that, or 1200 dpi.

Again, if you're only printing words, your printer's memory is no big deal. However, if you have illustrations, you'll find this requires a lot of memory. Make certain the printer has a minimum of 4MB of internal memory. By the way, you can usually add memory if you need more capability later.

I hope I have convinced you that you should invest in a computer and that I've given you some ideas about what you'll need. Now here's some good news. Many commercial printers and office-supply stores have computers and ancillary equipment that, for a fee, you can use, instead of buying your own. Now understand, this is a temporary stopgap. Sooner or later, you're going to have to get your own. And one additional big reason is discussed in the next chapter: the Internet.

16

WHAT THE INTERNET CAN DO FOR YOU IN CONSULTING

The Internet has revolutionized the way consultants of all types do business. Company research that once required multiple telephone calls and interviews, plus trips to the library and the purchase of various directories now takes only a few minutes. Product information that took hours of expensive research time to uncover is now at your fingertips. Brochures, pictures, and other material, once so expensive, can now be made available instantaneously to potential clients at no additional cost to you. A direct mail campaign to potential clients, which used to take weeks of preparation, hours of envelope stuffing, and several days or more in the mail—plus money for printing, envelopes, and postage—now can cost little and be available to hundreds, or even thousands of prospects, in a few seconds. How can this not be revolutionary? In this chapter, we're going to look at two major ways of taking advantage of this technology: research and marketing.

What Is the Internet?

The Internet is nothing more than a worldwide network of computer systems that links you with other parties simultaneously via telephone or cable-line modem. The significant aspect of this is the number and location of these parties; they are located all over the world. The estimates of the numbers of individuals on this "party line" range up to 100 million or more, and the number is growing by millions every month. I've heard that approximately a billion people will be online by the time this book is published. With a billion people seeking products and information, having needs and wants for their businesses, and producing information, news, and advertising, that's a lot of potential for a consultant for getting information, and reaching any target audience, including someone interested in your services.

What Do You Need to Get Online?

To get on line, you need your computer, a modem, a connection to the Internet, and a Web browser such as Microsoft Internet Explorer or Netscape Navigator. The connection comes from a company like AOL (America Online), Prodigy, or numerous others. These folks are constantly competing for your business, which is why you may have received free disks or a CD-ROM in your mailbox offering you free hours and an automatic connection when you use the disk or CD-ROM. When you buy a new computer with a modem, you'll probably have both a browser and a connection company all loaded up and ready to go. All you have to do is agree to their terms (you pay extra for the service) and follow the directions provided, and you're on. You'll probably will also want a separate phone line if you use a phone modem and not cable or remote access. Otherwise your time online will interfere with your phone calls and visa versa.

Researching on the Internet

In the chapter on research, I mentioned starting at the library. In a library, we use the library's catalog index, which may be on a card or on at computer terminal. We search catalog indexes on the Internet as well. These catalog indexes are called search engines. Your library's catalog index may list forty thousand entries; however, a search engine may have 100 million, probably more!

There are many search engines. Some are specialized for certain areas of interest; some search the whole Web. Even with a 100 million or more entries, I've found that what one search engine can't locate for you, another can.

The Search Engines

Here are a few of the major search engines along with their Web addresses:

AltaVista: http://www.altavista.digital.com
Archie: http://www.alpha.science.unitn.it/cgi-bin/archie
Galaxy: http://www.galaxy.com
HotBot: http://www.hotbot.com
Internet Sleuth: http://www.isleuth.com
Lycos: http://www.lycos.com
MetaCrawler: http://www.metacrawler.com
UltraSeek: http://www.ultra.infoseek.com
WebCrawler: http://www.webcrawler.com
Yahoo!: http://www.yahoo.com

How to Use the Search Engines

The best way to find out about these search engines is to do a search. There are four easy steps:

1. Type the Internet address into your Web browser software.
2. Enter a word or word group having to do with your research topic into the entry box on the engine.
3. Click the button on the engine that begins your search.
4. Review your results and further investigate those matching documents (listed as electronic links that you can inspect by clicking with your mouse) that look good. If you receive no "hits," repeat steps two through four using different words.

Let's go through the search process. We'll use the Yahoo! engine. First, we want to type in Yahoo!'s electronic address. So we enter: http://www.yahoo.com. Then we'll hit the Enter key on the computer. That gets us to Yahoo! You should see the same screen as shown in Figure 16-1.

Figure 16-1. Initial Yahoo! Web page.

Auctions · Messenger · Check Email

YAHOO!

What's New · Personalize · Help

Yahoo! Mail
free from anywhere

PEPSI **SHAQ VS. CINDY?**

NordicTrack
Get Free Shipping

| consulting | **Search** | advanced search |

Y! Shopping - Apparel, Books, Computers, DVD/Video, Luxury, Electronics, Music, Sports and more

Shop Auctions · Classifieds · PayDirect · Shopping · **Travel** · Yellow Pgs · Maps **Media Finance/Quotes** · News · Sports · Weather
Connect Chat · Clubs · Experts · GeoCities · Greetings · Invites · **Mail** · Members · Messenger · Mobile · Personals · People Search
Personal Addr Book · Briefcase · Calendar · **My Yahoo!** · Photos **Fun** Games · Kids · **Movies** · Music · Radio · **TV**   **more...**

Yahoo! Auctions - Bid, buy, or sell anything!

Categories		**Items**	
· Antiques	· Computers	· PlayStation 2	· Palm Pilots
· Autos	· Electronics	· MP3 Players	· Lincoln Pennies
· Coins	· Sports Cards	· Hello Kitty	· Cameras
· Comic Books	· Stamps	· Kate Spade	· Longaberger

In the News
· Four Texas prison escapees arrested; fifth commits suicide
· Hijack of Yemeni plane foiled
· DR Congo readies for president's burial
· Calif. faces more power shortages
more...

Arts & Humanities
Literature, Photography...

News & Media
Full Coverage, Newspapers, TV...

Marketplace
· Yahoo! PayDirect - send and receive money online
· Get your own Web domain
· Y! Travel - buy tickets, check arrival times

Business & Economy
B2B, Finance, Shopping, Jobs...

Recreation & Sports
Sports, Travel, Autos, Outdoors...

Computers & Internet
Internet, WWW, Software, Games...

Reference
Libraries, Dictionaries, Quotations...

Broadcast Events
· 12pm ET : Sundance Film Festival
· 7pm : Purdue vs. Indiana
· 7:30pm : Syracuse vs. Notre Dame
more...

Education
College and University, K-12...

Regional
Countries, Regions, US States...

Entertainment
Cool Links, Movies, Humor, Music...

Science
Animals, Astronomy, Engineering...

Inside Yahoo!
· Y! Movies - Snatch, The Pledge, The Gift, Last Dance, Traffic
· Y! Invites - plan your Bowl party
· Y! Ski & Snow - get the latest snowfall info
· new! Play free Fantasy Golf

Government
Elections, Military, Law, Taxes...

Social Science
Archaeology, Economics, Languages...

Health
Medicine, Diseases, Drugs, Fitness...

Society & Culture
People, Environment, Religion...

Local Yahoo!s
Europe : Denmark - France - Germany - Italy - Norway - Spain - Sweden - UK & Ireland
Asia Pacific : Asia - Australia & NZ - China - HK - India - Japan - Korea - Singapore - Taiwan
Americas : Argentina - Brazil - Canada - Chinese - Mexico - Spanish
U.S. Cities : Atlanta - Boston - Chicago - Dallas/FW - LA - NYC - SF Bay - Wash. DC - **more...**

More Yahoo!s
Guides : Autos - Careers - Health - Living - Outdoors - Pets - Real Estate - Yahooligans!
Entertainment : Astrology - Events - Games - Movies - Music - Radio - TV - more
Finance : Banking - Bill Pay - Insurance - Loans - Taxes - Live market coverage - more
Local : Classifieds - Events - Lodging - Maps - Restaurants - Yellow Pages - more
News : Top Stories - Business - Entertainment - Lottery - Politics - Sports - Technology - Weather
Publishing : Briefcase - Clubs - Experts - Invites - Photos - Home Pages - Message Boards
Small Business : Biz Marketplace - Domain Registration - Small Biz Center - Store Building - Web Hosting
Access Yahoo! via : Pagers, PDAs, Web-enabled Phones and Voice (1-800-My-Yahoo)

Make Yahoo! your home page

How to Suggest a Site - Company Info - Copyright Policy - Terms of Service - Contributors - Jobs - Advertising

Copyright © 2001 Yahoo! Inc. All rights reserved.
Privacy Policy

Let's say we want to research the consulting field. In step two, we enter the word "consulting." Then we hit the search button. The results are shown in Figure 16-2, which shows only the first page. Because the term "consulting" is so broad, not only are there 227 matches, but each represents just a part of consulting. For example, the first line only displays a link to companies that do computer consulting.

Maybe that's what we are primarily interested in, so we'll follow that link. We use our mouse again to point and click on this link. This takes us to what you see in Figure 16-3; the first of thirty-seven pages of listings of companies doing computer consulting.

If we are interested in looking at the first one, 3 Village Computer Consulting, we click on this link as we did earlier. This takes us to 3 Village Computer Consulting's Web page, as shown in Figure 16-4.

Now if these results weren't what we were looking for, we'd want to do a more advanced search. So we'd go back to Yahoo!'s initial page (Figure 16-1) and click on the words "advanced search." This gives us some options for different search methods, help, and so forth, as is shown in Figure 16-5.

From this example, you can see how easy it is to find and research prospect clients on the Internet as well: Just type in your target market and see what comes up.

Evaluating and Using Your Results

That's all there is to it. You can print out things you find. You can also copy information with your computer and electronically "paste" them into other documents. Of course, you should be careful to credit anything you use with footnotes and also be careful not to run afoul of copyright laws protecting others' intellectual property. Material on the Internet is just like printed material in this respect.

Sometimes you have to work with different but related words to find what you want. Sometimes you need to try different search engines. But there is so much information out there that I've come to believe that you can find just about anything—it's just a matter of doing the research. No wonder government security agencies were concerned a few years ago when they located accurate instructions on how to build an atomic bomb!

Figure 16-2. The result of searching for "consulting" on Yahoo!

Figure 16-3. One of thirty-seven pages of companies doing computer consulting.

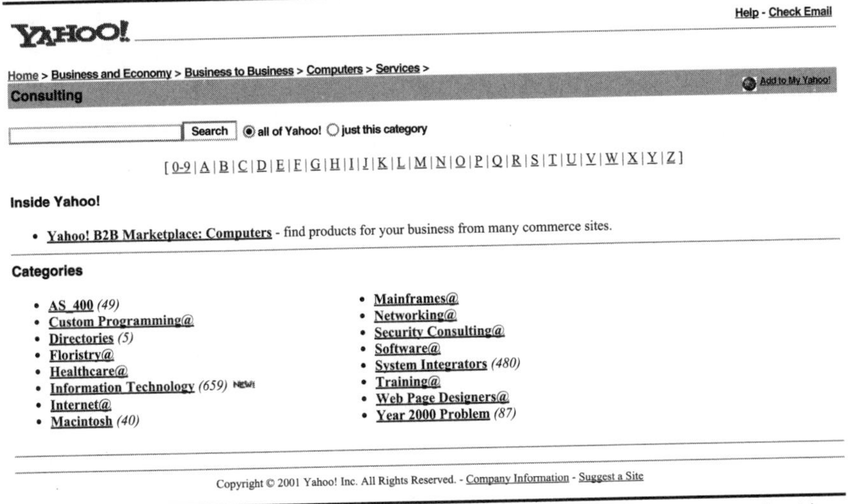

Reproduced with permission of Yahoo! Inc. © 2001 by Yahoo! Inc. Yahoo! and the Yahoo! logo are trademarks of Yahoo! Inc.

Figure 16-4. 3 Village Computer Consulting's initial Web page.

3 Village Computer Consulting
9 Peters Path - Setauket, NY 11733
516-941-3027
516-246-8232 fax
gbarry@3vcc.com

**The Big Technology Advantage
for Small Business**
- The 3VCC Advantage
- SecurityNet Plus
- Project Consultation
- FlexPacks
- About 3 Village Computer Consulting
- Request for information

Figure 16-5. Advanced search options using Yahoo!

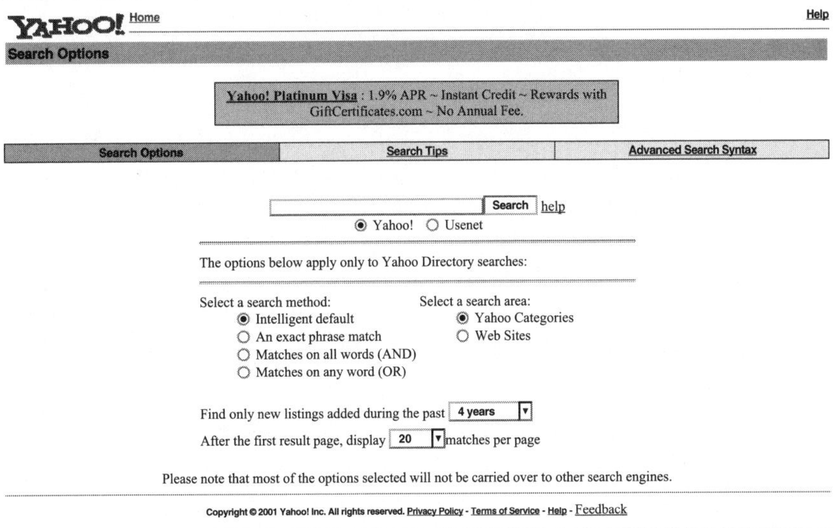

Some Books on Researching on the Internet

For an in-depth look at researching on the Internet, try the following:

- *The Information Specialist's Guide to Searching and Researching on the Internet & The World Wide Web* by Ernest Ackermann and Karen Hartman (Abt Content)
- *The Internet Research Guide*, rev. ed. by Timothy K. Maloy (Watson-Guptill Publishers)
- *The 10 Minute Guide to Business Research on the Net* by Thomas Pack (Que Education and Training)

Marketing on the Internet

In the summer of 1999, a movie that cost $50,000 to make beat out *Star Wars Episode I* in per-screen average sales, taking in an average of $26,500 at every screening. The movie was *The Blair Witch Project*. Made by Hollywood "nobodies" with no well-known actors and actresses, the movie became a blockbuster and grossed millions of dollars. What was the secret? The Web site (see http://www. blairwitch.com) and Internet marketing.

If the Internet can do this for a film, what can it do for a consultant? Plenty, but you've got to be smart about it and know what you're doing.

Internet "Freeways" for Marketing

At the present time, there are three main Internet "freeways" that are useful for the consultant in marketing. These are: (1) the World Wide Web, (2) the Usenet, and (3) e-mail.

Let's look at each in turn.

The World Wide Web

The World Wide Web (www) consists of a giant freeway of home pages, catalogs, electronic stores, and much much more. It is in color and has graphics, sound, and even video.

Now to place a color advertisement of multiple pages in a magazine and run it month after month would cost you a fortune. Never mind that a magazine does not have the flexibility of sound or video. Only the largest of corporations can afford such advertising, and even they are very selective. But on the Web, even you and I can afford to do it, and we can compete with the giants of our industry. In fact, I'm going to show you how you can do this for only a couple of hundred dollars a year.

How to Establish Your Own Web Site

There are alternatives to paying someone several thousand dollars or more to develop your site. One way of developing your own Web site is to do it yourself. No, you don't need to be a computer programmer with years of technical know-how or a room full of experts. There are computer programs available that will walk you through the steps. Several years ago, I bought the CD-ROMs *Instant Web Pages* and *Web Ware* from MEI/Micro Center (1100 Steelwood Road, Columbus, Ohio 43212-9972; toll-free 1-800-634-3478) for only $14.97 each! I'm sure there are many other similar and maybe even better programs around today. Most programs I've priced recently will run you from a little under one hundred to several hundred dollars.

Many universities also conduct courses on this subject. Two years ago I attended a four-hour course during which the instructor walked us through step-by-step, and we actually built our own site during the course. You may also find a student or professor willing to build a Web site for you at a university at a cut-rate price.

My Web site, http://www.stuffofheroes.com, was developed to help promote my book *The Stuff of Heroes: The Eight Universal Laws of Leadership*. A student, who was also an instructor of the subject at a community college, developed my site. Currently, I'm converting the site, but keeping its name, to promote my seminars and workshops. I'm trading consulting services with an established computer consultant; I'm consulting on marketing and strategy in exchange for the redevelopment of the site, so it's a win-win situation for both of us. And that's another way of getting your site developed at no cost, through barter.

Once You Have Your Site Developed,
Then What Do You Do?

Your next step is to pick a name and get an Internet Service Provider, or ISP, to put your site up on the WWW. Pick a name that's easy to remember and to get to. There's a lot of mystery built into picking a name, more than I think is necessary. There are a number of folks saying that they know the "secret" of getting your Web site to be one of those first twenty that come up out of the thousands that are also offering similar products or services with the search engines, as we saw before. Your domain name is supposed to be part of the secret. I think it's all a lot of hooey. For these "experts" to be correct, they would have to have fewer than twenty clients in any field anyway, even if they had the secret. Why twenty? Because that's usually the default for the number of cyberlinks to sites that will be called up on your screen when you do a search. If your site is listed as number 21 out of 10,007 that are related to the search word, you are out of luck. The truth is, there are so many folks doing business on the Internet in every field, that if you're depending on the search engines as a marketing tool to get you business, better stick to trying to win the lottery. Your odds are better.

I would suggest a name that's short. That way, whenever you give it out, face-to-face in casual conversation or more formally in a speech, people will remember it, whether they write it down or not.

Contrary to "the rules," I don't think it's important to include words that will be picked by search engines because I think the Web is so saturated that relying on business reached through search engines has got to be the wrong way to attract prospects to your Web site.

Registering Your Domain Name

Once you have a name, you must register it with what is called InterNIC. They will also give you your domain address called a Universal Resource Locator, or URL. Among other things, registration prevents duplication of domain names. I registered with Network Solutions, Inc. (P.O. Box 17305, Baltimore, MD 21297-0525;

toll-free 888-771-3000). You can also register electronically (http://rs.internic.net). At the time I registered, the cost was $70 for two years.

Now back to the ISP. There are hundreds, and you can locate them through a search. My ISP is Solo Web Hosting services at http://www.websolo.com. You can register on the Internet, and they advertise that they can activate you in ten minutes. They offer a free domain name check at their site and will register your name for you with InterNIC. Their current charges are from $6.95 per month for their basic package of unlimited Web space and usage to $25.95 per month, which includes not only the basic package but also other services, including an unlimited nationwide dial-in account.

There are other services that may be of interest to you. For example, if you sell a product, you'd want your customer to have the ability to order using a credit card. If you sold written information, giving your customer the opportunity to download the information on the spot saves you postage and printing costs, and let's your customer get the material instantly. These and other services are all available at a nominal additional cost to you. You just have to check with the potential ISP and see what they provide.

Why Not a Cybermall?

Cybermalls, or virtual malls, have been heavily promoted with full-page newspaper advertisements on weekends, free seminars, videotapes, and you name it. The idea sounds good on the surface. Just like regular shopping malls, you open a store on a cybermall. The cybermall develops your site, and you pay yearly "rent" for it. Most offer some sort of "training," really consulting to help you with marketing questions. And most cybermalls bundle various services together: e-mail boxes, free virtual banners advertising your service, and so on. Costs are high in comparison with an ISP—as much as a thousand dollars or more a year, compared with $100 to $200 for an ISP.

Is it worth the additional costs? For most consultants, I would say no. The mall theory is that (1) people come to visit the mall and stop in and buy your services just like a regular shopping mall, and (2) customers come for one thing and see your listing and go to visit your site too. This is called "spillover."

First, I believe the psychology of visiting a regular shopping mall is not the same for a virtual mall. People go to a regular mall partly for a good time. They go to see what's new, they socialize, they have lunch, and they may even go to a movie. For many it's a "day at the mall," and they "shop until they drop." Those that visit a cybermall are usually looking for something specific. Few have the time to spend all day at a cybermall without the socialization with friends, spouse, or girlfriend/boyfriend that goes along with it. So even though the cybermall may be well promoted, and most are not, you're not going to get much business due to "walk-in business" and the fact that you are in "a mall." Also, as a consultant, how many consultants do you see with storefronts in real malls?

Regarding spillover, it's more of the same. Unlike the thrill of the chase in a day of buying, cybermall buyers will probably get what they want and get out. You'd have to be pretty lucky for someone to see the business listing on their way out and start looking for a consultant. Buying consulting services simply is not an impulse purchase.

How Should You Market on the World Wide Web?

The key to Web marketing is promotion, both online and offline. You've got to get people to your Web site. You can't rely on the search engine to do it for you. Remember the thirty-eight pages of computer consultants when we researched consulting earlier in this chapter? There is so much competition on the Web for any business or service that trying to build a business based on a search engine is ludicrous.

Publicity: The Number One Secret for Marketing on the Web

Hot!Hot!Hot! was a Web site that sold salsa over the Internet. The owners sold their business a couple years ago. They began in 1994, so Hot!Hot!Hot! was one of the first businesses to attempt to sell anything online. It became hugely successful and is one of the folk heroes of the Internet. Now as it happens, the salsa business

was located in Old Town, Pasadena, near my home, and I participated in some consulting for the owners of Hot!Hot!Hot! in their
new business. They told me that half of their salsa business came
from their Web site and the other half from their storefront.

The key even in those days was not a search engine. It was
publicity. One of the owners had majored in public relations in
college. She tirelessly promoted the business and the Web site
through articles she wrote and interviews she gave to newspapers
and magazines about the uniqueness of the business and what was
then the uniqueness of Web site marketing.

As a consultant, you've got to do the same thing. Make your
Web site marketing synergistic with your other marketing efforts.
Put your Web site address on your business cards, stationery, bro-
chure, and anything else printed having to do with your business.
Whenever you talk to anyone, mention your Web site address.
That's why you want it simple like "stuffofheroes."

Using Banners

Banners are the color advertisements you see floating around
all over the Web. You click them, and they send you to the associated Web site. The key here is to spend your advertising dollar for
banners only where prospective clients hang out. Amazon.com, the
online bookseller, puts banners all over the Web. But each banner
is specific to the topic of the Web site in which it appears. Even
so, probably much of their advertising dollar is wasted because
frequenters of some Web sites are probably not buyers of books. In
your case, if you did consulting for a certain industry, you could
put a banner in that industry's trade association Web site, and
you'd probably get some business.

You can get no-cost banner advertising by putting someone
else's banner on your site. One way is to find noncompetitive but
compatible sites and offer a one-for-one exchange. There are also
banner exchange services. If you use them, it may not be a one-for-
one exchange. That is, you may need to carry two ads for every one
of yours. The reason is that these companies make their money by
selling those extra ad impressions to companies willing to pay for
more exposure. Here are some banner exchange services to try:

- http://www.linkexchange.com
- http://www.smartage.com
- http://www.worldbannerexchange.com
- http://www.bannerco-op.com

You can have banners created at www.worlddesignservices.com or by using programs at the sites listed above.

Cyberlinks

Cyberlinks are electronic links connecting one Web site to another. You "point," using your mouse, at a particular link and click. Presto, you're taken to that Web site.

Like much of marketing on the WWW, it's a case of using proven concepts in another environment. Find noncompeting consultants and offer to exchange links. In other words, in your Web site will be a cyberlink describing their consulting service and linking your site with theirs. On their site, you will describe your service, and there will be a similar link.

Again, we're talking about a win-win situation for everyone. The other consultant gets clients they wouldn't normally get, and so do you. Moreover, the clients win too, because you can build a directory of these links that can attract people to your Web site simply to use it to look for a unique type of consulting that you may not offer.

Give Information Away

The concept of giving information away seems to confirm the law that whatever you give away comes back to you many times over. That's the concept of the newsletter described in Chapter 3. As a matter of fact, you can put your newsletter on your Web site. If you come out with a new edition every month or so, you'll get some people returning every month to read the newsletter. If you do this make sure to also promote your newsletter on your site.

You can put articles you have published on your Web site. Of course, you can put all the information in your brochure on your Web site. The reality is that your Web site is one big brochure with unlimited space and no printing or mailing costs.

One interesting twist for articles and the like is not to put the article or newsletter on your Web site directly, but to put a link whereby your client or prospect can download this information to his or her computer. That way, you also can build a list of prospects by their e-mail address. This list is extremely valuable for Internet marketing, as we'll see below.

Usenet Marketing

The Usenet is a collection of interactive discussion groups, also called newsgroups. People participate by reading "postings" done by others and maybe by adding their own in response. Some Usenet newsgroups are screened for what is allowed to be posted and what is not. In others, it's a complete free-for-all. Newsgroups have their own protocol and etiquette that you need to master before you market on them. Mass-marketing your services through postings would be ill-advised. Called "spamming," it can get you banned by some Internet service providers (ISPs) and many won't do business with you once you do it. It's important to know the culture of the newsgroup you're dealing with before you begin to market.

You can reach newsgroups through your browser. Here are a few directories to begin with:

- Internet Newsgroup Directory: http://internetdatabase.com/usenet.htm
- Liszt's Usenet Newsgroup Directory: http://liszt.com/news/
- Newsgroup Index: http://ben-schumin.simplenet.com/news index/

E-Mail Marketing

E-mail is electronic mail, you type in a message, press a button, and it is instantly sent anywhere in the world. Now, what if you had the e-mail addresses of one thousand or ten thousand potential clients? You hit one button, and zap—you send your message to these one thousand or ten thousand potential clients instantly, and it doesn't cost you a cent. Pretty good, right? There must be a catch. Well, there is, but it is a small one. If your message is unwelcome, that's "spamming," just as with the newsgroups. Trust me, spam and you are going to regret it.

So, it looks like catch-22. We have this wonderful method of direct marketing that is instantaneous and costs nothing, but if we use it, we're dead. So what can we do? There are three solutions. They all depend on sending our advertisement only to someone we are certain wants it. How can we do this? Here are the three methods:

1. Do our research, offer something free, and make certain it is something the recipient is going to be interested in. A good example is contained in Figure 16-6. This is an advertisement I received by e-mail advertising free information on relationship marketing.
2. We can ask visitors to our Web site if they would like to receive additional updates about our consulting activities periodically. Those that answer yes get put on our e-mail mailing list.
3. We can rent e-mail lists of people who have specifically requested information about the kinds of products or services we are offering. These names are collected by others and rented to us.

If you use either option two or three, you should note in your advertisement that this was information they specifically requested. That's just a little reminder to them to let them know that you are not "spamming."

Following are some sources for e-mail lists:

○ http://www.catalog.com/vivian
○ http://www.copywriter.com/lists
○ http://www.listz.com

Figure 16-7 shows Listz' topic list of e-mail lists. In total 99,095 lists are available!

I know you're wondering about prices. As this is written, the going rate is ten to thirty cents a name. However, I've also seen highly specialized lists for a lot more, and other lists for a lot less.

Figure 16-6. An e-mail advertisement.

Dr. William A. Cohen

From: <Jonlowder@aol.com>
To: <wcohen@calstatela.edu>
Sent: Friday, August 06, 1999 3:48 PM
Subject: Relationship Marketing Curriculum

Dear Professor Cohen,

I was browsing your school's website and noticed that you are a marketing professor and I thought you might find the resources at the Relationship Marketing Resource website valuable for your curriculum.

At our website you will find all the information you need about our newsletter, Relationship Marketing Report, our article reprint packages, and our marketing evaluation software.

Relationship Marketing Report is a newsletter that shows you how to build relationships with your customers leading to:
    —increased customer loyalty and retention
    —higher sales
    —more referrals
RMR brings you advice from the top experts in marketing on how to increase profits and acquire new customers for your database.

The article reprint packages include the Loyalty Marketing Package, Lifetime Value Package, Customer Segmentation Package, and Database Marketing Package. These are greater resources for covering any of these topics in depth.

Our marketing program evaluation software includes simple and inexpensive marketing computation software. The software that we are now offering is:
    —Customer Lifetime Value with and without Database Marketing Programs
    —Direct Mail Response Analysis
    —Media Cost Calculation sheet for Lifetime Value Maximization
    —Inquiry and Lead Value Calculation Chart

If you think any of these products may be useful for your curriculum, or if you would like more information please visit our website at www.relationshipmktg. com/college/colleghome.htm. You can also call us directly at (888) 219-4648.

Best regards,

Jon Lowder, President
Marketing Publishers Inc.
Publisher of Relationship Marketing Report
www.relationshipmktg.com www.booksaboutmarketing.com
Phone: (703) 494-1914 email:jlowder@dc.jones.com

Figure 16-7. Liszt topic list of e-mail lists.

Liszt, the mailing list directory   Powered by **topica**

Find: [   ] [   ] [   ]   **Help**

Arts (206 lists)
Crafts, Television, Movies

Books (102 lists)
Writing, Science_Fiction

Computers (250 lists)
Hardware, Database, Programming

Education (112 lists)
Distance_Education, Academia, Internet

Humanities (254 lists)
Philosophy, History, Psychology

Music (216 lists)
Bands, Singer-Songwriters, Genres

News (50 lists)
International, Regional, Politics

Recreation (366 lists)
Games, Autos, Sports

Science (97 lists)
Biology, Astronomy, Chemistry

Business (178 lists)
Finance, Jobs, Marketing

Culture (298 lists)
Gay, Jewish, Parenting

Health (271 lists)
Medicine, Allergy, Support

Internet (78 lists)
WWW, Business, Marketing

Nature (123 lists)
Animals, Environment, Plants

Politics (96 lists)
Environment, Activism

Religion (111 lists)
Christian, Jewish, Women

Social (100 lists)
Regional, Religion, Kids

Save Big Money with Special Offers in Your Areas of Interest!

☐ Autos
☐ Animals & Pets
☐ Books
☐ Computer Hardware
☐ Consumer Electronics
☐ Developers
☐ Entertainment
☐ Fashion & Apparel
☐ Food & Drink

☐ Games & Toys
☐ Gifts
☐ Graphics & Design
☐ Health & Fitness
☐ Home & Garden
☐ Internet
☐ Investing
☐ Movies
☐ Music

☐ News & Info
☐ Science & Technology
☐ Small Business
☐ Software
☐ Sports & Outdoors
☐ Travel
☐ Women & Family
☐ Extra Great Deals

[your_email_here]   ⦿ HTML   ◯ Text   **Join**

Home • **About Liszt** • **Advanced Search** • **Submit, Edit, or Delete a List** • **Advertiser Info**

Some people even give their lists away free in return for signing up for some other service that they are offering.

Using E-Mail to Get Coverage for Your Consulting Practice

Clearly you can get a lot of mileage through publicity to media that will promote your business using e-mail. However, again you must be careful to avoid "spamming" or your publicity will backfire. Paul Krupin publishes *The U.S. Media E-Mail Directory* and can be reached at http://www.owt.com/dircon. He wrote a very useful article on getting news coverage, published on the Web by Hanson Marketing. Their Web site carries a lot of useful information for consultants at http://www.hansonmarketing.com.

Krupin says that the "Golden Rule" for e-mail promotion to the media is to target and personalize. He gives ten "commandments" for sending e-mail to the media:

1. Think, think, think before you write. What are you trying to accomplish? Will a media professional publish it or toss it?
2. Target narrowly and carefully. Go for quality contacts, not quantity.
3. Keep it short—no more than three to four paragraphs filling one to three screens.
4. Keep the subject and content of your message relevant to your target.
5. If you are seeking publicity for a product or service or want to get reviews for a new book or software, use a two-step approach. Query with a "hook" and news angle before transmitting the entire news release or article.
6. Tailor the submittal to the media style or content.
7. Address each e-mail message separately to each individual media target.
8. Reread, reread, and reread and rewrite, rewrite, and rewrite before you click to send.
9. Be brutally honest with yourself and your media contacts—don't exaggerate or make claims you can't prove.
10. Follow-up in a timely manner with precision writing and professionalism.[1]

Why Not an E-Mail Newsletter?

You can easily develop your newsletter and distribute it by e-mail. That way, you save all sorts of printing and mailing costs. Or you can use both forms for increased effectiveness.

E-Zinez.com publishes an entire free handbook on how to publish an e-mail newsletter at http://www.e-zinez.com. Another Web site to check out is that of All Real Good Internet. They have a lot of resources and information for publishing an e-mail newsletter. Their URL is: http://www.allrealgood.com/emailpublishing/resources/create.shtml. Here are a few of their dos and don'ts:

o Review your intention and content. It must provided needed information, not be a brag sheet.
o Make it attractive and in the simplest format for your readers. Usually simple ASCII text within the body of the newsletter is best.
o Keep it short, with an Internet address readers can go to for more information.
o Include easy unsubscribe information with each newsletter.
o Don't send your newsletter out unsolicited.
o Don't send it out too frequently. Once a month is a good starting point.[2]

Books on Internet Marketing

For additional reference, here are three books on Internet marketing:

o *Advertising on the Internet* by Robbin Lee Zeff, Brad Aronson, and Bradley Aronson (John Wiley & Sons)
o *Business-to-Business Internet Marketing* by Barry Silverstein (Maximum Press)
o *The Consultant's Guide to Getting Business on the Internet* by Herman Holtz (John Wiley & Sons)

The potential for doing research and promoting your practice on the Internet is incredible. Yet many consultants do not take advantage of the opportunity it presents. Integrate online marketing and research with traditional methods and you will find your productivity much increased and far more "bang" for each marketing dollar you spend on your practice.

Now, we're ready to start. Let's take a look at how to run our consulting business in Chapter 17.

Notes

1. Paul J. Krupin, "Ten Tips for Using E-Mail to Get News Coverage for Business," http://www.hansonmarketing.com/guest2-ahtml.
2. "Create Your Own E-mail Newsletter," http://www.allrealgood.com/email__publishing/resources/create.shtml.

17

HOW TO RUN YOUR CONSULTING BUSINESS

No matter how excellent you are technically as a consultant, unless you are a good business manager you will not realize your full business potential. Your business can even go bankrupt because of your failure to sustain a profit. Therefore, don't skip this chapter. I will explain the various forms of business organization including sole proprietorships, partnerships, and corporations. I will include information on business licenses, resale permits, fictitious name registration, use of credit cards, stationery and business cards, and insurance and personal liability. I will also tell you about other important topics, such as how to keep your overhead low, what expenses to anticipate, and what records you should maintain.

Selecting the Legal Structure for Your Consulting Firm

There are several different structures recognized by law from which you can choose for your consulting practice. These are the sole proprietorship, the partnership, and the corporation. Each structure has its own advantages and disadvantages, and you should select the one that is most suitable for you.

The Sole Proprietorship

The sole proprietorship is a business structure for a company that is owned by only one person. All you need to do to establish a sole proprietorship is obtain whatever business licenses are required in your local area. This makes it the easiest of legal structures to set up. It is also the one most frequently used for many types of small businesses and certainly one that you should consider for your practice.

Advantages

1. *Ease and speed of formation.* With the sole proprietorship, there are fewer formalities and legal requirements. Sometimes you need only visit your county clerk, fill out a simple form, and pay the license fee, which is generally $200 or less. In most cases, there is no waiting period; you can satisfy all legal requirements the same day you make your visit.

2. *Reduced expense.* Because of the minimal legal requirements, the sole proprietorship can be set up without an attorney, so it is much less expensive than either a partnership or a corporation.

3. *Total control.* Because you have no partners and your business is not a corporation, complete control of its management is yours; as long as you fulfill the legal requirements, you run your business as you see fit. Except for your clients, you have no boss. You and the marketplace make all the decisions. This has the additional advantage of responsiveness: You can usually respond much more quickly to changes in the marketplace.

4. *Sole claim to profits.* You are not required to share your profits with anyone because you are the sole owner. The profits are yours, as are all the assets of the business.

Disadvantages

1. *Unlimited liability.* While you own all assets and can make all decisions in a sole proprietorship, you are also held to unlimited personal liability. This means that you are responsible for the full amount of business debts and judgments against your business. This could amount to more money than you have invested in your business. If your business fails with you owing money to various creditors, those debts could be collected from your personal assets. Of course there are various methods of reducing this risk, for ex-

ample, through proper insurance coverage, which I discuss later in this chapter.

2. *No one to talk to.* In a sole proprietorship you are a one-person show, therefore, your own skills, education, background, and capabilities limit you. You may be able to get advice and counsel from friends, relatives, or business acquaintances, but no one is motivated by personal investment to give you this advice, nor will the giver suffer the consequences if the advice proves to be poor.

3. *Difficulty in absences.* Again, because there is only you, you will have to find someone to cover for you when you are sick or on vacation. Of course there are various ways around this limitation. You could agree to watch over the practice of some other consultant who works in the same area with the understanding that he or she will do the same for you when required. You could also pay someone to cover for you during your periods of absence. But no matter what solution you select, until you have employees working for you who can perform certain services for clients, it is a limitation that must be considered.

4. *Difficulties in raising capital.* Potential lenders see the sole proprietorship as represented essentially by one person. As a result, they feel the risk is greater than if there were more people involved, as in a partnership, or if you had a permanent legal identity, as in a corporation.

The Partnership

Legally a partnership can be entered into by simply acquiring a business license from your county clerk. However, unlike the sole proprietorship, I don't recommend that you attempt to do this by yourself; use the assistance of an attorney. Partnership definitions may vary in different states, and it is extremely important to document such obligations of each of the partners as investments and profits with a partnership agreement. Such an agreement should typically cover the following aspects of the practice:

- Absence and disability
- Arbitration

- Authority of individual partners in the conduct of the business
- Character of partners, including whether general or limited, active or silent
- Contributions by partners, both now and at a later time
- Dissolution of the partnership if necessary
- Division of profits and losses
- Salary, including draws from the business during its growth state or at any period thereafter
- Duration of the agreement
- Managerial assignment within the firm
- Expenses and how they will be handled by each partner
- Name, purpose, and domicile of the partnership
- Performance by partners
- Records and methods of accounting
- Release of debts
- Required and prohibited acts
- Rights of continuing partner
- Sale of partnership interest
- Separate debts
- Settlement of disputes

How a Partnership Differs from a Sole Proprietorship

It is important to understand the elements that differentiate a partnership from a sole proprietorship. A partnership features:

1. Co-ownership of the assets
2. Limited life of the partnership
3. Mutual agency
4. Share in management
5. Share in partnership profits
6. Unlimited liability of at least one partner

Advantages

1. *Ease and speed of formation.* As with the sole proprietorship, it is fairly easy and quick to establish a consulting business using the partnership structure.

2. *Access to additional capital.* In a sole proprietorship, the initial capital must come from your personal funds or loans from other sources. In the case of a partnership, you have at least one other source of additional capital for your consulting practice.

3. *Assistance in decision making.* It is said that two heads are better than one. With a partnership, you have at least one other person to help you analyze the various situations that you may come across in the management of the business, and another person to conduct the consulting work itself.

4. *Vacation and sickness stability.* When you have a partner, it's much easier to take a vacation or to have someone else handle clients when you are ill. Partners can cover for each other.

Like all other structures of business, partnerships have disadvantages too, and some of them are severe. In fact many attorneys recommend against a partnership because of potential problems later on. However, it should also be noted that many law firms themselves are organized as partnerships.

Disadvantages

1. *Liability for actions of partners.* All partners are bound by the actions of any one partner, and under normal circumstances, you are liable for the actions and commitments of any partner. Thus a single partner can expend resources or make business commitments, and all partners are liable whether or not they agree.

2. *Potential organizational disputes.* Organizations are made up of human beings. As a result, partners, especially equal partners, disagree. Even friends may find themselves at loggerheads if it is not clearly decided ahead of time, and in writing, who is the president, who the chief executive officer, who the vice-president, and so on. It has been said that for this reason, partnerships have all the disadvantages of a marriage with none of the advantages.

3. *Difficulty in obtaining capital.* Like a sole proprietorship, a partnership may be viewed as less stable than a corporation. As a result, in comparison to corporations, partnerships find it relatively more difficult to raise capital when and if needed.

The Corporation

Unlike a sole proprietorship or a partnership, a corporation is a legal entity separate and distinct from its owner. Also unlike the other two, a corporation cannot be viewed as a simple organizational structure. It is possible to set up a corporation without the aid of an attorney, but I don't recommend it. The reason is that state laws on corporations differ, and there are many trade-offs for the state you operate in that should be explained by an attorney. Also corporations that do business in more than one state must comply with the federal laws on interstate commerce and with the laws of the various states, which vary considerably. Further, you can limit yourself severely and may actually be in violation of the law if you deviate from the purpose of the corporation as set forth when you incorporate. Again, attorneys can be of great help here; in my experience, the basic forms found in books telling you how to form your own corporation often lead to problems down the road.

Advantages

1. *Limited liability.* In a corporation, your liability is limited to the amount of your investment in the business. This protects you from creditors or judgments against you, because you can lose only what you have invested and not your personal holdings outside of the business. However, the limited liability concept does *not* apply to corporations that offer professional services, and it is entirely possible that some consultancies may fall into that category.

2. *Relative ease in obtaining capital.* Many consulting firms need capital at one time or another for expansion or other purposes. Lenders of all types are usually more willing to make loans to an organization with a more permanent legal structure, such as a corporation, than to either of the other two basic types of structures. However, note that many banks may require the officer or officers of a small corporation to personally co-sign loans.

3. *Additional human resources.* A board of directors is required for a corporation. As long as qualified board members are appointed, more help is available to you as an integral part of the business than is the case with either a partnership or a sole proprietorship. It should also be noted, however, that a one-person corpo-

ration is in the same boat as a sole proprietorship should the owner be absent, no one will be there to cover.

4. *Credibility to clients and the industry.* A corporation, because of its permanent legal status, generally has more credibility with potential clients. Admittedly, at some point in the lifetime of your firm this becomes a very minor advantage, because your firm's reputation, whether you've incorporated or not, will be the primary factor. But at the start, incorporation can be of some importance.

Disadvantages

1. *Additional paperwork and government regulations.* There is a fair amount of paperwork and many more regulations associated with the corporation than with either of the other two structures.

2. *Reduced control.* A corporation must have a board of directors. There are additional local, state, and federal government regulations to contend with. Business activities thus tend to be much more restricted than in the simpler types of business structures. Also, the corporation cannot diverge from its mission statement without an amendment to its corporate charter.

3. *Expense information.* The corporate structure is the most expensive to form, because of the need to use an attorney. It is also slower to set up.

4. *Inability to take losses as deductions.* If you lose money in your business with either a partnership or a sole proprietorship, you can take these losses as deductions for personal income tax purposes. With a corporation, losses sustained in the current year cannot be used to reduce other personal income. However, a corporation's loss may be carried forward or back to reduce another year's income. There is an exception in dealing with corporation losses; it involves setting up a special type of corporation, a possibility you should discuss with your accountant or attorney.

5. *Income taxes.* Many years ago, favorable income tax treatment would have been considered an advantage of incorporating. But that was when the maximum rate of federal income tax on corporations was 46 percent of net profits, while maximum personal income tax was 50 percent. Earlier yet, personal income tax was as high as 90 percent. Because tax laws change frequently, always check with an accountant.

Currently, income taxes are usually a disadvantage of the corporate form because of double taxation. Corporate profits are taxed once through the corporation itself as a legal entity. However, Uncle Sam gets a second bite through your salary or when profits are distributed to you as a shareholder. If profits are high enough, this may not be an important factor to you. You could be building your practice and then taking your money out when you sell the practice. However, if profits are not that high, you'll be losing money through taxation instead of saving it. You should check the latest tax laws to judge the trade-offs.

The S Corporation

The S corporation is a particular type of corporation created especially by Congress to benefit small companies. At the option of the corporation, it can have its income taxed to the shareholders as if it were a partnership. Why is this a good deal? First, it permits you to avoid the double-tax disadvantage of taxing corporate income. Second, it lets you offset business losses incurred by the corporation against your personal income. The net result is that you have the advantages of incorporating without the taxation disadvantages.

To qualify as an S corporation, you must meet certain requirements. These are:

1. There may be no more than ten shareholders, all of whom are individuals or estates.
2. You cannot have any nonresident alien shareholders.
3. You must have only one class of outstanding stock.
4. All shareholders must consent to the election of S corporation treatment.
5. A specified portion of the corporation's receipts must be derived from actual business activity rather than passive investments.

Because of higher corporate taxes under changing tax laws, it may be better not to incorporate at all if your practice is enjoying high profits. So be sure to consult with your accountant before making the decision to be treated as an S corporation.

Other Legal Necessities

Once you decide on a form of business structure, you still have a few other legal details to take care of.

Obtaining a Business License

As noted earlier, unless you incorporate, you generally need only local business licenses, either municipal or county or both. The licenses may require that you conform to certain zoning laws, building codes, and other regulations set forth by local health, fire, or police departments. However, usually these restrictions are minimal and fairly easily met in the case of a consulting practice. Certain permits may be required for certain types of consultancies or activities that are considered hazardous or in some other way detrimental to the community. But if you are required to obtain such a permit, you will be so informed when you purchase the business license. Again, for a consulting practice, usually this is not required.

Some states require licensing for certain occupations, which may affect certain types of consulting practices. Again, if that is the case, you will be so informed when you get your local business license. For example, most states require personnel recruiters who place job applicants to be licensed. For complete information, contact your state's Department of Commerce.

There are also federal licensing requirements for some businesses that could affect certain types of consulting, such as an investment advisory service. Again, you will usually be informed if you need an additional license when you get your local business license. But to be absolutely certain, contact the U.S. Department of Commerce, which can be found under the "U.S. Government" listing in your local telephone directory.

The Resale Permit

If your state has a sales tax, it also has a state board to control and collect the tax. Usually this board will allow you to secure a resale permit.

The resale permit has two purposes. First, it assigns you duties as an agent of the state to collect sales tax. Second, it allows you to purchase items you intend to resell to someone else without paying the tax yourself. If there is sales tax in your state, you must either give your resale permit number to a vendor or you must pay the tax. If a fee is required to obtain a resale permit, the agency involved will inform you at the time you apply for it. Frequently this agency requires security from you in the form of a cash deposit against the payment of future state tax on the products that you will sell. This amount can be sizable, as much as several thousand dollars in some states. If you fail to pay any sales tax due, the state can deduct this amount from your deposit. Thus it is protected even if you go bankrupt. Bear in mind that in most states, there is no sales tax on professional services, only on the sale, rental, and repair of tangible personal property. You need to check your state's regulations.

It is definitely not to your advantage to tie up several thousand dollars of your hard-earned cash merely to satisfy a security deposit for a resale permit. In some cases in which the deposit is high, installment payment arrangements can be made. However, the amount of money required—if any—depends on the information you provide at the time you obtain the resale permit. Minimum requirements are usually determined when certain conditions are met. These situations include: if you own your home and have substantial equity in it; if the estimated monthly expenses of your consulting practice are low; if your estimated monthly sales are low; if you are presently employed and your business activities are part-time; if you have no employees other than yourself; and if you have only one place of business. As I said before, services are usually not taxed, only products. But if products are part of your business or an adjunct to your consulting practice, you should obtain a resale permit if there is a state tax in your state.

Fictitious Name Registration

Fictitious name registration is required if you use any name in your practice other than your own. If you use a business name that includes names other than yours or your partners', implies the existence of additional partners, or indeed implies anything that your practice is not, you will need fictitious name registration.

Thus "James A. Smith" is a perfectly acceptable business name that does not require fictitious name registration as long as your name is actually James A. Smith. However, "James A. Smith and Associates" requires fictitious name registration. There are some fictitious names that you usually cannot use at all. You cannot, for example, call yourself a university or research center or use other descriptions that imply a nonprofit corporation unless you are one. Most states will prohibit you from using the title Doctor, Reverend, or Professor unless you meet certain legal requirements. But other than those types of restrictions, most "doing business as" names are acceptable as long as you obtain the proper registration. Interestingly, consulting firms may take advantage of fictitious name registration; law and CPA firms may not.

Fictitious name registration is usually very easy; it should not be considered a major problem in setting up your consulting practice. First, find out the law in your state by contacting someone such as the country clerk. Typically there is a small registration fee of less than $50 and another small fee, perhaps $30 to $50 dollars, for publication of your registration in a general circulation newspaper distributed in the area in which you intend to do business. Once publication is accomplished, you file the affidavit with your county clerk's office. In many cases, the newspapers can handle the entire matter for you. The form is simple, and filling it out takes only a few minutes. Many states allow you to obtain more than one fictitious name on the form. For some types of consulting practices, this could be useful; it allows you to test certain products under names other than your client's or the regular business name of your practice. Then, if the product fails in the marketplace, it will have no effect on either your or your client's image.

Fictitious name registration is in force for a predetermined fixed period, which varies by state; five years is typical. In many cases, newspapers will write you ahead of time offering to handle the whole renewal business for you. In this way, they secure publication of the form in their newspaper.

Clients' Use of Credit Cards

Credit cards, such as Visa and MasterCard, are becoming increasingly useful for the professional consulting practice. In fact, many other professionals, such as doctors and dentists, now accept credit cards from their patients or clients. Accepting credit cards has two major benefits for you. First, it adds additional credibility. Companies or individuals that have not done business with you before will recognize the Visa or MasterCard name and will realize that those agencies investigated you before allowing you to use their services. Second, the consumer credit company will provide credit to your clients and will collect the money for you. Thus several thousand dollars in consulting fees can be billed and paid over a period of time without your being the collection agency. Of course there is a disadvantage to using consumer credit companies: You pay the company a certain percentage of each billing. Usually the higher your credit card sales, the lower the percentage the consumer credit company charges. The percentage involved is generally about 4 percent of the sale.

Stationery and Business Cards

It's extremely important that you get the highest quality business cards and stationery that you possibly can. These items represent you to your clientele and communicate a message about the type of firm you are. Get the most expensive you can afford. Your stationery should have at least 25 percent rag content, and the letters should be engraved. The raised print has a classic appearance. (A less expensive way to achieve this raised look is a process known as thermography.) The same is true of your business cards. If you do everything using desktop publishing, the raised letters won't be possible. This is a trade-off that you're going to have to consider. That is, the higher quality appearance of raised letters versus the increased expense and loss of flexibility.

If a logo is used, it should be simple and representative of the type of consulting you do. "High-class professional" is what you want your stationery and business cards to say.

Insurance and Personal Liability

As a consultant, you face certain risks, some of which you can insure against and some of which you cannot. For example, changes in economic and business conditions, the marketplace, or technology cannot be insured against. Any of these can change and hurt your business. However, other types of risks can be transferred through insurance. These include bad debts caused when subcontractors or clients go bankrupt, disasters caused by weather or fire, theft, liabilities from negligence and other actions, and death or disability of key company executives. You should think of insurance as a form of risk management. Do your risk managing in a four-step process.

1. *Identify* the risks to which your consulting practice will be subjected.
2. *Evaluate* the probability of occurrence of each risk. Also list the cost to you should this event occur and the cost of insurance protecting you against the risk.
3. *Choose* the best way to allow for each risk, whether to accept all or part of the risk or to transfer the risk through insurance.
4. *Control* the risk by implementing what you select as the best method.

The services of direct writers or agents are helpful in the risk-assessment process. A direct writer is a commissioned employee of the insurer; the business that he or she writes belongs to the insurance company. An agent, on the other hand, is an independent businessperson like you who has negotiated with the insurer to represent it for a given territory. The agent is also compensated on a commission basis.

There are advantages in both cases. An independent agent may represent many different insurers and so would be able to offer you a wider choice of coverage. Also, because the independent agent deals with these many different types, he or she may have greater knowledge in the overall field than a direct writer whose experience is limited to the employer company. However, direct writers may cost less, as their commission is less than that of the independent agent. Also, direct writers become specialists in their line, with in-depth knowledge and experience. This means that for a certain type of insurance of particular importance to you, this seller may know the finer details of the risk you are attempting to manage.

To locate direct writers or agents, consult your phone book or friends or acquaintances in business.

Keeping Overhead Low

One of the most important pieces of advice that I can give to you for managing your consulting practice is to maintain a low overhead. This means keeping costs that do not directly contribute to each and every project or to marketing to the absolute minimum. Many new consultants feel, for example, that they must have a fancy office at a prestigious address. If an address is indeed necessary to your success, you can usually rent a mail drop in an esteemed neighborhood. But usually this is not really an important factor in your being hired as a consultant. The fact is, most clients won't come to your office; usually you'll go to theirs.

Many years ago, when I was working for another company as director of research and development, I interviewed an individual who told me the following sad tale. He and several other senior executives in a major aerospace company resigned to form their own consulting practice. Each invested enough money to last many months they thought. Coming from a large company in which each had had an expensive office, elegant furniture, and a personal secretary, these new consultants found it impossible to control spending for what they considered minimum requirements. They acquired expensive offices in a high-rent area and outfitted them with rich mahogany paneling and thick, luxurious rugs. But that rich image didn't save this fledgling consulting firm from bankruptcy; in a few weeks, their money was depleted. On the other hand, I am acquainted with a wealthy search consultant who did half a million dollars in billing his first year out of his home. As his partner told me, he did hundreds of thousands of dollars in billings in his pajamas, but neither his clients nor the executives he placed ever knew.

Remember, at first you don't even need a secretary, only typing services. What you definitely don't need is a secretary sitting around with nothing to do except contribute to your ego.

For most consulting practices, it is better to consider a home office to start with, especially if you are beginning part-time. In my many years of consulting, I can count on one hand the number of times a client has visited the office that I maintain in my home. It happens usually if the client is in a start-up situation and thus has no office for me to go to. Occasionally the pressure of time will prevent you from traveling, and your client will come to you. One multimillion-dollar accountant calculated that because my billing rates were higher than his, it was less expensive for him to travel to my office than the other way around.

The Telephone

To keep overhead low and yet maintain a business telephone without a secretary, you have two alternatives: One is a telephone answering service; the second is to buy or rent a telephone answering machine. Again there are trade-offs to be made, advantages and disadvantages to both. The telephone answering machine is relatively inexpensive; a good, professional-quality machine can be had for several hundred dollars. The disadvantage is that some potential clients simply will not leave a message on an answering machine. However, I believe that if your answering message is carefully worded and if you promise to get back with the caller soon, you have the greatest probability of getting the message that you need to continue the business relationship.

Even though an answering service may cost more, it may not be as good. Some answering service operators are rude and inconsiderate and will leave your caller on hold for long periods of time. This can be worse than a machine, where at least you control the friendliness and professionalism of the voice doing the answering. If you do use an answering service, I recommend that you check on it periodically to ensure that the operator has the highest standards of professionalism and you are not losing clients through their rudeness or incompetence.

Should you have a special business phone for the home? Maybe not. Business telephones are usually more expensive than personal telephones. It's true that the business telephone does entitle you to a special listing in the Yellow Pages, and if you want a special advertisement, as discussed in Chapter 2, you need a business telephone in order to get one. However, another quirk in many telephone systems is that they will charge you more to connect a business telephone than a personal telephone. Yet you can have a personal telephone converted to the business telephone at little or no extra charge. If your practice is listed under your real name, and you don't need the Yellow Pages listing as a consultant, it makes little sense to obtain a special business telephone—as defined by telephone companies. There is nothing wrong with having a telephone company install an additional personal phone that you call a "business telephone." As long as you use it totally for business purposes, it should be deductible for tax purposes. If it is listed on your business card and your stationery, as far as your clients know, it is your business telephone.

Fax Machines

Fax machines are definitely in. With a fax machine, you can send or receive photographs, reports, or other documents. When you want to get or send something instantly, a fax machine is really handy. Now don't get the wrong idea. You can still operate with great efficiency without owning or using a fax machine. But after you begin to see a positive cash flow, it is a handy item to have. Fax machines are quicker than the mail. Because the information is transmitted right away over your telephone lines, you can save a lot of money over using overnight couriers. Of course, to a certain degree this advantage has been superseded by e-mail, which is even faster.

Anticipating Expenses

One of the biggest mistakes new consultants make is failure to anticipate expenses. Recognize ahead of time that certain expenses will be necessary to set up and run your consulting practice as a business. Plan ahead for these expenses when you estimate what being in business will cost. Typical consulting expenses may include:

- Water, electricity, and gas
- Office supplies

- Postage
- Automobile expenses
- Telephone
- Travel other than by automobile
- Promotional material, including brochures
- Entertainment
- Income taxes
- Subscriptions to professional journals
- Memberships in professional and other associations

There will undoubtedly be additional expenses depending on the type of consulting you do. Make sure that you forget nothing; anticipate them before you establish your practice.

Necessary Records and Their Maintenance

Good records are necessary for several reasons. You'll need them for preparing tax returns, measuring management effectiveness and efficiency, reducing material waste, and even obtaining loans. These are the essential records you should maintain:

1. Daily summary of income received. Figure 17-1 shows a sample form.
2. An expense journal (see the example in Figure 17-2) that lists your expense payments in chronological order.
3. An expense ledger summary (see Figure 17-3) in which cash and check payments are totaled by category, for example, rent, wages, and advertising.
4. An inventory purchase journal (if product is in any way a part of your practice) that notes shipments received, accounts payable, and cash available for future purchases, as shown in Figure 17-4.
5. An employee compensation record, listing hours worked, pay rate, and deductions withheld for both part-time and full-time employees, as shown in Figure 17-5.
6. An accounts receivable ledger for outstanding invoices, as shown in Figure 17-6.

Figure 17-1. Daily summary of income received.

Day/Date Item Sold or Service Performed	Amount	
Total amount received today		
Total amount received through yesterday		
Total amount received to date		

Tax Obligations

As the owner of a consulting practice, you are responsible for payment of federal, state, and local taxes. Because the federal taxes tend to be the most complex for new consultants, we'll look at them first. There are four basic types of federal taxes that you may run into: income taxes, Social Security taxes, excise taxes, and unemployment taxes. Let's look at each in more detail.

Figure 17-2. Expense journal.

Date	To Whom Paid	Purpose	Check Number	Amount	
		Total expenditures			

Figure 17-3. Expense journal summary.

Purpose	Total This Period		Total up to This Period		Total to Date	
Advertising						
Car and truck expense						
Commissions						
Contributions						
Delivery expense						
Dues and publications						
Employee benefit program						
Freight						
Insurance						
Interest						
Laundry and cleaning						
Legal and professional services						
Licenses						
Miscellaneous expense						
Office supplies						
Pension and profit-sharing plan						
Postage						
Rent						
Repairs						
Selling expense						
Supplies						
Tax						
Telephone						
Traveling and entertainment						
Utilities						
Wages						
Totals						

Figure 17-4. Inventory purchase journal.

Date	Inventory Ordered Carried Forward	Shipment Received/Date	Accounts Payable	Cash Available for Future Purchases
		Totals		

Income Taxes

The amount of federal taxes you owe depends on the earnings of your company and on your company's legal structure, as I discussed earlier in this chapter.

If you have a sole proprietorship or partnership, your other income exemptions and nonbusiness deductions and credits are also important factors. The tax formula used is generally the same as that for the individual taxpayer. The only difference is that you file an additional form (Schedule C of Form 1040, Profit or Loss from Business or Profession) that identifies items of expense and income connected with your consulting business. If your business is a partnership, the partnership files a business return (Form 1065), and you report only your share of the profit or loss on your personal return.

Figure 17-5. Employee compensation record.

Name _____ Social Security No. _____

Date	Period Worked (hours, days, weeks, or months)	Wage Rate	Total Wages		Deductions					Net Paid	
					Soc. Sec.	Fed. Inc. Tax	State Inc. Tax				
		Totals									

However, there is an important difference between being a sole proprietor or a partner and being a salaried employee working for someone else. As a sole proprietor or a partner, you are required by law to pay federal income taxes and self-employment taxes *as the income is received.* You do this by completing Estimated Tax for Individuals Form 1040-ES. This is an estimate of the income and self-employment taxes you expect to owe on the basis of antici-

Figure 17-6. Accounts receivable ledger (for consulting services billed but not yet paid).

Date	Customer/Client Name	Products/Services	Amount Owed	Payments Made/Date

pated income and exemptions. Payment of tax is made quarterly—
April 16, June 15, September 17, and January 15.

If you have a corporation, you must also pay income tax on its
net profits separate from the amount taken out for salary, which is
considered part of your personal income.

Every corporation whose tax is expected to be $500 or more is
required to make estimated tax payments. These must be deposited with an authorized financial institution or a Federal Reserve
Bank. Each deposit is made with a federal tax deposit coupon and
done in accordance with the instructions on the coupon. Estimated
tax is due by the fifteenth day of the fourth, sixth, ninth, and
twelfth months of your corporation's tax year. If any date falls on
a Saturday, Sunday, or legal holiday, the installment is due on the
next regular business day.

In order to operate your practice, it is extremely important
that you have the necessary funds to pay your income taxes on
time. Your accountant can help you work out a budget to allow for
this. You can also use the work sheet in Figure 17-7 developed by
the U.S. Small Business Administration.

Withholding Income Taxes

According to the law, you must withhold federal income tax payments for your employees. These payments are passed on to the
government periodically. The process begins when you hire a new
employee. He or she must sign a Form W-4, Employee's Withholding Allowance Certificate, listing any exemptions and additional
withholding allowances claimed. The completed W-4 is your authority to withhold income tax in accordance with the current
withholding tables issued by the Internal Revenue Service (IRS). If
an employee fails to furnish a certificate, you are required to withhold taxes as if he or she were a single person with no exemptions.
Before December 1 of each year, you should ask your employees
to file new exemption certificates for the following year if there has
been a change in their exemption status. At the end of each year,
you must furnish each employee copies of Form W-2, Wage and
Tax Statement. As you are aware if you have worked for someone
else, the employees must file a copy of this with their income tax
return. You, as the employer, must also furnish a copy of this Form

Figure 17-7. Work sheet for meeting tax obligations.

Kind of Taxes	Due Date	Amount Due	Pay to	Date for Writing the Check
Federal Taxes				
Employee income taxes and Social Security taxes	___	___	___	___
	___	___	___	___
	___	___	___	___
	___	___	___	___
Excise Taxes	___	___	___	___
Owner-manager's and/or corporation's income taxes	___	___	___	___
	___	___	___	___
	___	___	___	___
Unemployment taxes	___	___	___	___
	___	___	___	___
	___	___	___	___
	___	___	___	___
State Taxes				
Unemployment taxes	___	___	___	___
	___	___	___	___
	___	___	___	___
	___	___	___	___
Income taxes	___	___	___	___
Sales taxes	___	___	___	___
	___	___	___	___
	___	___	___	___
	___	___	___	___
Franchise taxes	___	___	___	___
Other	___	___	___	___
	___	___	___	___
	___	___	___	___
Local Taxes				
Sales taxes	___	___	___	___
	___	___	___	___
	___	___	___	___
	___	___	___	___
Real estate taxes	___	___	___	___
Personal property taxes	___	___	___	___
Licenses (retail, vending machines, etc.)	___	___	___	___
Other	___	___	___	___
	___	___	___	___
	___	___	___	___

W-2 to the IRS on or before February 28 of each year. For complete details, contact the office of the IRS in your area.

And don't forget to check with your state office to find out if you are responsible for withholding your employees' state income taxes as well.

Withholding Social Security Taxes

For Social Security taxes, you must deduct a percentage from each employee's wages. As an employer, you must match that sum. Check with the IRS for the latest rules and percentages.

The following kinds of payments are not subject to Social Security taxes:

1. Payments made more than six months after the last calendar month in which the employee worked.
2. Payments made under a workers compensation law.
3. Payments or portions of payments attributable to the employee's contribution to a sick-pay plan.
4. Most payments made to a state or local government employee. The third-party payer should contact the state or local government employer for instructions.
5. Payments made for medical care.
6. Payments (generally for injury) that are not related to absence from work.

Remitting Federal Taxes

Remitting federal taxes involves three steps: You must report the income and Social Security taxes you have withheld from the employee's pay, and you must *deposit* the funds you withheld. In the third step you match your employees' contributions.

Use Form 941, Employer's Quarterly Federal Tax Return, to report both Social Security tax and withheld income tax. This form is filed quarterly, but the taxes themselves are paid in advance. Social Security tax and income tax withholding must be deposited regularly in a bank if they exceed a certain amount. How often these deposits must be made depends on your tax liability.

If you owe less than $1,000 in tax at the end of the quarter, your deposit is made by the fifteenth of the month after the quarter ends.

If you withheld less than $50,000 during the twelve-month period ending last June 30, you must deposit tax monthly—by the fifteenth day of the next month—unless you meet the "less than $1,000" exception above.

Failure to deposit Social Security, also called FICA, and income tax withholding by the due date results in a 5 percent late payment penalty. You may also be charged interest on the unpaid deposit.

The due dates for Form 941 are April 30, July 31, October 31, and January 31. However, if you make timely deposits, you have ten extra days to file the returns.

The third step, matching the contribution, is done on Form 940. Any additional details are available from your local IRS office.

Excise Taxes

Federal excise taxes are due on the sale or use of certain items or transactions and on certain occupations. Normally, a consultant is not involved in excise tax. However, to be absolutely certain, again, check with your local IRS office.

Unemployment Taxes

If you pay wages of $1,500 or more in any calendar quarter or if you have one or more employees on at least some portion of one day in each of twenty or more calendar weeks, either consecutive or nonconsecutive, your consulting practice is liable for federal unemployment (FUTA) taxes. It doesn't need to be the same employee, and individuals on sick leave or vacation are counted as employees.

FUTA tax is reported annually on Form 940, Employer's Annual Federal Unemployment Tax Return, which is due by January 31 of the next calendar year. If you have made timely deposits, however, you have until February 10 to file.

When are deposits required? If at the end of any calendar quarter, you owe more than $100 FUTA tax for the year, you must make a deposit by the end of the next month.

FUTA tax is not withheld from your employees' wages. This is an out-of-pocket expense the employer bears.

FUTA tax is computed on the first $7,000 of wages paid to each employee during the calendar year. The tax rate varies, depending on the state in which you do business.

Obtaining an Employer Identification Number

An employer identification number is required for all employment tax returns filed with the federal government. You obtain this number by filing a Form SS-4 with your regional IRS center. At the same time, you can ask for your business tax kit, IRS 454; it has additional information on taxes pertinent to each particular business or consulting practice with which you may be involved.

State and Local Taxes

State and local taxes vary by area. Three major types of state taxes are unemployment taxes, income taxes, and sales taxes (see the discussion of the resale permit under "Other Legal Necessities" earlier in this chapter). Every state has unemployment taxes; the rules vary by state and may not be the same as those of the federal government. Local taxes from counties, towns, and cities may include real estate, personal property taxes, taxes on receipt of businesses, and so forth. For more information on all these types of taxes, contact your local and state governments.

Minimizing Tax Paperwork

As you can see, many of the required taxes concern employees. If you have no employees, the amount of paperwork is significantly reduced. Instead of hiring permanent staff for your company, try to retain individuals and pay them as consultants. There are some restrictions on how many hours or days someone may work for you and still be considered a consultant, so be sure to check on the current regulations if you do this.

For remitting all types of taxes, be certain to consult a good tax accountant. You will pay for the service, but this expert will save you far more in the long run.

Sources of Additional Information

Here are some books that may assist you in managing your consulting practice:

- *Accounting and Recordkeeping Made Easy for the Self-Employed* by Jack Fox (John Wiley & Sons)
- *Adams Streetwise Small Business Start-Up: Your Comprehensive Guide to Starting and Managing a Business* by Bob Adams (Adams Media Corporation)
- *The McGraw-Hill Guide to Starting Your Own Business: A Step-by-Step Blueprint for the First-Time Entrepreneur* by Stephen C. Harper (McGraw-Hill)

Epilogue

There is no question in my mind that you can become a successful consultant (either full-time or part-time) and make a valuable contribution to your clients and to society at the same time. Everything you need to know in order to market and put into practice your own expertise in any particular field has already been given to you in the pages of this book. The questions that remain unanswered are those that will arise as you begin actual work as a consultant.

This is as it should be, for certain aspects of your consulting work are unique not only to your category of consulting, type of industry, or geographic area but, more important, to your personality, style, and way of doing business. All totaled, the answers to these questions constitute your differential advantage over all the others doing identical work, and a sustained differential advantage over your competition will be the primary factor in your success.

A great adventure awaits you with many challenges, some disappointments, and the thrill of victory along the way. Further, your journey will involve not only monetary rewards but also the satisfaction of doing what you want and doing it well.

But no book, regardless of how complete or thorough it may be, can begin this journey for you. This you must do for yourself. Without your beginning, your action, your taking the steps toward starting your consultancy, there can be nothing. Therefore, the rest is up to you. I wish you the great success that only you yourself can achieve.

Appendix A

REFERENCES USEFUL TO CONSULTANTS

Note that some of the following references are out of print (OP). They are still useful, however, and you should be able to find them in a library or used bookstore.

General Consulting

Become a Top Consultant: How the Experts Do It by Ron Tepper (John Wiley & Sons).

The Complete Guide to Consulting Success, 3rd ed. by Howard Shenson (Upstart Publishing).

The Concise Guide to Becoming an Independent Consultant by Herman Holtz (John Wiley & Sons).

The Consultant's Handbook: How to Start & Develop Your Own Practice by Stephan Schiffman (Adams Media Corporation).

The Consultant's Manual: A Complete Guide to Building a Successful Consulting Practice by Thomas L. Greenbaum (John Wiley & Sons).

The Consultant's Survival Guide by Marsha D. Lewin (John Wiley & Sons).

Consulting: The Complete Guide to a Profitable Career, Rev. ed. by Robert E. Kelley (Scribner).

Consulting for Dummies® by Bob Nelson and Peter Economy (IDG Books Worldwide).

Flawless Consulting: A Guide to Getting Your Expertise Used, (Second Edition) by Peter Block (Jossey-Bass Publishers).

How to Become a Successful Consultant in Your Own Field, 3rd Ed. by Hubert Bermont (Prima Publishing).

How to Succeed as an Independent Consultant, 3rd ed. by Herman Holtz (John Wiley & Sons).

Million Dollar Consulting: The Professional's Guide to Growing a Practice, Rev. ed. by Alan Weiss (McGraw-Hill).

The Overnight Consultant by Marsha D. Lewin (John Wiley & Sons).

Shenson on Consulting: Success Strategies from the Consultant's Consultant by Howard L. Shenson, (John Wiley & Sons) (OP).

The 10 Hottest Consulting Practices: What They Are, How to Get into Them by Ron Tepper (John Wiley & Sons 1995).

Consulting for the Government

The Entrepreneur's Guide to Doing Business with the Federal Government: A Handbook for Small and Growing Businesses by Charles Bevers, Linda Christie, and Lynn Rollins Price (Prentice-Hall) (OP).

How to Sell to the Government: A Step-by-Step Guide to Success by William A. Cohen, (John Wiley & Sons) (OP)

The One-Hundred Billion Dollar Market: How to Do Business With the United States Government by Herman Holtz (AMACOM) (OP).

Marketing for Small Businesses and Consultants

Big Ideas for Small Service Businesses: How to Successfully Advertise, Publicize and Maximize Your Business or Professional Practice by Marilyn and Tom Ross (Communication Creativity).

Building a Mail Order Business: A Complete Manual for Success, 4th ed by William A. Cohen (John Wiley & Sons).

The Consultant's Guide to Getting Business on the Internet by Herman Holtz (John Wiley & Sons).

Expanding Your Consulting and Professional Services by Herman Holtz (John Wiley & Sons, Inc.) (OP).

Get Clients Now!: A 28-Day Marketing Program for Professionals and Consultants by C. J. Hayden (AMACOM).

Marketing Your Consulting and Professional Services by Dick Connor and Jeff Davidson (John Wiley & Sons).

138 Quick Ideas to Get More Clients by Howard L. Shenson and Jerry Wilson (John Wiley & Sons).

Selling Services: Marketing for the Consulting Professional by Paul O'Neil (Psi Successful Business Library).

Problem Solving for Consultants

Awaken Your Birdbrain: Using Creativity to Get What You Want by Bill Costello (Thinkorporated).

The Confident Decision Maker: How to Make the Right Business and Personal Decisions Every Time by Roger Dawson (Quill).

Consultation: A Handbook for Individual and Organizational Development, 2nd ed. by Robert R. Blake and Jane S. Mouton (Addison-Wesley).

Creative Problem Solving by Donald J. Noone (Barrons Educational Series).

Creative Solution Finding: The Triumph of Breakthrough Thinking over Conventional Problem Solving by Shozo Hibino, Gerald Nadler, and John Farrell (Prima Publishing).

Decision Traps: Ten Barriers to Brilliant Decision-Making and How to Overcome Them by J. Edward Russo and Paul J. H. Schoemaker (Fireside).

The Entrepreneur and Small Business Problem Solver, 2nd ed. by William A. Cohen (John Wiley & Sons).

Handbook of Business Problem Solving by Kenneth J. Albert, ed. (McGraw-Hill) (OP).

The Marketing Problem Solver by J. Donald Weinrauch (John Wiley & Sons) (OP).

101 Creative Problem Solving Techniques: The Handbook of New Ideas for Business by James M. Higgins (New Management Publishing).

Executive Search

Executive Recruiters Almanac, edited by Steven Graber (Adams Media Corporation).

Secrets of a Corporate Headhunter by John Wareham (Jove Publishing) (OP).

Secrets of the Executive Search Experts by Christian Schoyen and Nils Rasmussen (AMACOM).

Newsletters/Journals

The Consultant's Craft Newsletter
Summit Consulting Group
P.O. Box 1009
East Greenwich, R.I. 02818
Tel.: 800-766-7935
Email: summitconsultinggroup@compuserve.com

Consultants News
Kennedy Information
Kennedy Place
Route 12 South
Fitzwilliam, N.H. 03447
Tel.: 800-531-1026 or 603-585-6544
Fax: 603-585-9555
E-mail: subscribe@kennedyinfo.com

Consulting BizTips
New Ventures Publishing Group
123 World Trade Center, Suite 327
P.O. 420726
Dallas, Tex. 75342
Tel.: 972-227-5326
Fax: 972-227-6628
E-mail:coj@bizhowto.com

Consulting Opportunities Journal
New Ventures Publishing Group
123 World Trade Center, Suite 327
P.O. 420726
Dallas, Tex. 75342
Tel.: 972-227-5326
Fax: 972-227-6628
E-mail: coj@bizhowto.com

Journal of Management Consulting
The Journal of Management Consulting, Inc.
858 Longview Road
Burlingame, Calif. 94010-6974
Tel.: 650-342-1954
Fax: 650-344-5005
http://www.jmcforum.com
Email: jmc@jmcforum.com

Marketing Energizer Zine for Consultants
Hanson Marketing Group, Inc.
7903 Pine Road
Wyndmoor, Penn. 19038
Tel.: 215-836-5866
Fax: 215-836-4465
http://www.hansonmarketing.com/freezine.html

Useful Material for Consultants on the Internet

American Business Information
http://www.abii.com/
Order in-depth profile on any business, and get the address and phone
  number of any business.

American Express Small Business Exchange
http://www.americanexpress.com/smallbusiness/
Information on creating a business plan, managing a business, and expert
  advice on small-business problems.

American Demographics
http://www.demographics.com
Demographics of special interest to marketers.

Business Essentials Library
http://pasware.com/
Sections on business planning including sample plans, information on
  financing and marketing, plan outlines, and also answers to questions.

Commercial Services of the U.S. Department of Commerce
http://www.ita.doc.gov/uscs/
Numerous programs having to with export, including trade statistics
  abroad.

Dun & Bradstreet
http://www.dbisna.com/dbis/market/hmenu.htm
Tips for creating a marketing plan and more.

Fortune 500
http://pathfinder.com/@@nEp5NAYAo1fNhn6/fortune/1997/
specials/f500/index.html
Statistics and data on Fortune 500 companies.

Free Marketing Magazine for Consultants
http://www.hansonmarketing.com
Online help for consultant, marketing tips, and more.

Hoovers Online
http://www.hoovers.com/
Company information and profiles on more than 2,700 companies, both
    public and private.

The Internet Invention Store
http://www.catalog.com/impulse/invent.htm
Information on new products.

Internet Links to Free Advertising
http://www.linkcenter.com
http://www.freelinks.com

Kennedy Information Research Group
http://www.kennedyinfo.com
General information on consulting, such as trends and fees.

Linkexchange
http://www.linkexchange.com
Banner exchange; starting, promoting, and managing a Web site; selling
    online, and more.

The Market Research Center
http://www.airsearch.com
Links to any product or service category. Good source for information on
    competitive sites.

MCNI
http://www.mcni.com
Forums, free consultant listing, search service, book store, and more.

Promotion Clinic
http://www.promotion-clinic.ppa.org
Ideas, products, and promotion campaigns.

Small Business Advisor
http://www.isquare.com/
Advice and short reports for small businesses.

SMARTAGE
http://www.smartage.com
Graphics programs to create Web sites and banners, information on free
    advertising, building and selling an online store, and more.

Statistical Abstract of the United States
Numerous sites—use a search engine and look up Statistical Abstract of
    the United States.
Demographics of all types.

Trade Show Central
http://www.tscentral.com:80/html/ven_fac.html
Search directory for 33,000 trade shows worldwide.

U.S. Small Business Administration
http://www.sbaonline.sba.gov/
Information on starting a business, expanding one, local BA resources,
   shareware, and more.

World Inventors Trade Association
http://www.inventnet.com.au/invent/prod.htm
Information on new products from thirty-five countries.

World Trade Directories Sources
http://www.net-promote.com/wholesale-directories.html
Sources of trade directories for purchase of wholesale products
   worldwide.

Appendix B

SAMPLE CONSULTANT'S BROCHURE

Sample Brochure

I put the sample brochure in this appendix together myself. If you have a computer and a color printer you can do the same. The beauty of this brochure is flexibility and cost. Since you are printing these yourself with a computer printer, you don't need to pay anything until you have a prospective client and need a brochure. And, you pay only for what you need. Yet, the brochure is extensive and has everything in it. My brochure emphasizes my seminars on leadership. But it is flexible so that it can be personalized not only by subject matter but with the latest information and geared toward a particular client.

Here's what you do. Buy a package of letter-size folders. I like white, but any color will do. Also, buy a package of white, full-size labels, $8^1/_2 \times 11$. Avery size 5165 works just fine.

Using your word processing program, write and lay out the design for the front and back of your folder. The labels are self-adhering, so all you need to do is print them out and affix them to the front and back, respectively, of your folder.

Inside your folder you will find pockets on either side, plus a place to insert your business card. You can print out special business cards using your computer and printer as well. In the left-hand pocket, I put articles that I've written or that have been written about me. In the right side, I put letters from satisfied clients, a

partial client list, a short biographical background, and descriptions of my consulting, or in this case of my seminars. I also include
a black and white photograph. As I said, you can vary the contents
of the pockets according to your client and the situation.

Sample Brochure Cover

Here's an example of what the front cover of my brochure looks like.

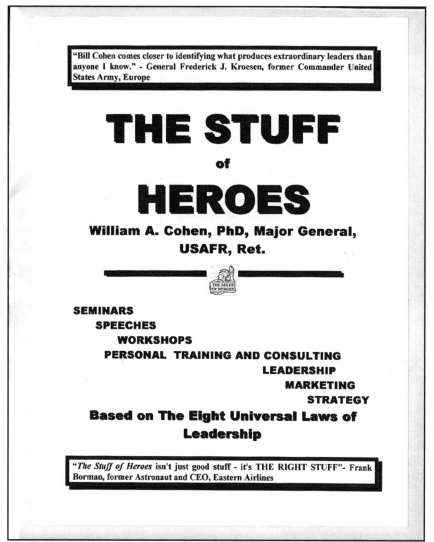

Sample Brochure Interior

Here (and on the facing page) is example of what the interior of my brochure looks like.

Profile of a Peak Performance Expert

Dr. Bill Cohen is Professor of Marketing and Leadership, former department chairman and Institute Director at California State University Los Angeles and is a retired major general from the U.S. Air Force Reserve. He has also taught at the University of California Los Angeles, University of Southern California and Claremont Graduate University.

Among his 35 books translated into 11 languages and over 100 articles resulting from his research, are the best selling books *The Stuff of Heroes* (Longstreet Press, 1998) and *The Art of Leader* (Prentice Hall, 1990). The latter was named a Best Business Book of the Year by <u>Library Journal</u>. The former was

nominated   998 by
Manageme   if world
class lead   ls and
admirals, p   ne 500
companies.   es and
universities
    Amoi   ilifornia
State Unive   / Forge
George Wa   (1985),
and the C   Award
(1996). He   399, he
was named   is from
around the   awards
include the   juished
Flying Cros   ak leaf
clusters.
    Dr. C   d trade

Appendix C

The Consultant's
Questionnaire and Audit

Part I: Organization

Company: _____

Division: _____

Address: _____

City, State, and Zip Code: _____

Web Site: _____

Other Division Locations: _____

_____

_____

_____

Company Officers and Other Key Executives: _____

_____

_____

_____

Primary Contact for This Engagement: _____

Title: _____

Address: _____

City, State, and Zip Code: _____

Phone Number: _____

Fax Number: _____

E-mail: _____

Backup Contact for This Engagement: _____

Title: _____

Address: _____

City, State, and Zip Code: _____

Phone Number: _____

Fax Number: _____

E-mail: _____

Note: Obtain relevant company organization charts

Part II: Production (For Manufacturers)

What percentage of production is:

_____% Job-order (custom) manufacture?

_____% Repetitive (standard) manufacture?

  100% Total

What percentage of production is:

_____% Private label for someone else?

_____% Sold under your own name?

  100% Total

Do you subcontract? _____

_____% If yes, what percentage of your total work?

Who are your major subcontractors? _____

_____

_____

_____

Are you satisfied with their work? _____

_____

_____

_____% What percentage of your production do you export?

What countries do you export to? What is the percentage of export to each country?

_____ _____%

_____ _____%

_____ _____%

_____% At what current percentage of production capacity are you now operating?

_____% What additional percentage could you add to total capacity (100%) in order to accommodate additional sales?

How many months would it take to reach this figure? _____ months

_____% What is the minimum percentage of capacity at which you must operate in order to break even?

How seasonal is your production?
_____ Not at all _____ Slightly _____ Fairly _____ Highly _____ Totally

At which season(s) is production at its peak? _____

At which season(s) is production at its minimum? _____

To what extent are your production operations regulated by governmental controls?

_____% Federal _____% State _____% Local

Who are your major suppliers? Are you satisfied with them?

_____ _____%

_____ _____%

_____ _____%

_____ _____%

Part III: Markets Served

If possible, give estimates for the following:

	Last Year	Three Years Ago
Total industry sales	$_____	$_____
Your sales	$_____	$_____
Your market share	$_____	$_____

	Last Year	Three Years Ago
Major competitor's share	$_____	$_____
Second-ranking competitor's share	$_____	$_____
Third-ranking competitor's share	$_____	$_____

_____% Consumer market   _____% Industrial market

Describe each consumer market or industrial market by SIC code.* List your products, or services, the channels used to distribute them, and your approximate percentage share of each market.

Market	Products	Channel(s)	Market Share

*This is a code developed by the federal government to describe products and services and the companies that offer them.

List your major competitors.

Name and Address	Strongest Markets	Why strong in these markets?	Strongest Products	Why strong with these products?

What new competitors have entered the marketplace in the past three years? _____

_____

_____

Have any done unusually well? If so, in what markets, with what products, and why? _____

_____

_____

_____

Part IV: Products

Approximately how many different individual products do you manufacture? _____

$_____ What is the dollar amount of your average sale (to your end customer)?

How many times is your average product purchased by the same customer in a single year? _____

_____% Approximately what percentage of your customers are repeat customers?

What is the average purchase life of your customers? _____

Why do they stop buying from you? _____

_____

_____

_____

Which of your products have the highest margins? _____

_____

_____

_____

Do you sell any "loss leaders"? List them below:

_____

_____

_____

_____

_____

_____

Has their effectiveness ever been tested against that of other items? If so, which items, and how?

_____   _____

_____   _____

_____   _____

_____   _____

_____   _____

_____   _____

_____   _____

_____   _____

_____   _____

List your products below by sales and profits:

Product	Annual Sales	Annual Profits
_____	$_____	$_____
_____	$_____	$_____
_____	$_____	$_____
_____	$_____	$_____
_____	$_____	$_____
_____	$_____	$_____

Have you considered dropping those products that account for low profits? If low-sales/low-profit products are being retained, indicate why:

_____

_____

_____

_____

_____

_____

_____

_____

_____

_____

_____

Do you have an ongoing new-product research and development program? _____

When was your last new product introduced? _____

When was your last major product modification introduced? _____

How do you do new-product research and development?
_____ In-house
_____ Subcontract

Why do you do new-product research and development?
_____ Meet the competition

_____ Counter product obsolescence
_____ Reduce production costs
_____ Reduce material costs
_____ Enter new markets
_____ Increase sales
_____ Other _____

_____

How do you screen potential products for development? _____

_____

Part V: Marketing Research

Do you have an ongoing market research program? _____

Do you have correct information on:
_____ Who's buying your products?
_____ Why they're buying?
_____ Where your products are being bought?
_____ Who's making the purchase decision?
_____ How to best reach your customers through advertising?
_____ The effectiveness of advertising programs?
_____ Your competitors' products?
_____ Your competitors' strategies?
_____ Potential markets?
_____ Relative effectiveness of different channels of distribution?
_____ New applications of your products?
_____ Export potential?
_____ Related products demanded by your customers?
_____ Relative effectiveness and efficiency of salespeople?
_____ Packaging effectiveness?
_____ Pricing sensitivity?
_____ Image and positioning of your product relative to others?
_____ Publicity possibilities?
_____ Operating ratios in your industry?

What trade associations do you belong to? _____

_____

_____

What trade magazines or journals do you subscribe to? _____
_____
_____

Do you use the market research available from associations and magazines? _____

Do you use the market research available from the Internet? _____

If you make use of internally generated market research, which organizations within your company provide this research, and what research do they provide? _____
_____
_____
_____
_____

What outside organizations have assisted you in doing research?
_____
_____
_____
_____

Part VI: Market Segments

Consumer Market

What segments of the market do your present customers represent?
_____
_____
_____
_____

Are your products more:
_____ Habitual purchase?
_____ Impulse purchase?
_____ Planned purchase?

In your market, which are the most important factors for buying?
_____ Price   _____ Features   _____ Appearance
_____ Quality   _____ Performance   _____ Other _____
_____
_____

Who influences the decision to buy your products?
    _____ Men   _____ Lawyers
    _____ Women   _____ Religious leaders
    _____ Children   _____ Mechanics
    _____ Doctors   _____ Contractors
    _____ Dentists   _____ Tradespeople
    _____ Educators   _____ Fraternal or social groups
    _____ Beauticians   _____ High-income or influential people
    _____ Barbers   _____ Others _____

Industrial Market

Who makes the purchase decision for your product? If more than one
individual, indicate all. _____
_____
_____
_____

Outline the sequence of events as to how this decision is made. Include
other factors or individuals influencing this decision. _____
_____
_____
_____
_____
_____

Part VII: Pricing

How do you decide on the price for your products? _____
_____
_____
_____

What's your warranty policy? _____

_____

_____

_____

What's your service policy? _____

_____

_____

_____

Any other special policies of importance? _____

_____

_____

_____

Pricing Checklist

Examining Costs, Sales Volume, and Profits. The questions in this part should be helpful when you look at prices from the viewpoint of costs, sales volume, and profits.*

Pricing and Costs. The company that sets the price for an item by applying a standard markup may be overlooking certain cost factors that are connected with that item. The following questions are designed to help you gather information that should be helpful when you are determining prices on specific types of items.

	Yes	No
1. Do you know which of your operating costs remains the same regardless of sales volume?	_____	_____
2. Do you know which of your operating costs decreases percentagewise as your sales volume increases?	_____	_____
3. Have you ever figured out the break-even point for your items selling at varying price levels?	_____	_____

*This section (which continues until the beginning of Part VIII) is adapted from Joseph D. O'Brien, *A Pricing Checklist for Managers,* published by the U.S. Small Business Administration.

		Yes	No

4. Do you look behind high gross margin percentages? (For example, a product with a high gross margin may also be a slow turnover item with high handling costs. Thus it may be less profitable than lower-margin items that turn over fast.) _____ _____

5. When you select items for price reductions, do you project the effects on profits? (For example, if a food marketer considers whether to run canned ham or rump steak on sale, an important cost factor is labor. Practically none is involved in featuring canned ham; however, a rump steak sale requires the skill of a meat cutter, and this labor cost might mean little or no profits.) _____ _____

Pricing and Sales Volume. An effective pricing program should also consider sales volume. For example, high prices may limit your sales volume, while low prices may result in a large but unprofitable volume. The following questions should be helpful in determining what is right for your situation.

		Yes	No

6. Have you considered setting a sales volume goal and then studying it to see if your prices will help you reach it? _____ _____

7. Have you set a target of a certain number of new customers for next year? _____ _____
    If so, how can pricing help to get them? _____

8. Should you limit the quantities of low-margin items that any one customer can buy when such items are on sale? _____ _____
    If so, will you advertise this policy? _____ _____

9. What is your policy when a sale item is sold out before the end of the advertised period? Do you allow disappointed customers to buy the item later at the sale price? _____ _____

Pricing and Profits. Prices should help bring in sales that are profitable over the long haul. The following questions are designed to help you think about pricing policies and their effect on your annual profits.

		Yes	No
10.	Do you have all the facts on costs, sales, and competitive behavior?	____	____
11.	Do you set prices with the hope of accomplishing definite objectives, such as a one percent profit increase over last year?	____	____
12.	Have you set a given level of profits in dollars and in percentage of sales?	____	____
13.	Do you keep records to give you the needed facts on profits, losses, and prices?	____	____
14.	Do you review your pricing practices periodically to make sure that they are helping to achieve your profit goals?	____	____

Judging the Buyer, Timing, and Competitors. The questions in this part are designed to help you check your practices for judging the buyer (your customer), your timing, and your competitors.

The Buyer and Pricing. After you have your facts on costs, the next point must be the *customer*—whether you are changing a price, putting in a new item, or checking out your present price practices. Knowledge of your customers helps you determine how to vary prices in order to get the average gross margin you need for making a profit. (For example, to get an average gross margin of 35 percent, some retailers put a low markup, 10 percent for instance, on items that they promote as traffic builders and use high markup, sometimes as much as 60 percent, on slow-moving items.) The following questions should be helpful in checking your knowledge about your customers.

		Yes	No
15.	Do you know whether your customers shop around and for what items?	____	____

		Yes	No

16. Do you know how your customers make their comparisons?   _____   _____
    ☐ By reading newspaper ads?
    ☐ Store shopping?
    ☐ Hearsay?
17. Are you trying to appeal to customers who:
    ☐ Buy on price alone?
    ☐ Buy on quality alone?
    ☐ Combine the two?
18. Do any of your customers tell you whether your prices are in line with those of your competitors?   _____   _____
    ☐ Higher?
    ☐ Lower?
    ☐ Competitive?
19. Do you know which items (or types of items) your customers call for even though you raise the price?   _____   _____
20. Do you know which items (or types of items) your customers leave on your shelves when you raise the price?   _____   _____
21. Do certain items seem to appeal to customers more than others when you run weekend, clearance, or special-day sales?   _____   _____
22. Have you used your individual sales records to classify your present customers according to the volume of their purchases?   _____   _____
23. Will your customers buy more if you use multiple pricing (for example, three for thirty-nine cents for products with rapid turnover)?   _____   _____
24. Do your customers respond to odd prices more readily than to even prices, for example, ninety-nine cents rather than one dollar?   _____   _____
25. Have you decided on a pricing strategy to create a favorable price image with your customers? (For example, a retailer with eight thousand different items might decide to make a full margin on all medium or slow movers

Yes   No

while featuring—at low price levels—the re-
maining fast movers.)   _____   _____

26. If you are trying to build a quality price image,
do your individual customer records, such as
charge account statements, show that you are
selling a larger number of higher-priced items
than you were twelve months ago?   _____   _____

27. Do your records of individual customer ac-
counts and your observations of customer be-
havior in the store show price as the important
factor in their:
☐ Buying?
☐ Service?
☐ Assortments?
☐ Some other consideration?

Time and Pricing. Effective merchandising means that you have
the right product at the right place, at the right price, and at the right
time. All are important, but timing is the critical element for the smaller
retailer. The following questions should be helpful in determining what
is the right time for you to adjust prices.

Yes   No

28. Are you a "leader" (rather than a "follower") in
announcing your price reductions? (Followers,
even though they match their competitors, cre-
ate a negative impression on their customers.)   _____   _____

29. Have you studied your competitors to see
whether they follow any sort of pattern when
making price changes? (For example, do some
of them run clearance sales earlier than others?) _____   _____

30. Is there a pattern to the kinds of items that
competitors promote at lower prices at certain
times of the month or year?   _____   _____

31. Have you decided whether it is better to take
early markdowns on seasonal or style goods or
to run a clearance sale at the end of the season? _____   _____

Yes   No

32. Have you made regular annual sales—such
    as anniversary sales, fall clearance, or holiday
    cleanup—so popular that many customers wait
    for them rather than buying in season?   _____   _____
33. When you change a price, do you make sure
    that all customers know about it through price
    tags and so on?   _____   _____
34. Do you try to time reductions so they can be
    promoted in your advertising?   _____   _____

Competition and Pricing. When you set prices, you have to consider how your competitors might react to your prices. The starting
place is learning as much as you can about their price structures. The
following questions are designed to help you check out this phase of
pricing.

Yes   No

35. Do you use all the available channels of infor-
    mation to keep you up-to-date on your com-
    petitors' price policies? (Some useful sources of
    information are: things your customers tell you;
    competitors' price lists and catalogs, if used;
    competitors' advertising; reports from your sup-
    pliers; trade paper studies; and shoppers em-
    ployed by you.)   _____   _____
36. Should your policy be always to:
    ☐ Try to sell above or below competition?
    ☐ Or only to meet the competition?
37. Is there a pattern to the way your competitors
    respond to your price cuts?   _____   _____
38. Is the pricing of your leader competitors affect-
    ing your sales volume to such an extent that
    you must alter your pricing policy on individual
    items (or types of items) or merchandise?   _____   _____
39. Do you realize that no two competitors have
    identical cost curves? (This difference in costs
    means that certain price levels may be profit-
    able for you but unprofitable for your competi-
    tor or vice versa.)   _____   _____

Practices That Can Help Offset Price. Some companies take advantage of the fact that price is not always the determining factor in making a sale. They supply customer services and offer other inducements to offset the effect of competitors' lower prices. Delivery service is an example. Providing a comfortable shoppers' meeting place is another. The following questions are designed to help you take a look at some of these practices.

	Yes	No
40. Do the items or services you sell have advantages for which customers are willing to pay a little more?	_____	_____
41. From personal observation of customer behavior in your store, can you estimate about how much more customers will pay for such advantages?	_____	_____
42. Should you change your services so as to create an advantage for which your customers will be willing to pay?	_____	_____
43. Does your advertising emphasize customer benefits rather than price?	_____	_____
44. Are you using the most common nonprice competitive tools? (For example, have you tried to alter your product or service to the existing market? Have you tried stamps, bonus purchase gifts, or other plans for building repeat business?)	_____	_____
45. Should policies on returned goods be changed so as to better impress your customers?	_____	_____
46. If you sell repair services, have you checked out your guarantee policy?	_____	_____
47. Should you alter assortments of merchandise to increase sales?	_____	_____

Part VIII: Distribution

How much of your product line is:
_____% Manufactured by you?
_____% Manufactured for you by someone else?
  100% Total

Is your distribution:
_____ Regional? In what areas? _____
_____
_____

_____ National? What are your strongest areas? _____
_____
_____

_____ International? What are your strongest foreign countries? _____
_____
_____

What systems of distribution do you use? _____
_____
_____
_____
_____

How do you subdivide your product lines in your sales organization?
_____ Geographic territories   _____ Type of customer
_____ Type of product   _____ Other _____

How do you decide on methods of distribution and which distributors
to use? _____
_____

Part IX: Selling

Do your salespeople, agents, or distributors have exclusive territories?
_____
_____
_____

How many people do you have selling your product, and what are
their responsibilities? _____
_____
_____
_____

How do you compensate your salespeople? _____

_____

_____

_____

Do you offer any special sales incentives? _____

_____

_____

_____

Who prepares your product catalogs? _____

_____

_____

_____

What aids to selling do you, your distributor, or your agent provide to people selling your product? _____

_____

_____

_____

Do you provide any type of formal sales training? Explain type, subjects, length of programs, etc. _____

_____

_____

_____

How frequently do you hold sales meetings or conferences? What subjects are covered? _____

_____

_____

_____

What branch offices do you maintain? _____

_____

_____

_____

How do you select or recruit your agents and salespeople? _____
_____
_____
_____

How do you set sales quotas? _____
_____
_____
_____

What trade discounts do you offer? _____
_____
_____
_____

What terms of sale do you use? _____
_____
_____
_____

Do you grant any special concessions or offers to stimulate sales? ____
_____
_____
_____

_____% What is your percentage of returned goods?

_____% What is your percentage of goods returned due to damage?

_____% What is your percentage of bad debts?

What is the average time for collection of amounts owed to you? ____

How frequently do your salespeople send in reports? _____

How do you maintain your sales records? _____
_____
_____
_____

What is your ratio of sales made to number of calls made? _____

Are your "cold calls" supplemented by any other type of communication such as direct mail? _____
_____
_____
_____

How do you control your salespeople's activities? _____
_____
_____
_____
_____

What percentage of your salespeople's time is spent on:
_____% Planning?
_____% Preparation?
_____% Travel?
_____% Calls on prospects?
_____% Calls on established customers?
_____% Other?
   100% Total

What are the following yearly gross sales figures of your salespeople?
$_____ Average gross
$_____ Lowest gross
$_____ Highest gross

$_____ What is the average amount spent on promotion activities
that back up sales per salesperson per year (total spent yearly
on sales promotion, advertising, and publicity divided by
number of salespeople)?

$_____ What is the average amount spent on sales activities per
salesperson per year (total spent on recruiting, training, expense accounts, and compensation divided by number of
salespeople)?

Part X: Advertising

What media do you use to promote to your customers? _____

_____

_____

_____

_____

_____

What advertising (including direct mail and telephone) have you done,
and what were the costs over the last year? What were the results?

_____

_____

_____

_____

_____

How were results measured for these ads? _____

_____

_____

_____

_____

_____

_____

Have you used the Internet for advertising? What were the results?

_____

_____

_____

_____

_____

_____

_____

_____

Do you have an advertising agency?

Name: _____

Contact: _____

Address: _____

City, State, and Zip Code: _____

Phone Number: _____

Fax Number: _____

E-mail: _____

Part XI: Promotion

What types of sales promotion have you done (discounts, coupons, contests, etc.), and what were the costs? What were the results? _____

_____

_____

_____

_____

_____

_____

_____

Part XII: Publicity and Public Relations

What type of public relations program did you engage in over the previous year, and what were the costs? What were the results? _____

_____

_____

_____

_____

_____

Part XIII: Management Operations

What type of planning does the organization do? _____

_____

_____

_____

_____

_____

How is budgetary control of operations planned and maintained? ____

_____

_____

_____

Part XIV: Financial Checklist: Are You Making a Profit?

Analysis of Revenues and Expenses. Since profit is revenues less expenses, you must first identify all revenues and expenses for the period under study to determine what your profit is.*

	Yes	No
1. Have you chosen an appropriate period for profit determination?	_____	_____

For accounting purposes, businesses generally use a twelve-month period, such as January 1 to December 31 or July 1 to June 30. The accounting year you select doesn't have to be a calendar year (January to December); a seasonal business, for example, might close its year after the end of the season. The selection depends on the nature of your business, your personal preference, or possible tax considerations.

2. Have you determined your total revenues for the accounting period?   _____   _____

In order to answer this question, consider the answer to the following questions.

$_____ What is the amount of gross revenue from sales of your goods or service (*gross sales*)?

$_____ What is the amount of goods returned by your customers and credited (*returns and rejects*)?

---

*This section (which continues until the beginning of Part XV) is adapted from Narendra C. Bhandari and Charles S. McCubbin, Jr., *Checklist for Profit Watching*, published by the U.S. Small Business Administration.

$_____   What is the amount of discounts given to your customers and employees (*discounts*)?

$_____   What is the amount of net sales from goods and services (*net sales = gross sales [returns and rejects plus discounts]*)?

$_____   What is the amount of income from other sources, such as interest on bank deposits, dividends from securities, and rent on property leased to others (*nonoperating income*)?

$_____   What is the amount of total revenue (*total revenue = net sales plus nonoperating income*)?

3. Do you know what your total expenses are?   _____   _____
    Expenses are the cost of goods sold and services used in the process of selling goods or services. Some common expenses for all businesses are:

    $_____   Cost of goods sold (cost of goods sold = beginning inventory plus purchases minus ending inventory)

    $_____   Wages and salaries (don't forget to include your own—at the actual rate you'd have to pay someone else to do your job)

    $_____   Rent

    $_____   Utilities (electricity, gas, telephone, water, etc.)

    $_____   Supplies (office, cleaning, and the like)

    $_____   Delivery expenses

    $_____   Insurance

    $_____   Advertising and promotion costs

    $_____   Maintenance and upkeep

    $_____   Depreciation (here you need to make

sure your depreciation policies are
realistic and that all depreciable items
are included)

$_____   Taxes and licenses
$_____   Interest
$_____   Bad debts
$_____   Professional assistance (accountant,
            attorney, etc.)

There are, of course, many other types of
expenses, but the point is that every expense
must be recorded and deducted from your revenues before you know what your profit is. Understanding your expenses is the first step
toward *controlling them* and *increasing your
profits*.

Financial Ratios

A *financial ratio* is an expression of the relationship between two
items selected from the income statement or the balance sheet. Ratio
analysis helps you evaluate the weak and strong points in your financial
and managerial performance.

	Yes	No
4. Do you know your current ratio?	_____	_____

The *current ratio* (current assets divided by
current debts) is a measure of the cash or near
cash position (liquidity) of the company. It tells
you if you have enough cash to pay your company's current creditors. The higher the ratio,
the more liquid the company's position, and
hence, the higher the credibility of the company. Cash, receivables, marketable securities,
and inventory are current assets. Naturally you
need to be realistic in valuing receivables and
inventory for a true picture of your liquidity,
because some debts may be uncollectible and
some stock obsolete. Current liabilities are those
that must be paid in one year.

Yes   No

5. Do you know your quick ratio?   _____   _____
       Quick assets are current assets minus in-
ventory. The *quick ratio* (or acid-test ratio) is
found by dividing quick assets by current liabilities. The purpose, again, is to test the company's ability to meet its current obligations.
Because it doesn't include inventory, quick ratio
is a stiffer test of the company's liquidity. It tells
you if the business could meet its current obligations with quickly convertible assets should
sales revenues suddenly cease.

6. Do you know your total debt to net worth
   ratio?   _____   _____
       This ratio (the result of total debt divided
by net worth, then multiplied by 100) is a measure of how the company can meet its total obligations from equity. The lower the ratio, the
higher the proportion of equity relative to debt,
and the better the company's credit rating will
be.

7. Do you know your average collection period?   _____   _____
       You find this ratio by dividing accounts re-
ceivable by daily credit sales. (Daily credit sales
= annual credit sales divided by 360.) This ratio
tells you the length of time it takes the company
to get its cash after making a sale on credit. The
shorter this period, the quicker the cash inflow
is. A longer than normal period may mean over-
due and uncollectible bills. If you extend credit
for a specific period (say, thirty days), this ratio
should be very close to the same number of
days. If it's much longer than the established
period, you may need to alter your credit policies. It's wise to develop an "aging" schedule
to gauge the trend of collections and identify
slow payers. Slow collections (without adequate
financing charges) hurt your profit, because you
could be doing something much more useful

Yes   No

       with your money, such as taking advantage of
discounts on your own payables.

8. Do you know your ratio of net sales to total
assets?   _____   _____

       This ratio (net sales divided by total assets)
measures the efficiency with which you are using
your assets. A higher than normal ratio indicates that the company is able to generate sales
from its assets faster (and better) than the average concern.

9. Do you know your operating profit to net sales
ratio?   _____   _____

       This ratio (the result of dividing operating
profit by net sales and multiplying by 100) is
most often used to determine the profit position relative to sales. A higher than normal ratio
indicates that your sales are good or that your
expenses are low, or both. Interest income and
interest expense should not be included in calculating this ratio.

10. Do you know your net profit to total assets
ratio?   _____   _____

       This ratio (the result of dividing net profit
by total assets and multiplying by 100) is often
called return on investment, or ROI. It focuses
on the profitability of the overall operation of
the company. Thus it allows management to
measure the effects of its policies on the company's profitability. The ROI is the single most
important measure of a company's financial
position. You might say it's the bottom line for
the bottom line.

11. Do you know your net profit to net worth ratio?   _____   _____

       This ratio is found by dividing net profit by
net worth and multiplying the result by 100. It
provides information on the productivity of the
resources the owners have committed to the
company's operations. All ratios measuring profit-

ability can be computed either before or after taxes, depending on the purpose of the computations. Ratios have limitations. Because the information used to derive ratios is itself based on accounting rules and personal judgments as well as facts, the ratios cannot be considered absolute indicators of a company's financial position. Ratios are only one means of assessing the performance of the company and must be considered in perspective with many other measures. They should be used as a point of departure for further analysis and not as an end in themselves.

Sufficiency of Profit

The following questions are designed to help you measure the adequacy of the profit your company is making. Making a profit is only the first step; making enough profit to survive and *grow* is really what business is all about.

		Yes	No
12.	Have you compared your profit with your profit goals?	___	___
13.	Is it possible your goals are too high or too low?	___	___
14.	Have you compared your present profits (absolute and ratios) with the profits made in the last one to three years?	___	___
15.	Have you compared your profits (absolute and ratios) with profits made by similar companies in your line?	___	___

A number of organizations publish financial ratios for various businesses, among them Dun & Bradstreet, (formerly, The Risk Management Association), the Accounting Corporation of America, NCR Corporation, and Bank of America. Your own trade association may also publish such studies. Remember, these published ratios are only averages. You probably want to be better than average.

Trend of Profit

	Yes	No
16. Have you analyzed the direction your profits have been taking?	_____	_____

   The preceding analyses, with all their merits, report on a company only at a single time in the past. It is not possible to use these isolated moments to indicate the trend of your company's performance. To do a trend analysis, you should compute performance indicators (absolute amounts or ratios) for several time periods (yearly for several years, for example) and lay out the results in columns side by side for easy comparison. You can then evaluate your performance, see the direction it's taking, and make initial forecasts of where it will go.

Mix of Profit

	Yes	No
17. Does your company sell more than one major product line or provide several distinct services?	_____	_____

   If it does, a separate profit and ratio analysis of each should be made: to show the relative contribution of each product line or service; to show the relative burden of expenses of each product or service; to show which items are most profitable, which are less so and which are losing money; and to show which are slow and fast moving. The profit and ratio analyses of each major item help you uncover the strong and weak areas of your operations. They can help you to make profit-increasing decisions to drop a product line or service or to place particular emphasis behind one or another.

Records

Good records are essential. Without them a company doesn't know where it's been, where it is, or where it's heading. Keeping records that are accurate, up-to-date, and easy to use is one of the most important functions of the owner-manager, his or her staff, and his or her outside counselors (lawyer, accountant, banker).

Basic Records

	Yes	No
18. Do you have a general journal and/or special journals, such as one for cash receipts and disbursements?	_____	_____

      A general journal is the basic record of the company. Every monetary event in the life of the company is entered in the general journal or in one of the special journals.

	Yes	No
19. Do you prepare a sales report or analysis?	_____	_____
a. Do you have sales goals by product, department, and accounting period (month, quarter, year)?	_____	_____
b. Are your goals reasonable?	_____	_____
c. Are you meeting your goals?	_____	_____

      If you aren't meeting your goals, try to list the likely reasons on a sheet of paper. Such a list might include areas such as general business climate, competition, pricing, advertising, sales promotion, credit policies, and the like. Once you've identified the apparent causes, you can take steps to increase sales (and profits).

Buying and Inventory Systems

	Yes	No
20. Do you have buying and inventory systems?	_____	_____

      Buying and inventory systems are two critical areas of a company's operation that can affect profitability.

	Yes	No
21. Do you keep records on the quality, service, price, and promptness of delivery of your sources of supply?	____	____
22. Have you analyzed the advantages and disadvantages of:		
a. Buying from suppliers?	____	____
b. Buying from a minimum number of suppliers?	____	____
23. Have you analyzed the advantages and disadvantages of buying through cooperatives or other such systems?	____	____
24. Do you know:		
a. How long it usually takes to receive each order?	____	____
b. How much inventory cushion (usually called safety stock) to have so you can maintain normal sales while you wait for the order to arrive?	____	____
25. Have you ever suffered because you were out of stock?	____	____
26. Do you know the optimum order quantity for each item you need?	____	____
27. Do you (or can you) take advantage of quantity discounts for large-size single purchases?	____	____
28. Do you know your costs of ordering inventory and carrying inventory?	____	____

The more frequently you buy (smaller quantities per order), the higher your average ordering costs are (clerical costs, postage, telephone costs, etc.), and the lower the average carrying costs are (storage, loss through pilferage, obsolescence, etc.). On the other hand, the larger the quantity per order, the lower the average ordering costs, and the higher the carrying costs. A balance should be struck so that the minimum cost overall for ordering and carrying inventory can be achieved.

| 29. Do you keep records of inventory for each item? | ____ | ____ |

These records should be kept current by making entries whenever items are added to or removed from inventory. Simple records on 3- by 5-inch or 5- by 7-inch cards can be used, with each item being listed on a separate card. Proper records will show, for each item, quantity in stock, quantity on order, date of order, slow or fast seller, and valuations (which are important for taxes and your own analyses).

Other Financial Records

	Yes	No

30. Do you have an accounts payable ledger? _____ _____
    This ledger shows what, whom, and why you owe. Such records should help you make your payments on schedule; any expense not paid on time could adversely affect your credit. But even more importantly, such records should help you take advantage of discounts that can help boost your profits.

31. Do you have an accounts receivable ledger? _____ _____
    This ledger shows who owes money to your company. It shows how much is owed, how long it has been outstanding, and why the money is owed. Overdue accounts could indicate that your credit-granting policy needs to be reviewed and that you may not be getting the cash into the company quickly enough to pay your own bills at the optimum time.

32. Do you have a cash receipts journal? _____ _____
    This journal records the cash received by source, day, and amount.

33. Do you have a cash payments journal? _____ _____
    This journal is similar to the cash receipts journal but shows cash paid out instead of cash received. The two cash journals can be combined if convenient.

34. Do you prepare an income (profit and loss, or P&L) statement and a balance sheet? _____ _____

Yes   No

These are statements about the condition of your company at a specific time; they show the income, expenses, assets, and liabilities of the company. They are absolutely essential.

35. Do you prepare a budget?   _____   _____

You could think of a budget as a "record in advance," projecting future inflows and outflows for your business. A budget is usually prepared for a single year, generally to correspond with the accounting year. It is then, however, broken down into quarterly and monthly projections.

There are different kinds of budgets: cash, production, sales, and the like. A cash budget, for example, shows the estimate of sales and expenses for a particular period of time. The cash budget forces the company to think ahead by estimating its income and expenses. Once reasonable projections are made for every important product line or department, the owner-manager has set targets for employees to meet for sales and expenses. You must plan to ensure a profit. And you must prepare a budget to plan.

Part XV: Materials to Ask For

- Sales brochures
- Price lists
- Public relations materials
- Product descriptions and photographs
- Special forms
- Annual report
- Financial statements
- Sample advertisements and promotional materials
- Information given out at recent trade shows
- Organizational charts

Appendix D

AN EXTENSIVE CONSULTING PROPOSAL

**A Proposal for a Project Planning and Control System
Procedure Development Program**

Submitted to:

[company name and address]

Attention: *[name]*

Submitted by:

Decision Planning Corporation
3184-A Airway Avenue
Costa Mesa, California 92626

All pages of this document contain information proprietary to Decision Planning Corporation. All data furnished in connection with this proposal shall not be duplicated, transmitted, used, or otherwise disclosed to anyone other than _____, and then only for the purpose of evaluating the quotation. This restriction is applicable to all sheets of this proposal.

Table of Contents

Description

1.0 Executive Summary

Decision Planning Corporation (DPC) submits this proposal to _____ _____ to develop project planning and control system procedures. The proposal contains a description of proposed services, associated schedule and costs, and DPC qualifications to assist _____ _____ in this program.

In order to facilitate evaluation of the subject matter, DPC has subdivided the proposal into four sections and two appendixes. Following is a brief description of each part.

EXECUTIVE SUMMARY	The Executive Summary section provides an overview of the proposed program and the proposed approach to accomplishing contract work. The section concludes with a description of DPC qualifications to perform the proposed tasks.
TECHNICAL PROPOSAL	The Technical Proposal section begins with a detailed description of work to be accomplished and products/services to be delivered to _____. In addition to defining program scope, Section 2.0 identifies responsibilities of _____ and DPC for development, review, and approval of individual products and services.
COST PROPOSAL	The Cost Proposal section contains a detailed estimate of labor hours and other elements of cost necessary to accomplish the proposed scope. This section also presents assumptions upon which the proposal is based, labor rates, terms and conditions, and other information necessary to fully understand the Cost Proposal.
MANAGEMENT PROPOSAL	The Management Proposal section begins with a discussion of the approach and methodology that will be used in accomplishing the statement of work. A summary schedule of events is also shown. The section closes with a detailed examination of DPC's project organization, in terms of both personnel to be assigned and the organization of personnel into the Project Team.
APPENDIXES	DPC concludes the proposal by providing two appendixes containing data that describe DPC's overall qualifications and performance

record. These appendixes are presented outside the body of the proposal in order to maintain proposal continuity and thus facilitate its
review. The subject appendixes are described
below:

Appendix A—DPC believes that its experience
and knowledge in providing
services offered in this proposal
are the foremost in the industry.
Appendix A, Relevant DPC Experience, provides a synopsis of
representative DPC accomplishments.

Appendix B—DPC is convinced that the qualifications and experience of the
staff proposed for this program
cannot be excelled by any of its
competitors. Appendix B, DPC
Staff Résumés, depicts career
accomplishments and the academic record of the DPC Program Team.

[*Appendix A and Appendix B have been intentionally deleted.*]

1.1   Program Background

_____ has initiated a corporatewide effort to upgrade
existing management information system hardware and software systems. In parallel with this effort, the engineering department has initiated
an effort to upgrade its project planning and control system by revising
existing procedures and/or developing new procedures that describe how
_____ organizes, plans, monitors, and controls project
work on its engineering and construction projects.

Decision Planning Corporation recognizes the desire of _____
_____ to have these procedures defined, written, and implemented as
soon as possible. The development of these types of procedures is normally accomplished in three distinct steps. The first step involves defining
the project planning and control system requirements. The second step
takes these general requirements and restructures them in the form of a

detailed system specification. The final step is the development of each procedure from the specification. Each procedure contains a logic diagram, narrative text, and instruction related to the fulfillment of the procedure requirements.

DPC is currently engaged with _____ to develop a customized training program on project planning and control concepts. This program is based on DPC's public seminar, which is currently being presented nationwide. DPC has, however, made substantial changes in the presentation material to be _____-specific. This training program provides a perfect base for developing system procedures. Having DPC execute the proposed procedures development program will assure _____ of maximizing its investment in the training program and make procedure implementation much easier.

1.2   Proposed Services

Decision Planning Corporation offers to accomplish the scope of work outlined below and defined in the Technical Proposal. To assure a clear and complete understanding of the work scope between _____ _____ and DPC, the proposed program has been subdivided into its component parts by means of a Program Work Breakdown Structure (PWBS) shown in [*Figure D-1*]. Following is a brief description of the elements of this scope at the second level of the DPC PWBS.

Figure D-1. Program Work Breakdown Structure.

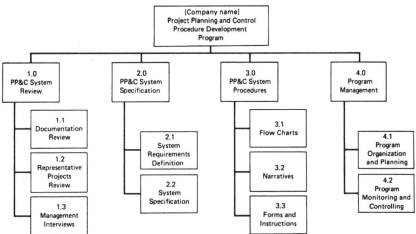

WBS Element 1	*Project Planning and Control System Review:* WBS Element No. 1 includes: a review of the existing _____ Project Planning and Control (PP&C) System documentation to gain an understanding of the current _____ project planning and control techniques; a survey of sample _____ projects to assure a clear understanding of planning and control needs of projects by size and type; and interviews with _____ management personnel to understand unwritten practices, procedures, working relationships, and attitudes.
WBS Element 2	*Project Planning and Control System Specification:* This WBS element includes activities related to defining requirements for organizing, planning, authorizing, monitoring, and controlling project work and resources, and preparation of a specification that will be the basis for preparing each procedure.
WBS Element 3	*Project Planning and Control System Procedures:* This WBS contains development of system procedures, including system flow diagrams, procedure narratives, and forms design and completion instructions.
WBS Element 4	*DPC Program Management:* This WBS element includes the organizing, planning, monitoring, and controlling of the work and resources necessary to assure the successful and timely completion of this engagement.

A detailed description of each WBS element is provided in Section 2.0, Technical Proposal. An overview of the approach DPC proposed for accomplishing the program work is shown in [*Figure D-2*]. DPC's work methodology is described in the form of a logic diagram depicting the relationship of WBS subelements. In Section 4.0, this logic diagram was used as a basis for development of a realistic program schedule.

1.3   Decision Planning Corporation Qualifications

Decision Planning Corporation has an outstanding record in the field of project management. Formed in 1972, Decision Planning Corporation has

Figure D-2. DPC approach for accomplishing program work.

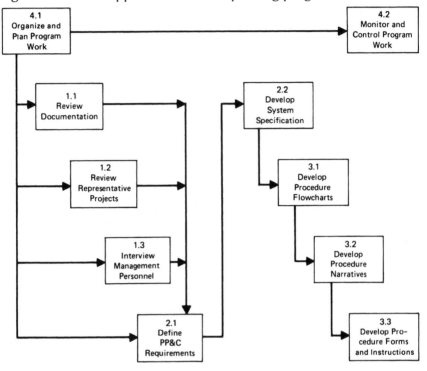

built a nationwide consulting practice and provided services to over one hundred organizations from a variety of industries and several branches of the federal government. Among DPC's clients are electric utilities, construction companies, architectural/engineering firms, reactor manufacturers, aerospace/defense contractors, the U.S. Departments of Energy and Defense, the Canadian federal government, and many other organizations. These organizations received assistance from Decision Planning Corporation in virtually every aspect of project management.

Appendix A indicates the extent of DPC's experience in the areas of project management relevant to this proposal. Of special interest to _____ _____ is the assistance provided to the Bonneville Power Administration, the Northwest Energy Corporation, the General Public Utilities Services Company, the Gas-Cooled Reactor Associates, and Southern Company Services. These engagements were performed in essentially the same environment and included the same scope of work as described in this proposal.

DPC personnel possess diverse experience in all aspects of project management, ranging from participation in the develop of original concepts of Integrated Project Management to achieving remarkable results in the management of projects utilizing these concepts. For this proposed work, Decision Planning Corporation has selected a team of experienced project management professionals. Each has extensive experience in project management control system design, documentation, training, implementation, and operation.

Their experience will assure that the _____ Project Planning and Control System Procedures will reflect the needs of the company and will be the correct combination of proper structure and practical knowledge of the needs of the project manager/engineer.

Decision Planning Corporation is uniquely qualified to assist _____ _____ on this program. Following is a summary of the benefits that will accrue to _____ by selecting Decision Planning Corporation for this assignment.

○ DPC is intimately familiar with the _____ project management environment. By selecting Decision Planning Corporation for this assignment, _____ will gain the benefit of DPC's extensive experience in the design, documentation, implementation, and operation of project management systems, thereby assuring that the PP&C procedures effort will be accomplished expeditiously.

○ DPC is an expert in project planning and control techniques of the electric utlity industry. DPC offers, as perhaps the only one of its kind in the United States, a public seminar entitled, "Project Planning and Control Within the Electric Utility Industry." _____ will gain the benefit of this know-how and experience in this engagement.

○ Decision Planning Corporation personnel contemplated for this assignment possess a balance of business and engineering backgrounds, thereby providing the disciplines necessary to conceptualize the system, utilizing a project manager's awareness of what is practical and what is not.

○ Decision Planning Corporation's experience with project management assignments in the project planning and control environment has extreme depth and breadth. Over the past five years, Decision Planning Corporation has assisted twenty major organizations involved in engineering/construction activities in the development, implementation, and operation of project management.

○ Decision Planning Corporation's entire corporate mission is dedicated to the business of assisting clients in the design, implementation, and operation of project management systems. Therefore, this effort is not secondary to other Decision Planning Corporation services. It is the central focus of its corporate experience and expertise.

In order to support the statements made and confirm the capabilities and performance records of Decision Planning Corporation, the following is a list of references provided to _____ for review.

[List of references intentionally deleted.]

2.0   Technical Proposal

Decision Planning Corporation proposes to provide the necessary services and related support to _____ in the conduct of a management system procedure development program outlined below. The program scope is presented in a modular fashion to enable _____ _____ to identify how those services are best suited to its present management needs.

SCOPE

The proposed scope of work involves the performance of ten (10) specific tasks. The individual tasks are structured as elements of a Work Breakdown Structure as shown in [*Figure D-1*]. The purpose of the Work Breakdown Structure is to define the deliverable products and services necessary to complete the program scope and to assure that the management of the engagement WBS is coded by a unique identification number. This number is used to identify the WBS element on all cost and schedule documents contained in this proposal. By using the WBS identification number, _____ may correlate all proposed cost and schedule information to the work scope defined for that element.

RESPONSIBILITIES

Since the WBS describes the products and services associated with management system procedure development, and not the responsibility for preparing the product or performing the service, an identification of the responsibilities for various tasks regarding each individual WBS element product/service is set forth in [Figure D-3]. The matrix contains the following information.

○ The vertical axis provides a listing of all WBS elements, products, and services.

○ The horizontal axis contains a listing of activities associated with product/service development.

Figure D-3. Responsibility matrix.

Responsibility Matrix		Responsible Organization						
		DPC				[Company name]		
Work Breakdown Structure Element		Execute	Review	Consult		Execute*	Review	Approve
Number	Description							
1.0	PP&C System Review							
1.1	Documentation Review	x						
1.2	Representative Project Review	x				x		
1.3	Management Interviews	x				x		
2.0	PP&C System Specification							
2.1	System Requirements Definition	x		x		x		x
2.2	System Specification	x				x		x
3.0	PP&C System Procedures							
3.1	Flowcharts	x	x			x	x	x
3.2	Narrative	x	x			x	x	x
3.3	Forms and Instructions	x	x			x	x	x
4.0	Program Management							
4.1	Program Organization & Planning	x						x
4.2	Program Monitoring and Control	x						x

*XXXX effort is expected to take one equivalent person.

    o Where axes intersect, a symbol is used to indicate responsibility for performance of the activity under consideration.

Activities associated with accomplishment of the proposed scope of work are identified as *execution, review, consulting,* and *approval.* Statements shown below describe program activities in terms of the content of work and deliverable products, where applicable.

EXECUTION   System review and analysis, flow chart preparation, development of procedures, and their presentation to the _____ personnel. All executed activities have clearly defined end products and/or services.

REVIEW   Analysis of results of execution activities for completeness and adequacy. Results of all reviews will be documented on the marked-up copies of program documentation, through memoranda, or by means acceptable to _____ _____ and DPC.

CONSULTING   Activities related to advisory program administration, management, and other "level of effort" work that does not result in a tangible end product.

APPROVAL   Work associated with formal acceptance of various products and services by _____ _____.

Decision Planning Corporation believes that material contained in this proposal presents a precise definition of the scope of work and responsibilities for its execution. It should be noted that the proposal quantifies the program scope to the maximum practical extent and avoids level of effort activities whenever possible. This provides a sound basis for management of the work scope and assures adequate visibility into the progress of each product.

2.1   WBS Element 1.0—Project Planning and Control (PP&C) System Review

Decision Planning Corporation will review _____'s PP&C System documentation, survey its project plans and reports, and conduct interviews with _____ management personnel, as needed. This effort will involve a three-step process. Each step is described below.

WBS ELEMENT 1.1   *PP&C Documentation Review:* DPC will review existing PP&C documentation and "take inventory" of current _____ practices associated with organizing, planning, authorizing, monitoring, and controlling labor, materials, and associated resources. This "inventory" will consist of the following:

a. Review of organization charts and position descriptions to develop an understanding of rules and responsibilities of people and organizations, and to identify the key interfaces of various project participants.

b. Review of other management policies, procedures, manuals, and related documentation to gain familiarity with current PP&C methods and practices.

c. Review of existing accounting and information systems to develop an understanding of: (1) labor distribution; (2) procurement/material commitments and distribution; (3) other direct costs distribution; and (4) other pertinent project and accounting information resources.

WBS ELEMENT 1.2   *Project Review:* DPC will review the character of the current engineering, construction, and maintenance projects. The review will consider a sample drawn from each of the major project groups—fossil plants, hydro plants, and transmission lines. The sample will be used to profile the project management requirements of _____ projects of each type and size. The review will address, as a minimum, the following:

a. Work Breakdown Structure and other project definition documents as presently exist.

b. Schedules throughout all levels.

c. Budget and/or expenditure forecasting documents.

> d. Work authorization documents, including contracts and purchase orders.
> e. Work progress/accomplishment and problem analysis documents/reports.

WBS ELEMENT 1.3   *Management Interviews:* Decision Planning Corporation will hold interviews with managers and other key personnel in engineering, project services, and other appropriate functional management areas to gain understanding of unwritten practices and procedures, working relationships, and relevant attitudes.

2.2   WBS Element 2.0—Project Planning and Control System Specification

Decision Planning Corporation will develop a specification for the enhancement of the _____ Project Planning and Control System. This specification will define criteria for organizing, planning, monitoring, and controlling project work and resources, and analyze _____ practices against these criteria.

WBS ELEMENT 2.1   *PP&C System Requirements Definition:* DPC (with the assistance of _____) will analyze project management practices identified in WBS Element 1.0 in light of existing project management requirements, and identify any additional requirements, as well as those which require further development. This approach will assure that the PP&C System reflects the state of the art in project management thought, as well as management style, values, and philosophy of _____.

WBS ELEMENT 2.2   *System Specification:* The results of the system requirements analysis will be documented in a System Specification. The specification will contain project management requirements and identity of the priorities that should govern the PP&C System procedure development. The report will also document the satisfactory features of the existing management systems so that eventual system modification effort can be undertaken with minimum change to existing practices.

2.3   WBS Element 3.0—PP&C System Procedures

Following the documentation of _____ system requirements, DPC, with _____'s assistance, will prepare the system procedures that meet those requirements.

WBS ELEMENT 3.1   *Flow Charts:* DPC and _____ will prepare graphic flow charts of the existing management practices. These flow charts will be compared to the requirements in the System Specification. Any shortcomings will be resolved jointly between DPC and _____. The outcome will be a flow chart of each intended procedure in the PP&C System. These flow charts will identify existing practices, modified practices, and any new practices and forms required to implement the practice. Upon completion of the flow charts, narrative explanations (text) of each step will be prepared. The flow charts and narratives will allow each reviewer to understand the flow and interaction of each step by viewing the graphical flow chart and understanding the contents of each step through review of the adjacent narrative. The ultimate goal is to assure that each intended procedure has consisted and clarified all necessary steps and interfaces.

A preliminary list of minimal system documentation follows:

- PP&C System Overview
- Work Definition and Responsibility Assignment Matrix
- Project Budgeting
- Project Scheduling Procedure
- Control Point Plan Development Procedure
- Authorizing Procedure

○ Performance Measurement Procedure

○ Baseline Measurement Procedure

○ Analysis and Forecasting Procedure

○ Change Control/Revision Procedure

○ Control Point Manager's Guide

The complete/final list of procedural documentation will be identified prior to any procedure development work. Each procedure will contain a flow diagram, flow diagram narrative, existing forms and/or new forms, narrative describing the purpose and scope of the procedure, definition of unique or new terms, and procedure requirements.

WBS ELEMENT 3.2   *Procedure Narratives:* Utilizing the flow chart narratives, DPC, with _____'s assistance, will prepare the series of procedures which will totally define the PP&C system.

WBS ELEMENT 3.3   *Forms and Instructions:* DPC will, if necessary, develop/revise PP&C forms and form instructions to be compliant with system procedure requirements. This task includes developing preliminary drafts, coordinating and reviewing preliminary drafts, and developing final drafts of both forms and form instructions.

2.4   WBS Element 4.0—Overall Program Management

In order to assure successful and timely completion of the proposed effort, this program must be organized, planned, monitored, and controlled effectively. The scope of work described below is designed to accomplish the above goals.

WBS ELEMENT 4.1   *Program Organization and Planning:* Near the outset of the program, DPC will finalize the following documents and submit them to _____ for review:

○ Work Breakdown Structure   [*Figure D-3*]

○ Organization Structure   [*Figure D-1*]

○ Detailed Program Execution
Network   [*Figure D-2*]

○ Program Schedule   [*Figure D-6*]

These documents will be designed to assure that all project activities have been thoroughly defined, assigned, and planned, and that adequate manpower is available for their accomplishment.

WBS ELEMENT 4.2   *Program Monitoring and Control:* DPC will continuously monitor the cost and progress of the program work and performance of DPC personnel. DPC recognizes that, during the execution of this program, a need may develop to alter the program scope, schedule, and/or budget. DPC will monitor the need for such changes, present them formally to _____'s management, and mutually agree upon the course of corrective action.

3.0   Cost Proposal

3.1   Estimate of Cost Elements

As described in Section 2.0, DPC has subdivided the _____ PP&C Procedure Development Program through three (3) levels of the WBS. The activities necessary to accomplish the statements of work were scheduled in a manner that considers the relationships and interdependencies of the various work elements.

DPC's cost estimate to perform the work described in Section 2.0 is shown in [*Figures D-4 and D-5*]. The figures show the labor and other resources necessary to accomplish each element of the DPC WBS. The labor categories depicted are: director of projects, senior consultant, and consultant. Estimates are shown in man-hours by labor category.

Decision Planning Corporation developed its cost estimate based on the labor rates shown below. [*Note that the rates have been intentionally deleted.*] These rates are based upon uniform market prices for services provided in substantial quantity to the general public. DPC labor rates are:

Director of projects	$____/day
Senior consultant	$____/day
Consultant	$____/day

The above rates are valid only for the resources shown and for a period of five months. If, during the course of this engagement, DPC is requested to provide services requiring special expertise in areas other than project planning and control, billing rates for such services will be negotiated with _____ at that time.

Figure D-4. Cost estimates by cost elements.

Estimate by Cost Elements	Labor*			Other					
	Director of Projects	Senior Consultants	Consultants	Airfare	Hotel/ Per Diem	Car Rental (Days)	Parking (Days)	Misc.
1.1 Documentation Review	8	8	10					
1.2 Representative Project Review	8	8	10					
1.3 Management Interview	8	8	12					
1.0 Total Review	24	24	32	3	13	5	13	3
2.1 System Requirement Definition	12	40	8					
2.2 System Specification	12	16	8					
2.0 Total System Specification	24	56	16	2	10	5	10	2
3.1 Procedure Flow Charts	4	80	120					
3.2 Procedure Narratives	3	120	160					
3.3 Procedure Forms and Instructions	3	40	56					
3.0 Total Procedures	10	240	336	9	43	24	43	9
4.1 Program Organization & Planning	16	24	12					
4.2 Program Monitoring & Controlling	16	24	12					
4.0 Total Program Management	32	48	24	2	10	5	10	2
Total Program	90	368	408	16	76	39	76	16

*Labor estimate is in man-hours.
Note: Use or disclosure of the data set forth hereon is subject to the restriction on the cover page of this proposal.

Other cost elements shown are estimated in units appropriate to the cost element. The cost elements and the units estimated are as follows:

Cost Elements	Unit of Estimation
Airfares	Round-trips from Costa Mesa to _____
Hotel/per diem	Days × number of on-site consultants
Car rental	Days × number of cars rented
Parking	Days × number of cars parked
Miscellaneous	Dollars per trip

Figure D-5. Cost estimates for proposed services.

Estimated Cost for Proposed Services		Labor				Other Cost Elements						Total Price
WBS Element	Quantity/Cost (Unit Price (Hr))	Director of Projects	Senior Consultants	Consultants	Staff Consultants	Airfare	Hotel/Per Diem	Car Rental (Days)	Parking (Days)	Mileage (100 mi.)	Visual Aids	
1.0 PP&C System Review	Q	24	24	32		3	13	5	13	3		
	$											
2.0 PP&C System Specification	Q	24	56	16		2	10	5	10	2		
	$											
3.0 PP&C System Procedures	Q	10	240	336		9	43	24	43	9		
	$											
4.0 Program Management	Q	32	48	24		2	10	5	10	2		
	$											
Total Program												

[Rates and costs intentionally deleted.]

At present, DPC anticipates that the only materials that may be required are the general office supplies, light graphics, and reproduction.

3.2   Cost Estimate Rationale

The cost estimate for the proposed services is based upon the following assumptions:

○ Timely completion and total cost of this program are dependent on the strict adherence of all participants to the project schedule.

○ _____ will provide office space and all necessary facilities for the DPC personnel while engaged in on-site services. On-site activities include approximately 60 percent of the total effort.

○ The term *site* refers to the _____ offices located at _____. Travel to locations other than the "site" shall be regarded as out-of-scope activity and shall be negotiated/billed separately.

○ Total project duration is assumed to be ten to twelve weeks.

○ DPC currently reimburses its personnel for lodging at cost and provides a food and incidentals allowance rate of $____ per day. For the _____ area, DPC estimates $____ per night, which represents the middle range of a single hotel room. The total of $____ per day has been multiplied against the estimated number of per diem days. [*Rates and costs have been intentionally deleted.*]

○ Substantial cost savings can be realized by taking advantage of airline discounts and/or price reductions. However, to take advantage of these reductions, a firm schedule must be established. As soon as a firm schedule is established, DPC will attempt to take advantage of all possible cost savings related to travel, reducing the overall travel-related expenses.

3.3   Cost Summary

The cost estimate for the proposed statement of work associated with procedure development has been summarized in [*Figure D-5*]. The total cost estimate is for all services/products described in Section 2.0. [*Cost has been intentionally deleted.*]

3.4   Invoice and Payment

DPC will invoice _____ each month for the costs incurred at the billing rates and actual expense costs incurred to date. Refer to [*Figure

D-6]. DPC anticipates payment will be received from _____ within thirty days of submission of the invoice.

All payments should be made to:

> Decision Planning Corporation
> 3184-A Airway Avenue
> Costa Mesa, California 92626

4.0 Management Proposal

This section describes the organizational approach that DPC uses on its consulting assignments, the specific team proposal for this program, and the schedule for accomplishing the statement of work.

4.1 Program Organization and Staffing

Decision Planning Corporation controls all of its assignments with a matrix organization as shown in [*Figure D-7*]. The left side of this chart depicts DPC officers, and the right side shows the organization of the Program Team.

DPC will appoint Mr. Richard Brodkorb as director of this program to provide for adequate interfacing with _____ management and to assure complete control of project resources. Mr. Brodkorb will be supported by a team that possesses a unique blend of technical and business management backgrounds chosen specifically for this assignment. All team members will not be utilized at the same rate; three team members are proposed in order to assure that qualified individuals are available to support peak periods. A synopsis of the proposed team members and their experience related to this assignment is presented below. A more detailed résumé on each member is included in Appendix B.

> [*Synopses intentionally deleted.*]

4.2 Staffing Restrictions

The proposed staff is available to support _____ within three weeks of the date of this proposal. However, should authorization to proceed be delayed beyond _____, 20___, DPC may be required to assign a portion of the proposed personnel to other engagements. If this occurs, DPC will replace the reassigned personnel with staff mem-

Figure D-6. Program schedule.

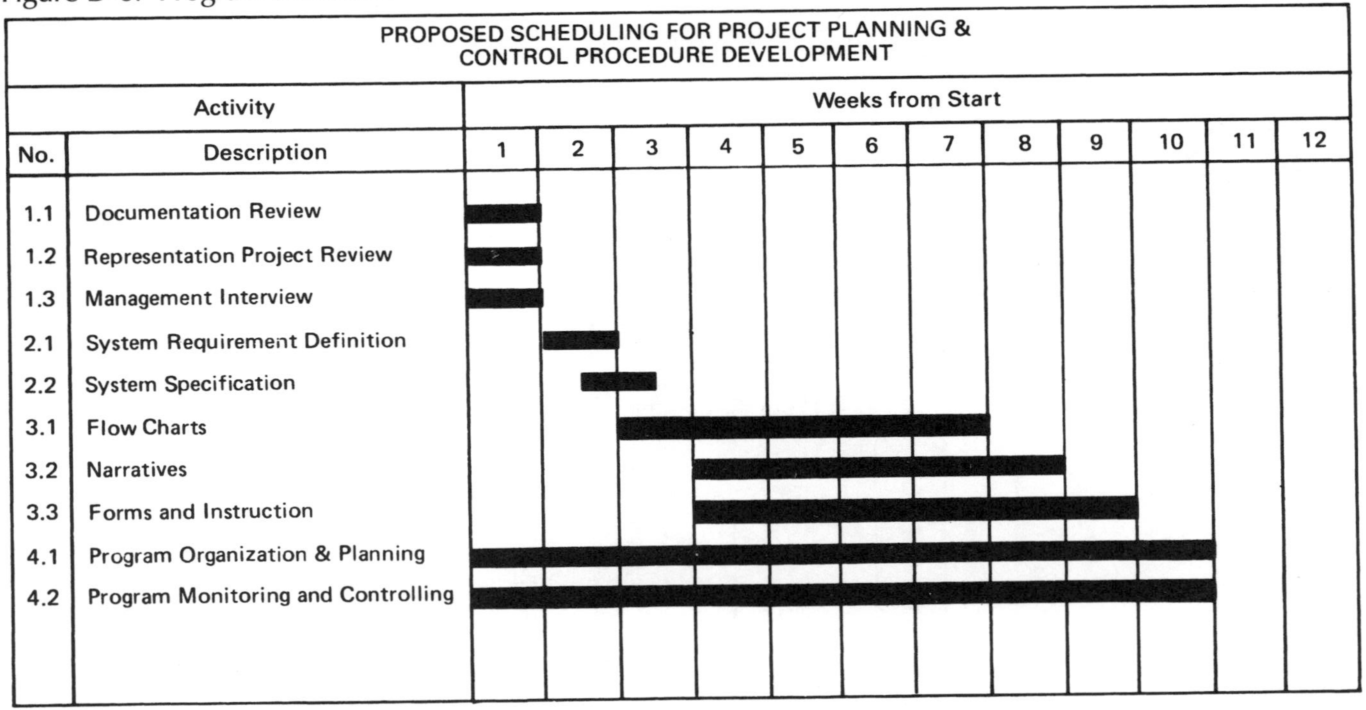

PROPOSED SCHEDULING FOR PROJECT PLANNING &
CONTROL PROCEDURE DEVELOPMENT

No.	Activity Description	Weeks from Start											
		1	2	3	4	5	6	7	8	9	10	11	12
1.1	Documentation Review	▮											
1.2	Representation Project Review	▮											
1.3	Management Interview	▮											
2.1	System Requirement Definition		▮										
2.2	System Specification			▮									
3.1	Flow Charts							▮					
3.2	Narratives								▮				
3.3	Forms and Instruction									▮			
4.1	Program Organization & Planning										▮		
4.2	Program Monitoring and Controlling										▮		

Figure D-7. DPC matrix organization.

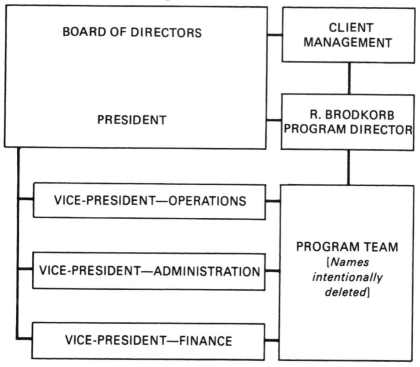

bers of equal qualifications. Replacements will be made with the approval of _____.

4.3   Program Schedule

The proposed schedule for accomplishment of the _____ Project Planning and Control Procedure Development Program is shown in [*Figure D-6*]. The schedule was developed in the framework of the Work Breakdown Structure [*Figure D-1*], and it depicts time phasing and duration of all activities identified in the Execution Logic Diagram [*Figure D-2*].

Rather than being oriented toward specific calendar dates, the schedule is constructed based upon working days and weeks after commencement of the engagement. A minimum of two weeks' advance notice should be given in order for DPC to support desired dates.

Appendix E

ASSOCIATIONS OF CONSULTANTS

Alliance of Health Care Consultants
Professional Practice Builders
1390 Willow Band Drive
Snellville, Ga. 30278-5805
Tel.: 770-978-7822
Fax: 770-978-7707

American Association of Consulting Pharmacists
1321 Duke Street
Alexandria, Va. 22314-3563
Tel.: 703-739-1300
Fax: 703-739-1500
E-mail: info@ascpfoundation.org

American Association of Political Consultants
900 Second Street, NE, Suite 217
Washington, D.C. 20002
Tel.: 202-371-9585
Fax 202-371-6751
E-mail: aapcmail@aol.com
Web site: http://www.theaapc.org

American Consulting Engineers Council
1015 15th Street, NW, Suite 802
Washington, D.C. 20005
Tel.: 202-347-7474
Fax: 202-898-0068
E-mail: acec@acec.org
Web site: http://www.acec.org

Association of Executive Search Consultants
500 Fifth Avenue, Suite 930
New York, N.Y. 10110
Fax: 212-398-9560
E-mail: aesc@aesc.org
Web site: http://www.aesc.org

Association of Image Consultants International
International Headquarters
P.O. Box 864
Middletown, Md. 21769-0864
Tel.: 800-383-8831
Fax: 301-371-8847
E-mail: aici@worldnet.att.net
Web site: http://www.aici.org

Association of Management Consulting Firms
380 Lexington Avenue
New York, N.Y. 10168
Tel.: 212-551-7887
Fax: 212-551-7934
E-mail: info@amcf.org
Web site: www.amcf.org

Association of Professional Consultants
777 South Main Street, Suite 57-304
Orange, Calif. 92868
Tel.: 800-745-5050
Fax: 800-977-3272
E-mail: apc@consultapc.org
Web site: http://www.consultapc.org

Council of Consulting Organizations
521 5th Avenue, 35th Floor
New York, N.Y. 10175
Tel.: 212-697-9693

Independent Computer Consultants Association
1131 South Towne Square, Suite F
St. Louis, Mo. 63123
Tel.: 800-774-4222
Fax: 314-487-1345
E-mail: membership@icca.org
Web site: http://www.icca.org

Institute of Certified Financial Planners
3801 East Florida Avenue, Suite 708
Denver, Colo. 80210-2544
Tel.: 800-323-4237
Fax: 303-759-0749
E-mail: institute@icfp.org
Web site: http://www.icfp.org

Institute of Management Consultants
1200 19th Street, NW, Suite 300
Washington, D.C. 20036-2422
Tel.: 202-857-5334
Fax: 202-857-1891
E-mail: office@imcusa.org
Web site: http://www.imcusa.org

International Platform Association
P.O. Box 250
Winnetka, Ill. 60093-0250
Tel: 847-446-4321
Fax: 847-446-7186
Web site: http://www.internationalplatform.com

International Public Relations Association
McCormick & Company, Inc.
18 Loveton Circle
Sparks, Md. 21152
Tel.: 410-771-7301
Web Site: http://www.ipranet.org

Medico Legal Consultants
Mainland Office
11727 Kiowa Avenue, Suite 101
Los Angeles, Calif 90049-6132
E-mail: mlegal@aloha.net

National Bureau of Cerified Consultants
(Formerly the National Bureau of Professional Management Consultants)
Management Consulting Center
2728 Fifth Avenue
San Diego, Calif. 92103
Tel.: 619-297-2207
Web site: http://www.national-bureau.com

National Speakers Association
1500 South Priest Drive
Tempe, Ariz. 85281
Tel.: 602-976-2552
E-mail: information@nsaspeaker.org
Web site: http://www.nsaspeaker.org

Professional and Technical Consultants Association
P.O. Box 4143
Mountain View, Calif. 94040
Tel.: 650-903-9305
E-mail: office@patca.org
Web site: http://www.patca.org

Public Relations Society of America
33 Irving Place, 3rd Floor
New York, N.Y. 10003-2376
Tel.: 212-995-2230
Fax: 212-995-0757
E-mail: hq@prsa.org
Web site: http://www.prsa.org

Turnaround Management Association
14800 Conference Center Drive, Suite 402
Chantilly, Va. 22021
Tel.: 703-803-8301 or 312-822-9700
E-mail: info@turnaround.org
Web site: http://www.turnaround.org

INDEX